SHOTS FIRED

ON PATROL WITH A CANADIAN STREET COP
BY
GARY CAMERON

CODE FIVE *PRESS*

Published in 1997 by Code Five Press

Canadian Cataloguing in Publication Data
Cameron, Gary, 1951-
Shots fired

ISBN 0-9699783-0-8

1. Cameron, Gary, 1951- 2. Police patrol-British Columbia-
Vancouver-Anecdotes 3. Vancouver (B.C.) Police Dept. I. Title
HV7914.C35 1997   363.2'32'0971133   C96-910900-8

Editor - Brian Scrivener
Copy Editor - Martine Bilodeau
Cover Design - Addison Graphics
Cover Art - Pat Cameron

Printed and Bound in Canada by Friesens

10 9 8 7 6 5 4 3 2 1

Preface

I was a constable with the Vancouver Police Department from 1975 to 1987. It was a very good time to be a street cop. I enjoyed putting crooks behind bars, and I loved the challenge and responsibility that was so much a part of police work. The thing I miss most about the job is, of course, the people I worked with. You soon find out what someone is really like when you watch how they handle police calls, especially the serious incidents. No police officer ever let me down when I needed backup.

I wrote this book to help people understand what I used to do for a living. I believe policing is an honorable profession, and I was privileged to work with many police officers whom I grew to respect and admire. Nevertheless, the reader should keep in mind that the opinions expressed in this book are strictly my own, and don't necessarily represent the views of the Vancouver Police Department or the men and women who work there.

I have not named the other members who attended the calls I describe in this book because it wouldn't be fair to inflict my version of these events on them. After all, like most good "war stories," mine seem to have gradually "improved" with time. I have also taken the liberty of changing relevant details of some of the calls I attended in order to protect the privacy of victims. Many laws and police techniques have changed since I left the job, so some of the arrests described herein would be handled differently now.

I couldn't have written this book without the help of some very important people. I want to thank Mark Forshaw, Bill Wellman, Peter Cruise and Hilda Palmer for reading this manuscript in its early stages and offering me encouragement. Any errors are, of course, my responsibility. I owe special thanks to my mother and father, as well as my brother and sister. They've been extremely supportive during the writing of this book. I would never have finished *SHOTS FIRED* had it not been for the wisdom, encouragement and love I received from my wife, who is truly the best thing that ever happened to me. Nothing is more important than family, not even the job.

Lastly, I want to pay homage to a member of the Vancouver Police Department who was killed in the line of duty just before I left the job. Sergeant Larry Young was a good street cop. He will be remembered, and he will be sorely missed.

Contents

Chapter One
COPS AND ROBBERS

"Why the hell would I want to wear a bulletproof vest anyway? Nobody ever fired a gun at me, for crying out loud. When I start worrying about getting shot, that's the day I leave this job!"

The veteran police officer laughed good-naturedly as one of the younger members was being measured for a bulletproof vest just before the shift began. He would have reason to regret his words before the end of the day.

As I left the station that afternoon, the radio operator informed us of a robbery-in-progress at a nearby supermarket. According to the store manager, who had called police from the safety of his upstairs office, the suspects were stealing money from several cashiers at gunpoint.

When a security guard tried to intervene, one of the robbers placed a revolver to his head and pulled the trigger. Although the employee heard a clicking sound from the weapon as the hammer fell, fortunately for him it did not discharge. The suspects pistol-whipped him until he collapsed, and then fled the store. The two robbers made their getaway in a waiting car just as our members arrived on the scene, so the chase was on. We soon learned that at least one of their firearms was in good working order, because the suspects fired several shots at the police during the pursuit. A Dog Squad member fired one round in return, but neither of the crooks was hit and the chase continued.

The senior policeman who had joked about bulletproof vests half an hour earlier was crouching beside his car as they drove past. He dove for cover in a nearby gutter just as the suspects fired one round that narrowly missed him. He didn't quit the job that day, but I never heard him joking about bulletproof vests again.

One of our motorcycle policemen also got involved. During the pursuit, the suspects pulled up beside him and pointed a revolver at his helmet. He was forced to drop his bike on its side so he could use it for cover until they moved on. I joined the chase as the suspects sped eastbound on Broadway. I followed two cars behind them until the traffic ahead stopped for a red light. The suspect's vehicle, with nowhere else to go, crashed into the rear of one of the stationary cars. Suddenly the high speed chase was over. I caught a momentary glimpse of a robber leaving his getaway car through the driver's side door as I emerged from my black and white.

As I drew my service revolver and started to give chase, I heard shots fired on my right. It was too late for me to stop running, so I continued on my way past the getaway vehicle until I ran into a man standing beside the car in front of it. Everything happened very quickly, of course. I didn't know if this was the man I was looking for, but I grabbed him anyway and placed him against a nearby car at gunpoint. I have no idea to this day what he said to me during the next few seconds. Whatever it was must have struck a responsive chord because I immediately released him and continued on my way. I joined another officer who had just collared a suspect in the middle of the intersection. I helped to handcuff him as we struggled on the hood of another car that had stopped at the red light. The driver stared open-mouthed through his windshield as we proudly dragged our catch back to my car.

The shots I'd heard when I ran past the getaway car were from other officers exchanging fire with the second suspect on the passenger side. He subsequently surrendered after he ran out of ammunition. By the time we returned to my police car he was in custody. Members recovered two handguns inside the getaway car, as well as a large amount of stolen money from the store. The passenger's revolver had functioned all too well, albeit inaccurately. The second handgun, which the driver had used on the security guard, was an ancient but still operable .45 caliber revolver. The suspects had loaded it with ammunition from a .45 caliber semi-automatic. For some reason, perhaps because of different-sized casings, the rounds hadn't seated properly in the cylinder. That mistake had apparently saved the security guard's life.

I searched our suspect again when we arrived at headquarters and found an expensive gold chain later used as evidence in another court case. He had stolen it during a jewelry store holdup in a different municipality. Then I guarded the prisoner in an interview room while the detectives put their case together. I tried to get a statement from him, but he was far too streetwise to discuss his involvement in the robbery. The remainder of our conversation was surprisingly civilized, however, considering the fact that we could well have been faced with the possibility of shooting one another only twenty minutes earlier.

His criminal record up to that point was already lengthy, with numerous arrests for assaults and robberies. He was a heroin addict with an expensive habit, so he stole to feed his arm. He and his accomplices were successfully prosecuted for several armed robberies that had occurred in Vancouver, including one where a store owner had been shot. After talking to the robber, and examining his criminal record, I believe there is no chance this individual will ever rehabilitate himself. Because society chooses not to permanently incarcerate dangerous career criminals, people like him return to pulling armed robberies after each short stint they serve inside prison. It was a miracle that no one was hurt that day, despite heavy gunfire from both sides. As for the gentleman I had unceremoniously pointed my gun at during the foot chase, I saw him interviewed on TV later that evening. It turned out that he was the driver of the car our suspects had rear-ended at the red light.

During his TV interview he was kind enough to compliment our police officers on how they handled the robbery arrests. I found out later that after I confronted him and then left to pursue the real suspect, two more officers had noticed him standing there and again threw him up against his car at gunpoint. This time he had faced a police shotgun. Fortunately, he was tactful enough not to mention all of this unpleasantness on TV.

What the TV reporter didn't realize was that the unfortunate bystander was actually a senior commissioned officer from another police force. The plainclothes officer must have been very pleased to see these particular crooks in handcuffs, because the squad he headed had been assigned to find them and take them out of circulation. In fact, the officer was on his way home after a busy but fruitless day of coordinating the search when the suspects rammed his car. That they hit his car, out of all the thousands of vehicles passing through the city that day, has to be one of the most bizarre coincidences I ever encountered on the job.

***

My career with the Vancouver Police Department almost ended before it had a chance to begin. It happened the day I graduated from Block One at the Police College. I was faced with a vexing dilemma as I drove home from the graduation ceremony because I had forgotten to visit the bank the day before. My wallet was empty and I needed money so I could join my classmates for a celebration that evening.

My problem was that I was wearing my police uniform for the first time ever in public. My bank closed in five minutes so I didn't have time to make it home, change, and then drive back. There were no instant teller machines in 1975, so I had to go directly to the bank and wait in line to withdraw some cash. I dreaded wearing my uniform inside the bank because I didn't want to be the object of curious stares, but there was no alternative.

As I stepped out of my car, a clean-cut gentleman in a suit approached from the direction of the bank's front door and yelled at me. "Where is he? Did you get him?"

He must have wondered why a policeman was driving an Austin Mini, although all he saw now was me wearing the familiar blue uniform. Obviously he expected me to play the role of policeman, despite the fact that I didn't really feel like a policeman at the moment. "Slow down," I said. "What are you talking about?"

"The guy who just robbed us! He just left the bank! He had a gun!"

This was real, not a training simulation! The complainant was an employee of the bank. He had just followed a robbery suspect out the front door as I was parking my car. The suspect could have walked south, east or west as he made his escape, although the employee was sure he'd turned in my direction. I hadn't noticed anything out of the ordinary as I pulled up, but of course I wasn't expecting trouble. If the witness' account was accurate, the suspect must have walked right past me as I was parking my car.

The employee used his thumb and forefinger to illustrate the diameter of the barrel of the suspect's handgun. The circumference of the circle looked howitzer-sized to me. That meant the weapon was not a pellet gun, which has a noticeably small bore. I knew then that this robbery suspect was carrying a real handgun, not an imitation weapon.

I took a quick look around the crowded parking lot. None of the pedestrians looked like bank robbers to me, although of course at this time I hadn't been given a detailed description of the suspect. What the hell does a bank robber look like anyway? As my eyes swept the parking lot one last time, I caught sight of a male in his twenties sitting in the driver's seat of a nearby parked vehicle.

I looked at him and he stared back unflinchingly. I didn't see any indication that he was nervous or frightened. I hesitated for just a second, wondering what to do next. My first instinct was to walk over to the car and talk to him, although at the time it never occurred to me to draw my service revolver. That could have been a fatal mistake. The holdup procedures I'd just been taught at the academy were still fresh in my memory, and I made the decision to step inside the bank and begin an investigation.

Admittedly I was a little scared, perhaps even more than a little scared, but I was far more frightened of screwing up the call than I was of getting shot. As the first policeman on the scene of a serious crime, policy dictated that I enter the bank, obtain a complete description of

4

the suspect and phone it in to the communications center. I walked into the bank to find the usual state of confusion that accompanies an incident like this. The bank manager locked the main doors behind me to prevent potential witnesses from wandering off, as well as to keep out curious bystanders.

Two unusually calm tellers, each carrying a piece of paper with a hastily scribbled description of the armed robbery suspect, approached me as soon as they recognized the uniform. I immediately phoned the communications center and relayed this vital information to the operators so they could broadcast it to units in the area. Without the written descriptions I would have wasted valuable time getting organized. I thanked them profusely for their help. In all the subsequent holdups I attended over the years, never again was I given such prompt and able assistance by bank staff. Although they always did the best they could, considering the frightening circumstances, most robbery victims are understandably very distraught after looking down the barrel of a handgun.

As soon as I finished my conversation with the communications operator, I hung up the phone and waited for the police to attend. The real police, that is, because I didn't really consider myself part of the department yet. I just wanted someone to take over the crime scene so I could leave. The sooner that happened, the better.

I did not have long to wait because a Dog Squad car raced up to the front of the bank within two minutes. The constable's canine partner was barking excitedly from the back seat, eager to catch a crook. As I approached his car, the constable looked me over curiously and asked me where my portable radio was. Because I had neither the time nor the inclination to tell him what I was doing there in the first place, I just shook my head. He helpfully tossed me his spare radio and drove off to search for the suspect. I had never used a portable radio before, so I just stuck it in my back pocket and returned to the bank to await further assistance.

Ten minutes later, detectives from the Robbery Squad (later changed to the Major Crimes Squad) arrived to begin their investigation. One of them immediately approached me since I was the only uniformed officer at the scene. "Okay, you're assigned to the call. I want to see your reports on my desk before you go off-duty today."

I attempted to explain to the detective that I wasn't really on duty, despite the fact that I was in full uniform and carrying a police portable radio. He looked me up and down, shook his head in bewilderment and then walked away. I followed him like a lost puppy because I

5

was concerned that I would screw up his investigation somehow. He tried to ignore me. I got the distinct impression he thought I was pulling his leg, and he was clearly not amused.

I gave up on him and began taking statements from witnesses. They were all documented in my first police notebook, which until today had only contained entries about simulated criminal investigations and training exercises. I thought my ordeal was over when the policemen officially assigned to the call finally arrived to take charge, but the original detective approached me again. "We think the suspect might have left prints on the counter. Arrange for the Identification Squad to attend."

I didn't dare touch the portable radio, so I hesitated, then replied, "Yes sir. I'll use the phone."

He gave me another puzzled look, and impatiently ordered me to use the portable radio because he was certain they were already on the road attending another call. Since I was not yet assigned to a patrol car, I had no call sign or any other means of identifying myself to the radio operator. Rather than arguing with the exasperated detective, I decided to use the serial number engraved on the exterior of the radio case as my call sign. I successfully transmitted his request, but only after some fumbling while I tried to find where the transmit button was. The operator was obviously intrigued at the use of this strange call sign, which consisted of a four-digit number that was not even close to any of the car numbers then in use. Nevertheless, she dutifully passed the message along to the Identification Squad.

By this time I wanted desperately to leave the bank, but I still needed money for the night's celebration. Consequently, I had no alternative but to join the long line of irate customers we'd confined inside the bank as potential witnesses. Even though I'd already written down their statements, they still had to wait until one of the tellers replenished her recently depleted cash supply and reopened her wicket. Only then could they complete their own financial transactions. They looked on, perplexed, as the policeman who had disrupted their schedules now joined them in line.

One of the tellers who had provided me with a written description when I first entered the bank eventually came to my rescue again. She walked over and led me by the arm to her wicket, which was now liberally coated with a film of gray fingerprint powder. I finally left the bank with the cash for my evening's entertainment safely tucked away in my uniform pants pocket, happy to have survived my first call as a policeman.

I have no idea whether the man I observed sitting in his car was actually a bank robber. Perhaps it is best that I didn't find that out the hard way. I was not used to carrying my service revolver; to get involved in a shoot-out at that stage of my career would probably have been a mistake. It takes years of experience to become a competent police officer, so at the time I thought and acted more like a civilian than a policeman. Maybe I should have at least taken down his license number, but the idea never occurred to me until later that night in the bar.

Since the suspect probably walked right past me as I got out of my car, I often wondered what went through his mind when he saw me. It was fortunate that he was not trigger-happy, because at that distance he couldn't have missed. I checked the file years later. No one was ever arrested for the offense, and the investigators never generated any information about the suspect's identity. The case will probably never be solved.

***

Vancouver has always had an alarmingly high number of bank holdups for a city its size. The reality is that most bank robbers are drug addicts, and we have more than our share of addicts here. Many use a fist stuck in a jacket pocket to simulate a weapon and then hand the teller a holdup note. Most of these suspects are eventually captured, usually through their own incompetence, but sometimes with the assistance of bank cameras and other security measures.

Having said this, it should be noted that not all bank robbers are as harmless as the losers mentioned above. On a regular basis, police run across heavily-armed individuals and well-organized criminal gangs that pose an extreme danger to the public and to the police.

There is no question that crooks could probably realize a higher return from less risky criminal activities. Often it seems to be little more than a matter of prestige that drives suspects to pull bank jobs again as soon as they finish serving time for their last holdup. Despite increasingly sophisticated security precautions taken by financial institutions, bank robbers just keep coming back for more.

The danger posed by these individuals was brought home to our department several years ago when one of our police officers was shot twice by a particularly vicious robbery suspect. The officer, who was flagged over by a witness, interrupted the suspect while he was making his getaway immediately after a bank holdup. The policeman was gunned down before he had a chance to return fire. Fortunately, the officer survived. The robbery suspect eventually killed himself as the police closed in on him, rather than face the consequences of his actions like a man.

Bank robberies are not without their share of risks for the offenders themselves. One of Vancouver's less fortunate robbers, a transient, first came to our attention when he was arrested by two skid road beat patrolmen. They found a loaded handgun tucked inside his belt as they searched him. He was sent to jail, but was almost immediately released on bail. That day, he walked into a Granville Street bank and held it up. His luck ran out inside a nearby fast food restaurant shortly after he fled the bank. When a determined policeman attempted to arrest him, he pulled out a weapon and pointed it at the officer. The robber died almost instantly after he was shot once in the chest. It was, in police jargon, a "good shooting". One of our local TV stations managed to get a close-up shot of the ghastly expression on the suspect's lifeless face as he lay sprawled against a serving counter. They showed that film clip repeatedly on their nightly newscasts over the next few years whenever they needed to spice up a crime story.

***

One of our officers drove down a lane near Davie Street during a quiet day shift in the late seventies. Two pedestrians walking toward him split up as he passed. Out of curiosity he watched them in his rearview mirror as he negotiated the rest of the congested alley. His diligence was rewarded when he caught sight of them panicking suddenly and running away. At the same time, he heard a report of a holdup alarm from a nearby bank over his police radio.

One suspect disappeared immediately. The policeman gave chase on foot as the other suspect ran between two apartment buildings and ducked around a corner. The officer, fearing an ambush, wisely decided not to follow him right away. He took advantage of what little cover there was behind some shrubs growing around an apartment building doorway. He then edged cautiously toward the corner.

His precautions were justified. Seconds later the gunman emerged from his hiding place and opened fire. He had apparently been waiting there to ambush his pursuer but had become impatient. The robbery suspect fired two shots at the policeman and fled. Both shots narrowly missed. Investigators later recovered bullets embedded in the wooden trim of the doorway where the fortunate policeman had taken cover. The suspects were eventually identified after committing other offenses.

***

I made my first bank robbery arrest almost by remote control.

In fact, I didn't even see the suspects until after they were already in jail. It began with the routine check of a well-known heroin addict on the Granville Street Mall.

I hadn't been a policeman for very long, but one of the first things I learned was to recognize a hype, or heroin addict. At that time the Granville Street mall was heavily populated with addicts. As a group they were very much involved in the full spectrum of criminal activities, so a policeman interested in making arrests would usually meet with success just by checking drug addicts between radio calls. If there were arrest warrants outstanding, the addict went to jail. Because addicts frequently carried illegal drugs, weapons or stolen property of some type, a quick frisk often turned up enough evidence for a charge. At the time, the Charter of Rights existed only in the twisted imaginations of a few civil libertarians and naive politicians, so the evidence of a criminal offense obtained during a justifiable, routine street search was usually admissible in court.

Identifying a drug addict is not as difficult as it might seem. It is not so much that they all look alike. At any given time there are thousands of addicts in the Lower Mainland, from all levels of society. Many live a relatively normal existence and never set foot in the skid road area. Most of the addicts that chose to become part of the heroin subculture that existed on Granville Street in the seventies tended to act, dress and talk in a similar, distinctive manner. It was easy to verify drug involvement by asking them a few simple questions and then checking their arms for "tracks," a term used to describe the scars caused by repeatedly injecting narcotics.

The first addict I checked that day was obviously very nervous, and for good reason. Although it was a warm summer day, he was wearing a hip-length leather jacket and carried another new and expensive-looking leather jacket. He couldn't explain how the second jacket had come into his possession.

It soon became obvious to me that the second jacket must have come from a local department store, so I accused him of shop-lifting. As I did so, I laboriously turned the sleeves inside out and claimed knowledge of a hidden serial number that would enable me to trace the garment back to the store. He denied the theft, of course, and I was temporarily at a loss about what to do next.

At this point another officer joined me and offered some timely advice on how to handle the situation. We agreed out loud that criminal charges were in order. The addict became despondent, and finally offered to exchange information for his freedom. He was currently on parole, which meant he could be charged with breach of his parole conditions if he was caught stealing. He had only just returned to the street after a lengthy stay in a federal penitentiary, and he did not want to go back inside again. Heroin withdrawal is a painful, unpleasant experience.

The best he could do was to promise to meet me the next day with some good information. We told him we wouldn't charge him with breach of parole right away, although we might change our minds if he disappeared overnight. This is not the recommended way to run an informant, so I knew the odds were he wouldn't show up tomorrow.

There was no doubt in my mind that he'd stolen the jacket. He had conceded that by virtue of his failure to provide us with a reasonable explanation for its origin. However, there was still insufficient evidence to proceed with formal charges at this stage of the investigation unless I could find out which store the jacket had been stolen from. We sent him on his way and I seized the second jacket and placed it in our property office so that at least it could be returned to its rightful owner, if indeed the theft was ever reported to the police.

I showed up early for the meet. Much to my surprise, the informant arrived right on schedule. He was nervous, and clearly did not want to go back to jail. Having renewed his love affair with heroin since his latest release, he had good reason to value his freedom.

He got right to the point. He claimed to be in possession of important information about two bank robbers, but refused to reveal more until I guaranteed I was not going to send him back to jail because of the stolen jacket. I promised him truthfully that I had no intention of doing so, and he readily accepted my word. He then pulled out his address book and made a point of showing me an entry he'd made there, as if it were proof of his veracity.

He pointed to two names, both French Canadian. According to the informant, they were staying in one of the better hotels in the West End. The address was still valid, he claimed, because he'd just been up there the night before to sell them heroin. The two suspects had apparently hired female companions for the evening, so they were in a good mood that night. In fact, during the drug transaction they had bragged about the amount of money they'd stolen during their last bank job.

As I pulled out my notebook and began copying down the room number from his address book, he warned me that he'd deliberately transposed two digits of the room number when he originally made the entry, ostensibly for security reasons. He readily provided what he guaranteed to be the correct room number, and then left in order to score some heroin to soothe his rattled nerves.

Of course I had some real concerns about the accuracy of this information. His little trick with the room number left me even more uneasy. If it turned out he was lying, I would at the very least look like a fool. Even worse, if the room was actually occupied by innocent tourists, and detectives mistakenly kicked in their door because of my information, we could end up with a civil suit for false arrest. The potential for disaster seemed obvious even to an inexperienced police-man like myself.

First of all, it seemed too easy. I knew from experience that almost everyone I dealt with lied to me, even if they had no reason to be untruthful. On the other hand, why would this informant have gone to all the trouble of fabricating a story for me? He could just as easily have skipped the meet and avoided me for the next week or so, hoping that eventually I would forget about the theft charge.

I decided to forward the information to the robbery squad and then crossed my fingers. They sent word to my sergeant the next day that the robbery suspects were now in custody. The detectives had kicked in their hotel room door and interrupted a drug party funded by proceeds from the robber's last holdup. The arrests ended a crime spree that had included at least two hold-ups here in town, along with several others across Canada. Unfortunately I soon lost my informant when he was returned to jail on other, unrelated charges.

***

Most banks have security cameras installed to record the ac-tions of robbery suspects. The hold-up photos in the eighties were black and white and tended to be somewhat grainy and indistinct, although the quality seems to be improving lately. Nevertheless, they could still be very helpful to the investigators, especially if the suspect had made no effort to disguise his face.

I occasionally carried copies of some of the better quality holdup pictures inside my uniform hat while I patrolled the skid road area. I did this even though I was aware that the odds of identifying and arresting one of these robbery suspects from their bank pictures were next to nonexistent. In fact, it would be the golfing equivalent of scoring a hole in one.

Nevertheless, at the beginning of a particularly quiet month working day shift in the skid road area, I decided to try to capture at least one of the subjects featured in three of the best current bank pictures, all from recent downtown robberies. I stuck the photocopies in the visor of my car each morning and referred to them whenever I had a chance. Primarily, I guess, I just wanted to see if it could be done.

It turned out to be even more difficult than I'd anticipated. The biggest problem was driving in heavy city traffic while simultaneously examining thousands of faces on the sidewalk. The process was complicated by the need to avoid jaywalkers and other cars on the road.

I was shocked at how many of the thousands of pedestrians I drove by actually resembled my targets. In order to check out each possible suspect, I found that I had to stop my patrol car immediately and approach the individual on foot before he had a chance to disappear. That sometimes meant leaving the car parked in the middle of a busy street and crossing heavy traffic to get a closer look.

Several people looked so much like one of my suspects that I had to put the picture beside their faces to finally eliminate them. Some of these people were not amused by this procedure, but I made a point of showing the more amiable individuals the photo I was comparing them to. Most readily agreed that the resemblance was amazing. Once they understood what I was after, nobody walked away mad.

Near the end of the month, I found myself scheduled to work with a partner for the day, even though I usually worked alone at that stage of my career. I suspect he thought my plan to catch a bank robber was a little strange at first, but he soon entered into the spirit of the chase. Although we checked several individuals who fit the descriptions as we drove through the skid road area, none of them were bank robbers. After several hours of this, we were about ready to stop for a coffee when we spotted yet another potential suspect walking down a Gastown sidewalk.

We stopped immediately and approached him on foot. Although he did not try to run away, he looked very nervous and uncomfortable. He was a white male, about thirty-five years old, with gray, balding hair and a full beard and mustache. After a quick frisk to make sure he wasn't carrying a weapon, I compared him once again to one of the bank pictures I had been staring at all month. He seemed identical in every respect, although the quality of the photocopy was admittedly not the best.

We finally knew for certain we had our man after we compared the shirt he was wearing now to the description of the clothing worn by the suspect several weeks earlier during the holdup. Apparently he had not changed his wardrobe since then, because the clothing matched perfectly.

We arrested him and read him the official warnings as we

placed handcuffs on his wrists. During a thorough frisk we found two thick money rolls in different pockets. When confronted with this evidence, he readily admitted having committed the bank robbery. He told us that he had left for Vancouver Island after the holdup to lie low with friends until the heat died down. He had just stepped off the bus a few minutes before we stopped him, certain in his mind that no one would be looking for him after all that time.

A background check showed that he had a previous record for armed robbery, as well as a long history of mental illness. He had already spent time in mental institutions after committing similar offenses because he was always found to be unfit for trial due to insanity. This robbery charge was also dropped and he was subsequently sent to a hospital for further treatment. I imagine he's still holding up banks every time he leaves the institution.

***

Detectives traditionally become involved in criminal cases only after all the excitement dies down, because patrol members usually do the preliminary investigation of most offenses. However, on one occasion when a carload of our detectives drove by a bank on Hastings Street on their way to lunch, they had an opportunity to do some good, old-fashioned street policing. They couldn't help noticing a man wearing a ski mask run out of the bank's front door. He was in no mood to stop when they tried to arrest him.

They gave chase, of course, but lost sight of him as he sprinted into a low-rent housing complex. Their suspicions that the bank had been robbed were soon confirmed when they heard the holdup alarm call to that address on their police radio. Unfortunately, by that time the suspect had already disappeared.

My partner that day was fairly new on the job. Although he lacked experience, he was keen and best of all, in excellent physical condition. I was overweight and out of shape at the time, so we agreed that if we had to chase anyone on foot he was the designated runner. We monitored the situation over our radio and drove to the east side of the project to block off one of several convenient avenues of escape.

As we pulled into the parking lot, my partner spotted the suspect sprinting toward us, now minus his jacket and ski mask. He saw us at the same time, did a U-turn and ran in the opposite direction. We left our car and gave chase on foot.

Fortunately, my partner was able to keep up with him, because I soon dropped behind. Although the area was quickly inundated with blue uniforms, it was my partner who eventually tackled him and held him down until reinforcements arrived. I resolved to lose some weight as my heart stopped racing and I gradually recovered my breath.

I recognized the bank robber from several years earlier when he had been a very active pimp in the West End. After being found in possession of a number of stolen guns, he had spent several years in prison and had recently been released. He soon became addicted to heroin, which he paid for with the proceeds from various criminal activities. Today he looked like a man with one foot in the grave.

The holdup today had not gone well for him. The teller he tried to rob told him to go to hell and stubbornly refused to turn over any money. Running into a carload of detectives on his way out of the bank had been the last straw, and he returned to prison a broken and dispirited man.

***

On one particularly quiet night I covered another unit at a domestic dispute in a West End apartment. The boyfriend was very intoxicated, and I had a long conversation with him while the other officer chatted with his irate girlfriend. He was at that stage of drunkenness where he was indiscreet enough to want to impress us with his criminal bona fides. He began by hinting vaguely at his involvement in several bank robberies. Although his stories were not specific enough to use as evidence against him in court, he revealed enough to convince me he was telling the truth.

He then lectured us on the Vancouver Police Department's response to holdup alarms. It soon became obvious that he was quite familiar with our procedures. In fact, his detailed criticisms of our behavior were identical to those I'd heard many times from Vancouver police officers. I found myself nodding my head in agreement as he talked.

He went on to compare our holdup procedures with those of a city police force in Alberta, where they had the ability to shut down major intersections by remote control. This would effectively snarl all adjacent traffic routes immediately after bank robberies, thereby trapping the getaway car. It was an interesting and informative session.

When tempers finally cooled down, we did a quick search of the apartment and then left. It was strange to hear criticism of our work from the perspective of a drug addict and acknowledged bank robber. In fact, I always felt he would have made a fascinating guest lecturer at the police academy, although his drug habit probably left him little spare time for such niceties. We confirmed that he had an extensive criminal record. We also discovered that he had at one time been acquitted on charges of attempted murder after he fired a .45 caliber round through a Vancouver policeman's windshield during a bank robbery. The officer ducked just before the bullet entered the headrest behind him. Furthermore, we received information that the suspect habitually kept a loaded revolver under his bedside table, the one place we hadn't searched that night.

***

One of the most bizarre robberies I encountered seemed routine enough at first. I was assigned to take a holdup report at a bank in South Vancouver near the Oak Street Bridge. I arrived less than five minutes after the suspect left the scene. As I entered the building, I was greeted by a middle-aged lady who politely asked me if the bank had just been robbed. When I informed her she had guessed correctly, she smiled and said she had seen something that might be of assistance to our investigation.

She had become suspicious when she observed a man acting strangely after leaving the bank. She watched from a distance as the suspect jumped into his getaway car behind the bank, changed his clothing and then sped off. As a result, she was able to provide us with a description of the car and suspect, and she was even quick-witted enough to write down the license plate number. She was a perfect witness, something all too uncommon at a time when many people are increasingly reluctant to get involved.

I immediately transmitted the plate number and vehicle description over my radio to other units in the area. I also made certain that the information was passed on to police forces in the adjoining jurisdictions, because in the space of a few minutes the suspect could well have driven through several different municipalities. Once that was done, I placed my portable radio on a nearby desk and settled down to the monotonous task of interviewing witnesses and writing reports.

Gradually I became aware of increasing activity on our radio channel. Judging by the excited voices and snatches of siren noises I heard, there was obviously a car chase somewhere in our area. I ignored it, since I had more than enough to do already. Then I heard the sound of police sirens filtering into the bank though the front windows.

I found out later that one of our cars spotted the suspect vehicle soon after I gave our radio operator the description. The suspect refused to stop when they tried to pull him over, so they were now in pursuit. For some bizarre reason the chase had wound its way back through the city to the same bank he had robbed only ten minutes earlier. The suspect drove right by my location and finally dumped his getaway car in a front yard just a block away. It was truly a classic case of a criminal returning to the scene of the crime, although surely that couldn't have been his intent.

The robber was not ready to give up yet, however. He leapt from his car and started running. Our members pulled in behind him and gave chase on foot. They were quickly joined by a member of our dog squad, who released his German Shepherd to run the suspect down. The dog, in his eagerness to capture a bad guy, grabbed the first running figure that crossed his path. Unfortunately, that turned out to be one of our officers who was also hot on the trail of the crook. By the time the unlucky policeman separated the dog from his pant leg, the robber had used his head start to put some distance between himself and the local constabulary. The dog soon began tracking again and tried without success to pick up the trail from where the suspect had last been seen.

There were a lot of police cars in the area by this time, but I decided to leave my reports for a while and join the hunt anyway. It was too good an opportunity to pass up. While checking the lanes several blocks west of the bank, I came upon a man jogging toward me with a German Shepherd hot on his heels. I had obtained a brief suspect description earlier from witnesses, but I had only seconds now to compare the individual running toward me with that description. I had to make an immediate decision. This guy didn't look like a bank robber, but then again what the hell does a bank robber look like anyway? The dog was certainly not acting very aggressively toward the jogger, but it was common knowledge that some of our police dogs were less gung-ho than others. I drew my service revolver and ordered him to drop to the ground. He hesitated for a second, then decided not to argue and did as he was told. I cringed as he ended up face down in the middle of a mud puddle. I approached him carefully to get a closer look. After determining that he was unarmed, I had a short conversation with him that convinced me I had stopped the wrong man. He lived in the neighborhood, it turned out. He explained that he'd unwisely decided to walk his dog when he became curious about all the commotion outside, even though his instincts had warned him not to. I apologized and gave him my name in case he wanted to complain. Instead, he accepted my explanation and actually giggled as he began to relax a bit. When I left he was trying to scrape some of the mud off his clothing. He never did make an official complaint about his treatment at my hands.

The real bank robber remained at large for almost a week before he was finally arrested. We learned later that for several months he had been commuting to the Lower Mainland area from his home on Vancouver Island to pull bank heists. After each holdup he would take the ferry back to the Island and keep a low profile until he ran out of money to support his drug habit. Then he would return to Vancouver and rob another bank. He always changed his clothing immediately after leaving the bank, and then took several other precautions he hoped would fool the police. His methodical behavior led to his downfall this time when he left his pants in the getaway car he had abandoned so hastily. In the pant's pocket was his British Columbia Driver's License, complete with a color picture and an address where he could be located. That one mistake eventually put an end to his series of unauthorized withdrawals.

Chapter Two
VIOLENCE

I grew up in a small city in Atlantic Canada. On Halloween night the local rowdies used to congregate in the downtown area, under the watchful eyes of the city constabulary, to raise a little hell. For the most part it was harmless fun and just a matter of letting off steam, especially when compared to other parts of the province where it was customary each Halloween to set fire to the area's historic wooden bridges. The practice was discontinued only when there were no more of these landmarks left to torch.

One year I happened to be standing near a good-natured policeman who was monitoring the Halloween festivities while conversing with a particularly attractive young lady. I watched out of the corner of my eye as one of the locals, emboldened by the contents of a mickey of bootleg liquor, pulled a tomato from his pocket and casually approached the cop from behind. He drew back his arm and drove the tomato with all his might into the unsuspecting policeman's neck. It knocked his hat off and stunned him momentarily.

I will never forget the range of expression on that young man's face during the next five seconds. First there came a look of exultation as he turned to one side and began to make his escape. That look of triumph melted away instantly, to be replaced first by horror, and then by frightened resignation. Another cop, anticipating the attack, had moved in from behind and collared the perpetrator before he had a chance to disappear into the crowd. His feet never touched the ground as he was picked up and thrown bodily into the back of a nearby paddy wagon. As the van left the scene, everybody agreed that this particular gentleman was in for an unpleasant evening.

Although I never had problems with the local police, it always seemed quite reasonable to me that somebody who picked a fight with a cop should be thumped resoundingly and sent on their way. In fact, I could not understand why anyone would be stupid enough to want to fight the police in the first place. The Chicago Democratic Convention aside, many young people from my generation still had respect for authority.

When I was in my teens, I heard stories about the infamous

Vancouver Police jail elevator from acquaintances who had traveled across Canada. It was a world that was foreign to me, but still I found the idea of becoming a policeman intriguing. For a while it looked like I was heading for an engineering career, although I had spent several years working as a bouncer at the local legion and in university pubs. After dropping out of university, I hitch-hiked around the country and across Europe. I was eventually offered a job with the Vancouver Police Department while in the middle of training to be a naval officer in the Canadian Armed Forces at the Esquimalt naval base. By the time I joined the department at age 24, I felt I was ready to handle the challenge of police work.

Still, the violence I experienced firsthand on the job came as quite a shock to me. I learned rather quickly that many people didn't share my small town concept of the policeman as someone you respect and obey. In fact, one of my first lessons was administered by an unassuming lady we arrested for shop-lifting on Granville Street. Store security caught her after a short foot chase and held her until our arrival.

I had no trouble talking her into the back of the wagon. Then when the security guard pointed out that she was still wearing the fur coat she'd just stolen, I tried to convince her to give it to me so I could return it to the rightful owner. Even though I was reasonable and polite, she angrily refused my request.

Policemen fresh out of the academy need time to develop a proper presence on the street. That presence consists of a self-confident and comfortable use of the authority that comes with the badge, mixed in with common sense and a good sense of humor. Perhaps I was still using the cocky, overbearing tone that recruits sometimes adopt until they learn to vary their approach and attitude with each situation. For whatever reason, the shoplifter quickly became very hostile and aggressive, and then began swearing like a longshoreman. When I finally gave up on negotiating and climbed into the narrow compartment to retrieve the coat, she went berserk, clawing bloody furrows down the left side of my face and ripping my glasses off while I tried without much success to fend off the blows.

My upbringing left me with an aversion to hitting women, but that inhibition soon disappeared when I heard her grinding my glasses into the metal wagon floor with her boots as she continued trying to scratch out my eyes. Unfortunately, every time I tried to subdue her, my elbow would connect with the confining walls of the wagon compartment. Another policeman reached in and grabbed her arm. We finally managed to get handcuffs on her after a violent and bloody struggle.

The other officers on the scene were very amused at the spectacle once the fight was over. Although I had to endure some mild ribbing, nobody else seemed surprised at the ferocity and viciousness of her attack. I eventually learned the hard way that women are by far the dirtiest, most vicious of fighters. In fact, most policemen have a great deal of respect for their fighting ability.

It is also an unfortunate fact of life that when citizens watch police scuffling with a woman, they inevitably sympathize with the female and are often quick to make a second-hand complaint against the officers involved, regardless of the circumstances. Driving back to the station at a crawl because I couldn't see the road without my glasses left me with a new respect for the fighting prowess of the fairer sex.

***

Another of my early altercations was a very humbling experience. It began when I got into a dispute with a prisoner I was moving from one floor of the jail to another, by way of the elevator. He was much smaller than me, and also much more obnoxious. As the elevator doors opened on the fifth floor, the two of us rolled out onto the concrete floor, all the while punching and kicking each other. I did my best to choke him, but unfortunately that left one arm free. My vision clouded as a lucky punch connected with my nose, causing it to bleed profusely.

Because I was on top, my nose spewed blood all over him. That amused the officer I was working with at the time so much that he had difficulty helping me out in any meaningful way. The drunk suffered no injuries, and went to his cell with a smirk on his face knowing that he had bloodied one of Vancouver's finest. My partner insisted on calling the rest of the jail staff to our floor in order to show them the bloody evidence of my fighting prowess, or lack of same. It was not one of my better moments.

***

People assume that police are highly trained in the art of self-defense, but when I went through the academy, nothing could be further from the truth. We learned a few simple come-along holds that were supposed to help us control someone resisting arrest. We were also taught how to handcuff a suspect. The rest of our time was spent running and swimming and doing pushups.

There is no easy way to train someone with a middle class upbringing to deal with the kind of vicious, crazed attackers he or she is certain to encounter on the job. Perhaps a highly-skilled expert in one of the martial arts might have a slight advantage on the street, but it takes many years of intensive training to achieve that level of expertise. There are no secret holds, moves or punches that offer a distinct advantage to a policeman in a fight, at least none that we were ever taught. It would be safe to say that many policemen are just as out of shape and unskilled at fisticuffs as the rest of the population. Although the training has improved a bit since I joined up, the most valuable lessons about self-defense are still learned on the street, the hard way.

The law does allow a police officer to use the minimum amount of force necessary to effect an arrest, and in the academy recruits are lectured exhaustively on the proper use of force under the Criminal Code. Unfortunately, real life situations allow a cop only seconds to react, and even less time to remember all the relevant legal precedents learned during training.

A wise police officer learns how to size up the situation immediately upon arrival at a call. There is seldom time for hesitation and polite greetings. I would always ask a simple question to whomever looked like he had the biggest problem. Any question would do. "How are you doing?" was my favorite. The answer, or the tone of his or her reply, would often give me a valuable hint as to what was coming next.

It is an unfortunate fact of life that a small percentage of the hundreds of incidents police are involved in daily will result in a violent altercation. Some people fight because they're drunk; some fight because they don't particularly feel like going to jail that day; some are just vicious animals who will hurt anybody who crosses their path.

Our only advantage in a fight is that we frequently, but not always, outnumber the bad guys. The fact that we are sober while most of our opponents are not is helpful. A recruit soon learns that one-on-one does not make for a fair fight, because it is always safer for both sides if the cops outnumber the crooks while fighting them. With enough help on hand to assist in the arrest, a policeman can use less-harmful tactics and still ensure his own safety. While there are some officers with boxing training who can pummel an opponent to his knees, all policemen must consider the fact that they wear a gun which can be used against them if it inadvertently leaves its holster during a fight.

After the first few altercations, an officer learns how to read situations more accurately and to anticipate trouble before it starts. There were times when my instincts warned me I was about to be clobbered by someone I was dealing with. A preemptive strike was then necessary to prevent a sudden alteration of my facial features. I found those kind of instinctive reactions to a perceived threat difficult, but not impossible, to explain months later in court.

Individual officers have to learn the hard way which techniques work best for them. For instance, while escorting unruly fighters out of crowded beer parlors, I discovered an effective way to control prisoners who were reluctant to cooperate. Often they had to be removed quickly and cleanly so that nobody else in the bar had an opportunity to join in. The easiest method was to grab them by the hair on the back of their head and steer them toward the nearest exit. Quite simply, wherever the head goes, the rest of the body must follow. The downside was that this tactic appears brutal to the general public, even though it is perfectly humane and harmless.

Although we were issued blackjacks when we joined the department, nobody ever carried them. For many years we weren't allowed to use wooden nightsticks, apparently because there was concern the media might make an issue of it. When nightsticks were finally issued, the beat patrolmen who needed them the most were still not allowed to carry them for over a year because of image concerns. Many of us preferred using heavy metal flashlights for protection anyway. I carried mine all the time. Just holding it in my hand, at the ready, was often enough to deter potential assailants.

***

Of course handcuffs are extremely useful for controlling suspects. As I gained experience, I made it a practice to handcuff everybody I arrested as soon as possible. Even those I did not perceive as a threat found themselves wearing steel bracelets until they arrived at the jail. I saw too many policemen punched by their prisoners when their attention wandered momentarily. The cuffs also made it more difficult for prisoners to run away, although more than one suspect has escaped from the police while handcuffed behind his back.

Handcuffs are not an infallible method of securing prisoners. It is not uncommon for budding Houdini understudies to secrete a handcuff key or lock pick on their person. An agile prisoner has no difficulty bringing his handcuffed wrists from back to front by slipping them under his legs. He then has limited use of his hands in front of him; which poses an increased risk to the police. Even if the cuffs remain on and behind a prisoner's back, a violent suspect can do a lot of damage with a head butt to the face. This is known to rugby players as a "Scottish handshake" when it is done face-to-face.

While still a rookie, I was assigned to transport a transsexual to jail after he was arrested for robbery. The arresting officer had handcuffed him before he was placed in the wagon as he was familiar with the prisoner's foul disposition and violent reputation. As I opened up the back door of the wagon at the rear of headquarters, he threw the handcuffs in my face, hitched up his skirt and attempted to make a run for it. We found out later he had used a broken pen refill to pick the handcuff locks.

I managed to grab him by one arm as he clawed at my eyes and fought desperately to break loose. I ended up swinging the prisoner bodily through the air in a circle, hoping that eventually a wall would intervene and knock the fight out of him. The door at the back of the station opened just at that moment. An unsuspecting police officer emerged to be suddenly confronted by the world's ugliest flying object spinning in his direction out of the darkness. In an effort to ward off this startling apparition, he reflexively threw up his fists. One of them connected solidly with the transsexual's forehead, knocking the fight out of him and ending the struggle.

The officer merely shrugged off the incident without even breaking stride. As I walked the prisoner into the well-lit jail lobby, I began to sense that something was wrong when he started screeching like an injured dog. A deep cut on his forehead sprayed blood in every direction as he screamed in my face, attracting a supervisor whose curiosity was now well and truly aroused. Fortunately, he recognized my prisoner and remarked that he was well aware of the prisoner's violent reputation.

The officer we'd met at the rear of the station approached me later on and mentioned in passing that if there was a problem I should just send the Internal Investigations Squad detectives to him for an explanation. As a rookie, I appreciated the offer far more than he may have thought. Even at that stage of my career I was aware that incidents like this could quickly mushroom into a nightmarish situation, even though we had done nothing wrong. As it turned out, this time there were no repercussions.

***

As far as I'm concerned, there is no such thing as a fair fight when someone demonstrates serious intent to harm a police officer. In the end, the only thing that matters is winning. Losing a fight with a dangerous suspect could mean being disarmed, and that could ulti-mately result in fatal injuries. I can remember seeing film footage of prison inmates practicing methods of disarming policemen during a face-to-face confrontation. Too many policemen are killed with their own weapons.

I didn't hesitate to use whatever methods were necessary to protect myself. I was confident that I could justify that use of force in a court room later, should that prove necessary. It should be pointed out that some violent tactics are, of necessity, used only sparingly by police officers. For example, hitting someone on the head is avoided except as a last resort because of the potential danger a head injury poses. Any injury to a suspect's head is often immortalized for posterity in a color mug shot, because anyone charged with a serious criminal offense is usually photographed and printed in the jail immediately after their arrest. Defense lawyers love to bring copies of those pictures into court in order to elicit sympathy for their clients.

Defending oneself from an attack by an aggressive suspect was, at best, a necessary evil. There was often a fine line between self-defense and the use of excessive force. It was important to remember that society, the courts and the department were always standing over your shoulder, waiting to pounce should there ever be the slightest indication that line was crossed.

I rarely had to resort to punching people in the face, even though during my twelve years on the job I was involved in literally thousands of altercations. One particular incident happened at the end of a busy night shift. I was exhausted by that time, but en route to the station I stopped to cover another officer assigned to a disturbance call at the front of an old house in the West End. The fight was over by the time we got there.

I stood on the stairs directly in front of a seated bystander, waiting for the assigned unit to obtain details for his report. I talked briefly with the bystander, but since he wasn't directly involved in the altercation, I focused my attention on the original suspects at the top of the stairs. Although the bystander was obviously drunk, he seemed docile and I was not expecting trouble from him.

Suddenly, for no reason, he kicked me from his sitting position. His foot caught me squarely between the legs, and the intense pain took my breath away. Even though I was tired, my reflexes were still intact. I instinctively reached way back and punched him solidly in the face. I heard his nose break and blood started dripping from both nostrils. The fight ended as quickly as it started.

I had no trouble putting handcuffs on him. He immediately apologized profusely for what he'd done, stating in a distinctly nasal voice that he had no idea why the incident had occurred. I was desperately tired, and I did not relish the idea of taking him to the hospital to get his nose straightened and then spending two hours writing the Crown Counsel reports. Therefore, I eventually decided we were even and let him walk away. He had no previous record, and the matter ended there.

***

Another violent incident was just as unpredictable. I stopped a prostitute who worked the Granville Mall area to question her about a recent trick rip-off. She was not usually belligerent when I checked her, although she and her pimp were notorious for hundreds of strong-armings they had perpetrated over the years. Most of their victims were originally her tricks. Her criminal career peaked but did not end during one subsequent incident where a seemingly docile victim had suddenly panicked in the middle of one of their tag-team robberies and acciden-tally ran her over with his car.

On this day I asked her first about the whereabouts of her pimp. I discovered that he was presently pumping iron during one of his annual vacations inside Oakalla prison. She took offense at my sugges-tion that she would soon join him there if I got my way, and showed her displeasure by suddenly flicking a burning cigarette butt into my face.

It bounced off my glasses as I ducked. At the same time, my reflexes took over and I threw a punch in her direction which connected with just enough force to quiet her down momentarily. The glancing blow did no noticeable damage to her face, but I'm sure it must have smarted. As she was put into the paddy wagon for a trip to the drunk tank, she regaled the wagon driver with a stinging assessment of my pugilistic skills. "This pig punches like a goddamn sissy. He couldn't even knock out a girl!"

***

Yet another incident occurred in front of a hostile audience. It was a typically busy Friday night and my partner and I were working the West End in plainclothes. We attended a riot in a downtown bar that involved a dozen or so drunken football players. Anyone who crossed their path was fair game, so there was lots of action, as well as lots of blood, in and around the bar.

As was usually the case in the early hours of Saturday morning, everyone in the downtown area seemed to be intoxicated. The bar was empty when we arrived. We located the football players by following blood trails down the sidewalk. To get their attention and defuse a potentially explosive situation, we then arrested their ringleader for drunkenness in a public place.

As the prisoner stepped reluctantly into the back of the wagon, he paused to turn and address the crowd. Although I believe strongly in

25

freedom of speech, the last thing I needed was an exhortation to his friends that they should rise up against the authorities. I was acutely aware that we were grossly outnumbered by drunken behemoths who were incapable of rational thought and thus dangerously susceptible to suggestion.

As the prisoner gathered his wits together to make a farewell call to arms, I cracked him gently on the top of his skull with just enough force to make him flinch. As he ducked, I nudged him with my foot into the compartment and closed the door behind him, effectively ending the uprising before it could be instigated. Without their leader, the crowd began to disperse almost immediately.

As I turned to leave, a face in the crowd suddenly jumped out at me. I saw the bloated features of a senior commissioned officer who was well known then as a strict disciplinarian. He was also reputed to be a man without a sense of humor.

Apparently he was in the middle of a divorce at the time. Rumors had circulated that he was so lonely at nights he would climb into his company car and drive to calls he overheard on his police radio, hoping to find some breach of discipline on the part of officers attending these calls. He looked me over carefully, as if memorizing my face, then walked away disgustedly with his nose in the air.

As I waited nervously for parade the next day, I was concerned that the high-ranking officer might have misinterpreted my love tap as use of unnecessary force. Sure enough, someone spread a rumor that he'd written a scathing memo to be read out on parade that day. I anticipated it with growing alarm.

The memo was anticlimactic. Instead of chastising me, he found something far more sinister to complain about. Several uniformed members who had covered our call, he wrote, had been seen without their hats on. He reiterated the vital importance of wearing hats and ties in order to preserve the image of the department, and promised that in the future, offenders would be severely disciplined. Since we had worked plainclothes, we were safe from any repercussions arising from the memo. We went out on patrol that night with a clear conscience, grateful that our ever-vigilant management team had once again shown us the importance of adherence to the all important dress code regulations.

***

Nostalgia, as they say, just ain't what it used to be. I have the distinct impression, however, that most of the fight calls we attended in 1975 were far less violent than the fights we broke up when I left the job a dozen years later. The beer parlor mini-riots were always loud and raucous, and there were often piles of broken glass and bodies on the floors when we arrived. Injuries in the seventies were usually superficial and the problems ended when we carted away the participants for a night in the drunk tank. Most of the miscreants awoke from their revelry with only a hangover, because a night in the tank did not mean they acquired a criminal record.

During my first year on the job I was called to the Hotel Vancouver lobby one evening to deal with a drunk annoying the staff. He turned out to be a logger about my size, very drunk but obviously in good physical condition. I was still learning how to be a policeman, so when he refused to leave after I asked him politely, I was temporarily at a loss for words. When I put my hand on his shoulder to escort him out of the lobby, the fight was on.

During the altercation that followed, a man in a fancy black suit approached me twice and asked politely if he could be of assistance. I had no idea who he was, but I turned down his help each time, stubbornly determined to make the arrest by myself.

The two of us wrestled on the floor of the hotel lobby for about ten minutes until his strength finally started to fade. We ended up fighting on the front stairs at the entranceway on busy Georgia Street with me sitting on top of him, banging his head repeatedly into the concrete so I could get him handcuffed. I got one cuff on, but by this time I no longer had enough strength left to attach it to his other wrist. The man in the suit had disappeared and my fighter was still struggling, so I finally yielded to common sense and used my portable radio to have another car drop by and help me slip the last handcuff on.

I subsequently learned that the helpful man in the black suit was with hotel security. Apparently my stubbornness was the subject of much amusement when the area cars heard the story from him later after I cleared the call. I vowed then and there that I would never let my pride get in the way of requesting backup whenever necessary.

***

My partner and I received a call to St. Paul's Hospital emergency ward about a drunk annoying the staff. He had apparently entered the emergency ward the hard way by crashing through one of their glass doors. A nurse informed us that the drunk was a giant of a man, and that he was waiting for us around the corner. His size was indeed intimidating. He was also twice as drunk as he was huge, and three times as stupid. He stood defiantly with his back to the wall and introduced himself by informing us that he did not, under any circumstances, feel

27

like going to jail tonight.

We did not want to fight this man, and there weren't enough policemen working in the entire city to carry him off to jail. It was time for Officer Friendly to take control of the situation. In a very pleasant tone of voice, I said, "We're going to give you a break tonight. We're going to handcuff you in the front instead of behind your back, but only because you're such a nice guy."

Very gently, but as quickly as possible, we placed the cuffs around one meaty wrist and then the other as he tried to make up his mind how to respond to our polite request. The handcuffs were barely big enough to fit. The drunk was bewildered by this gentle treatment, having obviously expected a brawl. Before he could form the intent to object, he found himself securely handcuffed and under arrest.

The prisoner almost flattened the tires of the wagon he stepped into. The load was so heavy we felt obliged to warn the driver that his front end would be a little light for this trip to the drunk tank. We seized a rifle and replica revolver that the drunk had hidden inside his pickup truck.

***

During the time we walked a beat on the Granville Mall, my partner and I were always conscious of projecting the proper image to the criminal element we dealt with. This was especially important inside some of the seedier beer parlors. While a liberal activist might describe a policeman's tough demeanor as machismo or power-tripping, we knew that our safety often depended on the way we handled different situations. Many of the patrons inside these beer parlors were openly hostile to the police, and they always outnumbered us. What that meant was that if someone made a point of confronting us, he had to be dealt with firmly and appropriately.

Our reaction to a direct challenge to our authority was always watched carefully by everyone present. The rare policeman who showed fear, or who failed to back up another member during an altercation, soon acquired a bad name on both sides of the Thin Blue Line. He would inevitably run into problems on the street with trouble-makers who were more than willing to take advantage of any weakness in his character. At the same time, other policemen who learned of his reputation were reluctant to depend on him at calls he covered.

It is often said that you can smell fear, and there is much truth in that. I have seen people so surprised upon being confronted suddenly by the police that they lost control of their bowels. In fact, a police dog sometimes follows fear scent when tracking a criminal fleeing on foot after the commission of a crime. Therefore, a policeman learns to disguise any overt signs of his own fear, or lack of confidence, in order to gain the respect of the people he is dealing with. A lone policeman confronting an unruly mob will be watched closely by potential trouble-makers for any sign of weakness. It is often only the officer's calm demeanor and authoritative bearing that allows him to influence their behavior. Should he fail to project an image they can respect, or at least fear, he will quickly find himself trampled underfoot. This posturing, by the way, is sometimes mistakenly perceived as arrogance when it slips out during a routine traffic stop.

When I was first assigned to a walking beat with a regular partner, a drinker inside one of the toughest bars in our area soon put us to the test during an otherwise quiet walk-through. As we approached the exit door to leave, a full beer bottle sailed over our heads and disintegrated against the juke box. By the time we turned around, the place was as silent and peaceful as a monastery. I'd never before seen so much feigned innocence or lack of expression, and it was clear that a spontaneous confession on the part of the culprit was unlikely. Nor was there any possibility of obtaining fingerprints off what little was left of the broken bottle.

I've been hit in the face with a beer bottle, and I can vouch for the painful damage it can cause as it shatters. Had we walked out of there without taking any action, our nightly visits to that premise would have deteriorated rapidly into one confrontation after another. The regulars would soon spread the word that we failed to respond to this challenge to our authority. We had to do something, but we had no idea who threw the bottle. Our alternatives were, to say the least, limited.

Without further ado, we immediately walked up to the likeliest looking candidate, slapped handcuffs on him and dragged him out of the bar. At the same time, we made it very clear to everyone that this particular individual had been selected at random to atone for the sins of the guilty party.

He proclaimed his innocence immediately, but we explained to him that someone had to go to jail for the offense as an example to others who might contemplate repeating that type of behavior. He heartily agreed that it was wrong to throw bottles at the local beat cops. Understanding our concern, he thought the matter over for a moment and then promptly fingered one of his fellow patrons as the culprit. We removed the handcuffs and sent him on his way. Of course he wouldn't have been charged with anything anyway. We found the man who'd actually thrown the bottle at us making his way out the back door moments later, and put him in jail when we uncovered outstanding warrants for his arrest.

Undoubtedly this arbitrary abuse of our authority would not meet with the approval of most lawyers. It certainly would have been difficult to explain had the man we originally arrested complained. Neither of us felt very good about what we'd done, but the thought of fighting our way through that bar each night to regain lost respect made the alternative we'd chosen much easier to live with.

Coincidentally, the alleged suspect in that case turned out to be a crook we had arrested once before. We hadn't recognized him at first because he fancied himself as somewhat of a chameleon and had changed his appearance since we'd last checked him. He also fit the profile of a bank robbery suspect on the loose at the time, so we sent his name to the detectives in case he was responsible.

***

When you see so much real-life violence as a cop, it is easy to forget that most citizens judge police-related incidents in terms of what they've seen in television cop shows, or perhaps their childhood fights in the schoolyard. I lost track of the number of times I'd be struggling with a fighter, perhaps a drunk or some unruly miscreant resisting arrest, only to hear bystanders complaining angrily about police brutality. In fact, I have been involved in several altercations where I was doing my damnedest to subdue a violent suspect, only to have bystanders who had nothing to do with the incident march up to demand my badge number so they could make an official complaint about my conduct. At first I was surprised by this reaction, and more than once I searched my soul trying to identify what, if anything, I was doing wrong.

Was this a legitimate arrest? Yes. Was I using too much force? No. Had I caused the problem in the first place? Never. Well, almost never. I do have a sense of humor, after all, and I have always felt free to express my opinion, no matter how distasteful that might have been to the person I was addressing. Inevitably some people objected to my remarks, and a few individuals unwisely expressed their disagreement by throwing a punch. Nevertheless, I didn't deliberately instigate fights.

Was I lacking in public relations skills? All modesty aside, the answer to that would have to be a resounding no, although I suspect one or two of my supervisors might disagree. I disliked most of the crooks I dealt with, and I had difficulty disguising my contempt for them. However, on more than one occasion I turned potentially controversial situations into minor public relations coups for the department.

For instance, I once covered a policeman who still had much to learn about tact during an arrest at a crowded beach. He had tried to collar two rambunctious drunks by himself, and the fight was on. By the time I got there, he was in deep trouble. The crowd, for whatever reason, was decidedly hostile toward him, and nobody was offering to help. I knew it was not going to be an easy call when disgruntled citizens began asking for my badge number before I even arrived at the policeman's side. Breaking my portable radio over the head of one of the culprits as I subdued him did not make me any more popular with this crowd.

By the time we dragged these two jerks into the back of my wagon, indignant Vancouverites were actually lining up to complain about our behavior. It looked like the Internal Investigations Squad waiting room was going to be pretty crowded come Monday morning. Then one of the suspects started kicking loudly against the back doors of the wagon while screaming obscenities and threats at us and at the curious bystanders around us. I noticed that almost everyone in the group involuntarily took a step backward as soon as the disturbance started. The crowd went silent and their concern was evident when one citizen asked timidly, "What did they do, officer?"

"Murder," I replied with my straightest face, knowing the miscreants inside the wagon would forgive for this outrageous slur on their character by the time they sobered up. Now some people in the crowd were actually cringing each time the suspects banged on the wagon doors. One woman asked in a concerned voice, "Can they get out of there?"

I sucked in my beer belly and placed my hands on my hips in a woefully inadequate imitation of John Wayne. "Don't worry, ma'am. They're going straight to jail. You have nothing more to fear from them."

There were no more complaints from this crowd, and some of them even wandered by to congratulate us on our arrests. Many said, "You couldn't pay me enough to do your job," a phrase I was to hear thousands of times during my career.

**

Another incident that could have turned into a disaster for me happened during a particularly beautiful spring day. I was assigned to cover other units who were checking out a report that a drunk was annoying passersby in an East End neighborhood. As I pulled up, the drunk punched a policeman who was interviewing him and then bolted for freedom. My endurance during a foot pursuit was always limited at best, but I took a short cut with my car and managed to catch him in the middle of some bushes.

A struggle ensued, and my quarry, to be frank, got the worst of it. As I fought to handcuff him, I could hear a woman circling the bush area, screaming at the top of her lungs, "The cop's beating him up! I can hear him beating the guy up! Everybody come and be a witness!"

When we emerged from the bushes, my prisoner, a career criminal I recognized from previous arrests, looked somewhat the worse for wear. The lady was soon joined by her husband. Encouraged by the arrival of reinforcements, she planted herself in front of us and screamed in my face. "You beat him up! I can see the marks, pig! I knew it! I want your badge number! I'll have you fired for this!"

The prisoner ignored her, but I was furious. "Nobody got beat up here, lady. You make a false allegation about me, and I'll sue you for everything you're worth. I hope you don't mind losing your house."

I saw her husband put his hand on her shoulder to leave, but she was having none of it. She turned to the prisoner and pointed in my direction. "This pig beat you up, didn't he? I know he did!"

I will admit to feeling a sensation of impending doom. At this point the drunken villain could have accused me of carrying out the Lindbergh kidnapping and she would have cheerfully verified the allegation.

The prisoner fixed her with an icy stare. "Nobody got beat up, lady. Now why don't you piss off and mind your own business." Her husband dragged her away, and I could hear her yelling threats against me all the way to her house.

As I turned to the prisoner, my hostility toward his previous antisocial behavior receded. "You know you could have caused me problems. Why didn't you?"

He laughed. "I did something stupid with that other cop because I was drunk, and I got what was coming to me. I got no complaints. You were just doing your job." The wagon driver pulled up at that point, and I had him drive my prisoner home to sober up.

***

I had similar problems while working by myself one day in the skids. I was flagged down by a citizen who pointed out two drunks who had just rolled an elderly Chinese gentleman for the contents of his wallet. The bloodied victim was seated on a nearby curb. The two suspects started off in different directions as soon as they saw me. I grabbed each by an arm and the fight began. I tried to control them both and ask for assistance on my portable radio at the same time, but it

32

wasn't long before I realized I was in trouble.

Not one bystander offered to help. I started hearing the usual cries of "police brutality," even though all the elements of the scenario in front of them should have been enough to convince even the most cynical of citizens that, in this instance, I was wearing the white hat. The innocent victim was still sitting there, bleeding from his forehead. There was a witness beside us who was yelling that the old man had been robbed. The odds of two against one should have made me the underdog. Regardless, the verbal abuse continued until the suspects were finally overpowered and locked inside the paddy wagon.

***

Polls show that an overwhelming majority of our citizens support the police, but I think it would be more accurate to state that they appreciate having someone to do their dirty work for them. Clearly most of our citizens enthusiastically endorse the work that police officers do, at least up to the point where something goes wrong. Then they generally prefer to wash their hands of any further responsibility, in my opinion.

***

I'm sure most responsible citizens believe that any form of violence is unacceptable in our civilized society, but in real life some justifiable assaults never make it to a courtroom. I attended a service station on the corner of Terminal and Main Street at around three in the morning for an assault call. There was a trail of broken street signs and overturned newspaper boxes leading to the scene. I found two battered and bloodied victims on the pavement, waiting impatiently for medical help and whining for the police to take some type of action against their attackers.

It took a while to sort out what had really happened. Eventually we were able to determine that our two victims, both very drunk and obnoxious, had vandalized the neighborhood as they walked home from a bar. Both had lengthy criminal records. When they reached the service station, they stopped to hassle two young couples pumping self-serve gas for their car. When the intrepid duo picked a fight, the two young ladies locked themselves in the car and their companions set out to defend their honor. They were both college athletes, and in short order they literally kicked the stuffing out of the two drunken rounders.

I met the victims at the hospital later as they were sobering up and licking their wounds. Between sobs and moans they arrogantly demanded that their attackers be jailed immediately. It was difficult to keep a straight face as I tried to explain to them how slowly the wheels of justice turned, and how I wouldn't even want to take a statement from them until they sobered up. I promised I'd be in touch, and for all I know they are still waiting.

***

I encountered much the same situation in the largely-ethnic, working class neighborhoods of the East End. Junkies often broke into houses there at night while the occupants slept. Often the head of the household would awaken to find a burglar going through his belongings. Their first reaction was to take care of the problem themselves, and then call the police to clean up the remains. These homeowners had worked hard for what little they owned, and they were usually more than willing to defend their families with their lives.

By the time the police were notified, the burglar was usually quite pacified, albeit rather difficult to identify under the clotted blood. The conversations were usually much the same.

"Officer, I caught this guy breaking into my house and beat the shit out of him. What are you gonna do with him?"

"Oh, we'll be happy to put him in jail after he gets his face put back together in the hospital. Now, you say you were in fear for your safety and had to use minimal force to protect yourself from this man?"

"That bastard? I am not afraid of assholes like him. He broke into my house, so I beat the shit out of him. What's wrong with that?"

"No. No. No. What you mean is, you had to use force to defend yourself against him. Right?"

"Oh yeah, right. I see what you mean. You're right. But I guess he won't be breaking into any houses for a while, eh?"

"No, I wouldn't think so. Not until he gets off crutches, at any rate. Please feel free to call us again any time you find more customers." It was nice to play to an appreciative audience.

***

I ran into a similar situation where a rounder from the skid road area wandered into an East Indian restaurant and decided to dine and dash, or eat-no-pay as we used to call it. Unfortunately for him, the restaurant was staffed by militant Sikhs who, rumor had it, were receiving paramilitary training before returning to India to fight government troops. When I found him ten minutes later, he was at the bottom of a whirlwind of activity, similar to the tornado created by the Tasmanian Devil in a Bugs Bunny cartoon. I'd seen a similar tornado once before when a suspect we were chasing on foot inadvertently stumbled into the path of a carload of Drug Squad members.

When the action finally subsided, there were several athletic-looking Sikhs in turbans standing quietly beside their prisoner. He resembled a crumpled pile of debris on the ground. It was apparent that his knowledge of geography was second only to his skill in self defense when his only comment on the episode, in between spitting out newly loosened teeth, was, "But they're only Pakis. I didn't think they were that tough." Word circulated through the skids quickly, and I never did hear of another eat-no-pay at that restaurant.

***

Perhaps the most embarrassing off-duty incident I was ever involved in came early in my career. I stopped off at a corner store on my way home from a party. As I walked back to the milk cooler, a grubby-looking young man staggered into the store, knocking over displays and screaming obscenities. The girl behind the counter was frightened, so when I walked up to the till I advised her that I'd stand by while she called the police.

I didn't identify myself as a police officer because I didn't want to arrest this drunk on my own time. On the other hand, I couldn't leave her there alone with a violent drunk. Fortunately for me, the problem seemed to solve itself. Before she completed the call to 911, the drunk somehow managed to find his own way out, leaving a trail of stolen chocolate bars behind him.

I was relieved the matter had ended peacefully, having heard many times about the perils of getting involved in off-duty incidents. My reprieve ended when I emerged from the store and found the drunk lying on top of my Austin Mini in the parking lot, vomiting on the hood and urinating into his pants. I was tired and very reluctant to become involved, but I had to do something about him now. I pulled him off my car and deposited him on the sidewalk so I could make a clean getaway. He was still very aggressive, and he managed to kick me in the shins as I moved him.

Congratulating myself for handling the situation so deftly, I was about to limp back to my Mini when I caught sight of the drunk crawling groggily on his hands and knees across busy West Fourth Avenue, where a continuous stream of traffic threatened to end his promising drinking career. I couldn't leave him to his fate now, because as a cop I was technically on duty 24 hours a day. Had anybody witnessed me tossing him off my car, I would no doubt face some awkward questions at an inquest if a passing motorist subsequently ran him over.

I pulled him back onto the sidewalk as a car narrowly missed him. He objected, mumbling something about suicide. The fight was on, and we wrestled on the sidewalk for five minutes. At one point I grabbed his leg to prevent him from crawling back into traffic again. He then tried to jerk out of my grip. I suddenly found myself holding a plastic artificial leg, while he continued crawling into heavy traffic on his three remaining limbs.

I knocked some sense into the drunken amputee and pinned him to the ground until he finally passed out from his exertions. I then phoned for a wagon from the store, but I was told that they were all busy and I'd just have to wait my turn like everyone else. As they say, you can never find a cop when you need one. It was a good half an hour until I finally got rid of my prisoner. The incident became my favorite contribution when the conversation at coffee turned to the topic of off-duty arrests.

***

I know one Vancouverite who has an interesting war story of her own as a result of an incident she and I were involved in. She had picked up a young man in a bar and then offered to drive him home in her fancy sports car at the end of the evening. As she got to know him better during the car ride, she soon discovered that he was a jerk. Having had enough of his crude behavior, she pulled over at Main and Pender and ordered him to get out.

He refused, so she removed her car keys and walked one block to the police station at Main and Hastings for assistance. I happened to be at the Public Information Counter on another call when she walked in. I'd already spent a busy and violent Friday evening policing the skids, and the night was only half over.

She was very upset and frightened when she asked me to escort her back to her car and get rid of her unwanted passenger, and I really did feel sorry for her. I had reports to write, but I agreed to help, thinking that it would only take a couple of minutes.

As we walked south on Main, several bottles thrown in our direction exploded near us on the sidewalk. The projectiles had originated from a group of five or six drunks standing by the bus stop on the other side of the street. Had I been in a better mood, I would have called for additional units and arrested them. However, it was extremely busy at that time of night, and I was well aware that by the time cover arrived the suspects would be long gone.

Instead, I told her to stay where she was and then charged directly at the group. They obviously had not expected a frontal attack, and froze in their tracks. I barged into them at full speed and luckily managed to knock them all down at once like bowling pins. I didn't

36

stick around to savor my strike, and none of them tried to follow us as we started off again in the direction of her car. As we approached we could see her passenger door was open. The good news was that the unwanted guest was nowhere to be seen. The bad news was that in the five minutes she'd been away from the car, someone had ripped her stereo out of the dash, leaving a tangled mass of wires hanging where once a mighty Blaupunkt had blared. She was in shock by now, and just managed to choke out a quick thank you before driving off into the rather dubious safety of the night.

Chapter Three
HOT PURSUIT

There are few aspects of police work that consistently create more controversy than high-speed pursuits. When something goes wrong during a car chase, some in the media are quick to condemn the police while ignoring the fact that all too often there is no practical alternative. Unfortunately, no one has ever come up with a workable solution to the problem. The issue continues to receive regular and hostile exposure in the media as each incident makes headlines for two to three days and then fades away, only to be resurrected as background for the next pursuit accident story.

Those who would abolish police pursuits choose to ignore the fact that many dangerous criminals use vehicles as a means to escape arrest. If police are denied the option of chasing these suspects, then it becomes a simple matter for the crooks to increase the speed at which they travel during their getaway, thus virtually guaranteeing themselves immunity from capture.

Of course, many chases involve only minor infractions of the law. Typically an individual who has had a few drinks too many is caught speeding: if he decides he does not want to pull over and face the consequences, the chase is on. Critics of the police argue that in these instances the offender should be allowed to proceed once the vehicle's license plate number is noted. Theoretically, the driver can then be served with a summons at a later date, once the name of the registered owner is obtained from the Motor Vehicle Branch. This is not as simple as it sounds, because, in reality, once the pursuit is broken off, the probability of successfully prosecuting the individual driving the car is almost nil.

Often getting close enough to a speeding vehicle to read its license plate is not as easy as it sounds, since it is necessary to greatly exceed the offender's speed just to catch up. So even this plan necessitates a pursuit, however brief, in order to succeed. If the car subsequently turns out to be stolen, and car theft is definitely a growing concern these days, authorities have effectively forfeited any opportunity to bring the thief before the courts by prematurely halting the chase.

Some critics believe that police officers don't need to chase speeding cars because they can use their police radio instead. According to this argument, there is a viable alternative to high-speed pursuits so they should be banned outright. Even some policemen have repeated this stupid cliché to the media, leaving the public with the mistaken impression that police can avoid pursuits simply by keying their microphones. No one ever elaborates on what is supposed to happen next, although the cop presumably uses his radio to have another car apprehend the suspect vehicle, using some different but unspecified method that is safer than a high-speed pursuit. An alternative cited by some experts is the use of roadblocks.

In twelve years of police service, I have only heard of one chase that was successfully terminated with a roadblock. In that particular incident, a fleeing vehicle chose to attempt his escape by way of the Lions Gate Bridge toward the North Shore. Our members were able to alert the West Vancouver Police in time for them to block off all three lanes of traffic at mid-span. As the suspect proceeded northbound over the bridge, he was greeted by West Vancouver officers with shotguns. The only way he could escape was to jump into the harbor, which was hundreds of feet below. He chose to surrender.

One factor that proponents of the roadblock method ignore is that in a city like Vancouver, there are an infinite number of escape routes available to a suspect attempting to elude capture. There are usually only a few police units involved in most chases, so there is little chance of setting up an effective roadblock in time. Even if the police are lucky enough to cordon off the right roadway, it is easy for the suspect to drive onto the sidewalk or boulevard, bypass squad cars and spike belts, then continue on his merry way.

It would be simpler if police were permitted to use lethal force to terminate a potentially disastrous chase in order to prevent a tragedy that might involve innocent citizens. In that case, roadblocks only have to slow the progress of a speeding vehicle so that it can be disabled with a shotgun blast fired at the wheels. It is unlikely, however, that politicians would authorize such drastic tactics.

In short, roadblocks seldom work in a city environment. On the other hand, police patrolling highways may be able to use their special spiked barriers in some roadblock configurations if they have enough time to set up.

It is easy to explain why high-speed chases occur; it is difficult to justify the consequences when innocent people get caught in the middle. I have seen what happens when things go wrong during these incidents. The resulting carnage is difficult to forget. I know someone who was seriously injured as a result of his inadvertent involvement in a police chase. He happened to be in the wrong place at the wrong time when a policeman from another municipality attempted to pull over a vehicle which had passed him at high speed. Somehow the police unit collided with the bystander's car while trying to catch up with the violator. The violator got away. The bystander was less fortunate. He sustained serious injuries as a result of the collision, and now his life will never be the same.

I participated in many high-speed chases during my career, and I also experienced one police pursuit from the perspective of a frightened citizen caught in the middle. I was driving through another municipality one evening, en route to work, when I heard the roar of a car's engine through my open window just as I approached an intersection. Although the light was green for me, I instinctively slammed on my brakes. I came to a stop just as a car roared through the red light from my right, narrowly missing my front bumper by about a foot.

The driver, perhaps realizing at the last second that he was going through a red light, panicked and slammed on his brakes in the middle of the intersection. It was just enough to cause him to skid sideways in a cloud of tire smoke. He apparently changed his mind when he realized that he wasn't going to hit me, floored the gas pedal and continued on his way. I didn't get a good look at the license plate or the driver, so I was of no use as a witness.

I looked quickly to my right. Seeing nobody coming, I continued on my way after checking whether the light was still green. I just managed to clear the intersection as an unmarked police car roared through the red light, chasing the vehicle that had almost hit me. Some unmarked cars hide their sirens behind the radiator grill, making them less effective. Nevertheless, I should have seen it coming, and I didn't.

It was a valuable and enlightening experience for me. In fact, it helped to explain the stupid behavior of some of the motorists who ignored my emergency lights and sirens during chases. Quite often things happen so quickly that the average citizen just doesn't have time to react to the sound of sirens coming their way. My own close call certainly reinforced my healthy respect for the potential danger to the public during a high-speed pursuit.

I would love to provide an answer to the problem of police pursuits, but there is no easy solution. If police are forbidden to chase speeding cars, a number of new and equally dangerous scenarios will soon develop as crooks take advantage of a foolproof means of escape simply by using stolen, high-powered vehicles during the commission of crimes. Then nothing short of a serious motor vehicle accident will impair their chances of making a clean getaway.

The only alternative with any potential for success is the use of helicopters. These aircraft, along with pilots to man them, would have to be on standby at all times to assist in chases. This would be a very expensive proposition. For that reason, I suspect police helicopters will never be seriously considered by Vancouver, which has never been accused of being overly generous with equipment for its emergency services. Of course a helicopter can only monitor the progress of a speeding vehicle. It is still necessary to bring it to bay, and that invariably still involves a high-speed pursuit.

I saw a picture of one ingenious solution to the high-speed pursuit dilemma. A long-barreled .45 revolver had been incorporated into the dash of a mid-60's Texas Ranger police car, positioned so that it sat at hood level, pointing directly ahead through a small hole in the windshield. A policeman in a chase could merely reach over to his right and fire off six rounds into the suspect's trunk.

***

My first high-speed chase involved an impaired driver. My training officer and I found him speeding along Kingsway one night. He accelerated away from us when we tried to pull him over with our red and blue lights. It was a very short chase because seconds later, the driver lost control of his vehicle. He was trying to turn off onto a side street and plowed into a curb instead. No one was hurt, although he demolished his car's undercarriage, leaving the car a total write-off. After refusing a breathalyzer, he went to jail for the rest of the night.

***

Within a matter of days we had another short chase. My training officer pointed to a car stopped at an intersection. All I could see inside the passenger compartment was the top of a child's head, barely higher than the steering wheel. His driving was not bad considering that he could hardly reach the pedals. He was arrested after a short foot chase, but because he was a juvenile he was released to his parent's custody.

***

In the early hours of the morning, my partner and I left the West End to arrest a suspect in East Vancouver, well outside the boundaries of our assigned area. We monitored the East End radio channel, in addition to our own channel, during our passage through the area. As we approached our suspect's address, we overheard cars from South Vancouver switching channels to warn the East End radio operator that they were in pursuit of a stolen car, heading our way at a high rate of speed.

The stolen vehicle crossed East Broadway and neared our location at Nanaimo and First Avenue. We waited at the intersection after the pursuing unit radioed that the suspect vehicle was now eastbound on First from Commercial Street. We watched as the car and its two young occupants sped through a red light in front of us, still traveling eastbound and probably heading for a nearby entrance to the highway. Since they had left their original pursuers far behind, we decided to follow them.

The stolen car was an older Chevrolet, very popular with car thieves since it is easily hot-wired and the worn ignition switch can be operated by almost any Chev key. This car had a very powerful big-block engine, so we had trouble catching up to it. Had they taken the highway, they could have outrun us for sure. Instead, however, the suspects drove off the road into a field only a hundred feet short of the Highway One turnoff. The car bogged down in mud, so the two crooks abandoned it and fled on foot.

My partner and I, along with another officer who pulled in behind us, ran after them. The slower of the two suspects crossed the field and ran behind a house. My partner took one side of the house and I took the other. We tackled our suspect in the middle of the backyard. After a short struggle, we handcuffed the young car thief and turned him over to the police unit assigned to the call. The other suspect was soon apprehended nearby and placed in the wagon with his accomplice.

The Chevrolet turned out to be hot-wired, as evidenced by the tangle of loose ignition wires we found hanging under the dash. There were also three stolen car stereos in the back seat. The two suspects had a long history of stealing cars and had been involved in several previous car chases.

A Mountie from a neighboring detachment dropped by to help. When he heard the stolen car's engine roaring at full throttle, he checked under the dash and discovered the gas pedal jammed against the floorboard. The suspects had left the car in gear after it became mired in the field. It then dug its rear wheels deep into the soft ground until finally coming to rest on the frame. The vehicle continued spinning its tires at full throttle until the Mountie finally unraveled the spliced ignition wires to shut it off.

***

It would be fair to state that policemen have little affection for the City Hall bean counters responsible for purchasing police equipment. One year, an anonymous bureaucrat decided that our department should try out police cars with six-cylinder engines. Normally, our fleet uses eight-cylinder engines that are barely adequate to move full-size police cars through normal traffic. It did not take much common sense to understand that an under-powered vehicle just would not cut it in the real world of police work. Those of us who had to work in these cars knew the experiment was doomed to fail from the start.

Unfortunately, even though the six-cylinder cars were clearly unacceptable for police service, we were left to drive a number of dangerously-under-powered patrol cars for several years until they finally fell apart. In fact, one of these cars left the patrol division prematurely, after a frustrated policeman put the transmission in neutral and left the gas pedal on the mat until he finally heard terminally-destructive noises from under the hood.

Another policeman and I were assigned one of the six-cylinder cars during a particularly chilly night shift. We found it very difficult to pull over even routine speeders with this car. Because it accelerated so slowly, we had to reach inordinately excessive speeds just to catch up and then slam on the brakes at the last second to prevent overshooting the speeder. In the eight-cylinder police cars it was relatively easy to accelerate to the same speed as routine violators, clock them for several blocks, then pull them over safely.

Just before breakfast time we observed a taxi driving southbound on Oak Street. The cabby was obviously speeding, and we guessed he was on his way to a taxi stand in a nearby municipality to end his shift. I was driving, and decided to do a U-turn and issue him a speeding ticket.

The U-turn was uneventful, but accelerating up to his speed seemed to take forever. Meanwhile, the cabby saw us turning around and decided to make a run for it. After twenty blocks, we were still not close enough to get a look at his plates or his cab number. By the time we reached the Oak Street Bridge, our speed was just starting to match his, but I had to back off a bit because there were ice patches and I was afraid of losing control. Despite reducing my speed, I almost spun out as we turned at one of the bridge exits.

We were two blocks behind when the cab finally turned down a side street and ducked into a parking lot. By the time we followed him into the lot, the cab we'd been chasing was somewhere in the middle of dozens of other identical taxis. They were all parked in rows with their engines running because the drivers were changing shifts. I was, to put it mildly, a little upset when I stormed into their office and demanded to know the identity of the driver I had just chased all the way from Vancouver.

Everyone shook their heads and claimed to have no knowledge of any car chase. Several of the drivers exchanged knowing smirks which just infuriated me even more. I informed them in no uncertain terms that I would find the culprit, no matter how many of the company's drivers I had to ticket. One driver subsequently approached us outside and pointed out a cab he believed had just pulled in. He seemed a little unsure of himself, so we decided not to follow up the information. I drove off, licking my wounds and swearing vengeance against the cab driver and the city bureaucrat responsible for buying the six-cylinder car I was driving.

I phoned the police officer responsible for taxi permits in that municipality and requested that he check into the matter for me. By a happy coincidence, my first traffic stop the next night happened to be the same cab pointed out to us the evening before by the only cooperative cabby. This time the taxi driver jumped a red light when he saw there was no traffic coming and sped off down Granville Street at almost double the speed limit, oblivious to our presence behind him.

As I awarded him a matching pair of tickets, the cabby complained in a whining voice that the cops were always picking on him just because he was on parole for manslaughter. I knew the extra points from our encounter would probably lose him his license because he had already accumulated a long list of traffic violations since his recent release from jail. I was not surprised to get a phone call from the taxi squad the next day, telling me their sources had confirmed that this parolee was also the individual who had outrun me in the car chase. They canceled his taxi permit and ended his short but eventful career as a taxi driver for good.

***

Perhaps the most frightening chase I was ever involved in started with a broadcast that one of our cars was pursuing a green, older model Buick Riviera down East Hastings Street toward the skid road area. The speeds didn't sound excessive at first. When I heard that it was headed my way, I decided to sit at the intersection of Campbell and Hastings and wait for the chase to come to me.

At the intersection I momentarily considered doing a U-turn and then building up some speed in his direction of travel so I could take an active role in the pursuit. Before I could do so, the vehicle being chased came toward me over the Hastings viaduct with its lights out. It

44

is difficult under the circumstances to estimate just how fast the car was going, but my best guess is that he was doing well over a hundred miles per hour when he went through the red light I was stopped at. I was able to recognize it as a green Buick Riviera, but I could not make out the plate.

If I'd done the U-turn as soon as the thought occurred to me, I would have pulled directly into the Buick's path and it would have rammed me broadside. I could not possibly have survived the collision because of the incredible speed at which he was traveling. There weren't any police cars following him at that point because he was moving so quickly, and I didn't bother to take up the chase either. The Buick disappeared into the night.

I did, however, broadcast for the other cars to stay safely out of his way. At that speed, no one could hope to catch him anyway. Hours later, we managed to find the Buick, dumped on a side street. Unfortunately there was insufficient evidence to lay charges against the individual we believed had been driving during the chase. I took the liberty of rearranging his spark plug wires while I had a look under the hood, so I doubt he ever used this car to outrun the police again.

***

Not every stolen car stop turns into a car chase. Early in my career, while patrolling the West End one morning, I noticed a car with Alberta plates cruising the area. I'd seen the same car parked in front of my next-door neighbor's house recently. I'd begun to suspect that the person who was renting the house was dealing drugs after watching a steady stream of addicts visiting him at odd hours. I ran the plate on my computer and it came back as having been reported stolen.

The driver pulled over as soon as he heard my siren. I arrested everyone in the car, including my neighbor. The driver readily admitted that he alone was responsible for stealing the car back in Alberta. I released my neighbor after searching his house for further evidence. I almost had the opportunity to arrest him again a few months later, when the drug squad dropped by my house to ask if I wanted to join them in a search warrant attempt next door. Unfortunately, I was out of town at the time, but the raid was very successful. The heavy traffic I'd noticed in and out of the house at all hours dropped off dramatically after the occupants were all sent to jail.

***

At the beginning of my career, I used to check numerous license plates over the radio during my shift, which did not exactly make me popular with some of the male radio operators. Most were policemen on light duty who couldn't type and had difficulty entering the queries properly into the computer.

I was working the wagon one afternoon when I noticed a white convertible driving down Dunsmuir Street. The driver looked suspicious so I checked the plate to see if the car was stolen. The query took so long to process that I finally gave up. When the car turned left onto a side street, I stayed on Dunsmuir, a one-way street.

Seconds later, the radio operator informed me that the car had been reported stolen. I knew if I tried to circle around in rush hour traffic I'd never see him again, so I turned on the emergency equipment and did a quick U-turn. That was no easy task in the paddy wagon, because there were cars stuck in traffic all around me. I had to fight my way back against the flow of one-way traffic, while simultaneously trying to broadcast my location so a backup unit could attend.

In the process I wrapped the microphone cord around the steering wheel and shifter so tightly that I had to bend over to speak into the mike. The stolen car was also bogged down in heavy traffic, so I was able to pull in behind it a block later. Instead of sitting tight, the driver calmly emerged from the car with a "Who, me?" expression on his face.

Now I had to untangle the mike, put the gearshift into park, switch my siren off and work my way out of the driver's seat. At the same time I was also struggling to remove my service revolver from the awkward and outmoded holster that had been issued to me when I joined. Its leather cover completely concealed our weapons so that liberal Vancouverites would not be offended by the sight of our naked revolvers, but the design didn't function very well when you wanted to pull your gun in an emergency. Fortunately, the suspect only tried to talk his way out of the charge, rather than running or fighting for his freedom. He surrendered peacefully when his bluff was called.

***

One of my favorite cases involved yet another car, this one a brand new Corvette driven by a clean-cut gentleman from Quebec. I pulled him over on Granville Street near the mall, just after three in the morning. He was polite and cooperative, but I still had a feeling he was up to no good. When I checked his Quebec license and registration over the radio, I could find nothing out of the ordinary. My special interest at that time was checking Vehicle Identification Numbers, the unique serial numbers which are displayed prominently somewhere on or near the dash of most cars, usually on an engraved metal tag. I checked the Corvette's VIN on the computer, and it seemed to be legitimate.

It was a quiet night, so I had a chance to do a thorough job of checking out the car and its occupant. Although the driver displayed no visible signs of nervousness when I started paying extra attention to the Corvette's VIN, my instincts told me to keep looking. Something about the VIN tag did not seem right when I looked at it from outside the car. It was difficult to examine closely because, on the Corvette, it was positioned on the inside of the driver's side windshield post. My suspicions were confirmed when I used my knife to poke away at the numbers on the tag. Although it was supposed to be made from metal, part of it peeled away easily. The plate was covered with a strip of plastic Dyno tape, complete with an imprinted VIN which was only slightly different from the real one underneath it.

I placed the driver under arrest as everything about his story began to unravel. With the help of the Quebec Provincial Police, we learned that his driver's license, registration and insurance had all been stolen from motor licensing offices back east. When we fingerprinted him to determine his real identity, we discovered that he was a member of a notorious Quebec motorcycle gang. According to the Quebec police, he and his associates had stolen numerous expensive cars from car dealerships. They then transported the cars out west where they were sold as slightly used cars at bargain prices, usually to unscrupulous customers willing to overlook their suspicions. This Corvette, in fact, had been ordered by a Quebec policeman and stolen before he could take delivery.

The suspect eventually pled guilty to Quebec charges of auto theft, but not before one of the stolen auto squad detectives and I were flown to Quebec for the preliminary hearing. The situation we encountered in Montreal was difficult to comprehend. The people seemed less friendly than those I'd encountered while hitchhiking through Quebec in my youth. Only a few of the people we dealt with could or would communicate with us in English, although they were not overtly hostile toward us. The court system in B.C. seemed totally different to what little we were able to understand of the Quebec justice system.

It was fascinating to watch the court staff there try to put together a judge and court recorder who would admit to speaking sufficient English to understand our evidence. The stiff penalty finally handed out to the car thief, in part because of his horrendous record, well compensated us for the lengthy ordeal of the court case.

***

I arrived at the scene of a serious accident moments after it occurred. A young man driving a stolen car had decided for some reason to try to outrun the police. In the process he ran a red light. The occupants of the vehicle he struck broadside in the intersection were obviously badly injured, so we called for emergency ambulances to attend the scene. I looked inside what remained of the car he hit, and what I saw was like something out of a horror film. I made sure the car thief, who did not appear injured, also had a good look inside the car. Both occupants of the second car later died as a result of their injuries.

One of the passengers in the stolen car had a head injury that was pumping blood all over her blouse, so I placed a pressure bandage over the wound to stop the bleeding. I suspect she didn't even notice me, because she was hysterical and seemed to be extremely traumatized by the experience. It was truly a tragic incident. I'm not sure what, if anything, the police could have done differently, but I did a lot of soul-searching after this one.

***

Another car chase that ended unhappily involved two young men in a sports car. They had been out on the town that evening and became involved in a noisy dispute with several prostitutes at a skid road street corner. A neighbor called 911 to report the disturbance. As the police arrived, the young men immediately piled into their car and left the scene in a cloud of tire smoke. Apparently they tried to make a sharp right hand turn at high speed onto a dark side street, in order to elude the police. They lost control of the car instead. It spun and landed on its side, throwing one of the occupants, the only one without his seat belt fastened, through the open roof.

He crashed through a plate glass storefront window, sustaining serious head injuries in the process. I went into the store to check him out and found him lying on his side. There were dangerous shards of glass hanging just over our heads, so I grabbed a cardboard box and used it as a shield to protect us. There was no indication that he was dying at first, although there was some blood on his face.

Since I could see that he was still breathing, I knelt down beside him and said the usual ludicrous thing you say to seriously injured people. "You'll be okay. Don't move. An ambulance is on the way." A more experienced diagnostician standing nearby in a police uniform snorted in disagreement and walked away to check the other occupant.

At that point my patient emitted a death rattle, a sound that is difficult to describe but which seemed to me like someone gasping and at the same time swallowing for air that just wasn't there anymore. Blood suddenly began pouring out of several different openings from his skull and he died moments later. The victim was almost certainly brain-dead the moment he went through the window, according to the ambulance attendants.

The second occupant of the Corvette was not charged with any criminal offense because there was no evidence he'd been driving during the chase. I offered to drive him home on my way to notify the victim's next of kin. The young man was still in shock over his friend's death and had not been of much help to the investigators when they interviewed him immediately after the accident. He took an instant dislike to me, and eventually bailed out of my police car as we drove across one of the major bridges. I was relieved to see that he did not immediately jump off the bridge, and I left him there to make his own way home on foot.

Notifying the next of kin in this instance was one of the most difficult tasks I ever handled. The survivor had informed us that his deceased friend was the only son of a widow who had a history of heart attacks, so I arranged for an ambulance crew to come with me to the house while I broke the bad news to her. I did not think it would be right to burden her with details of the last few minutes of her son's life, so I simply told her that her son had died in a car accident.

These sudden death notifications are at times almost as hard on the policeman making them as they are on the next of kin. There is no way you can prepare yourself for the ordeal. In this case, the grieving mother took the news surprisingly well, although she was obviously heartbroken. I called her daughter and asked her to come over to take care of her mother, so I also had to tell her about her brother's death when she arrived.

***

A chase with a happier ending started just after midnight and wound its way from southern Vancouver to the East End. The members initiating the chase were following a stolen Corvette down side streets at high speed until it stopped momentarily as the passenger jumped out. The car then accelerated away from them again. One of the pursuing policemen, a recruit just out of the academy, chased the man on foot while his partner continued the car chase.

The speed they were traveling remained relatively high, despite the fact that the Corvette had two flat tires, the result of brief excursions off the roadway. Driving on the wheel rims did not seem to slow him down. When it appeared that the chase would be moving into an adjoining municipality, the RCMP working that area were notified by our radio operators.

The Mounties are very professional in the performance of their duties. They can always be counted on for prompt and able assistance, and they didn't disappoint us that night. One very determined Mountie parked his car on the boundary between our municipalities and waited patiently for the stolen Corvette. An effective roadblock would have been impossible to arrange at this location, but he didn't need any other cars for what he planned. With perfect timing and skillful driving he faked a move backwards as the stolen car approached, leaving just enough room in front of him for the vehicle to pass. As the car thief accepted his invitation, the Mountie surged ahead and tapped the Corvette's rear fender, sending it airborne over a curb.

The stolen car landed on the boulevard with enough damage that it was finally immobilized. Its driver still had some fight in him, however. He bailed out and started running through a nearby park. A female Mountie covering the chase observed the suspect running away and drove through the park after him. He was in no mood to surrender, so she pulled up beside him and skillfully bunted him into orbit with the back fender of her police car. By the time the suspect stopped rolling across the grass, one of our police dogs arrived to chew on him. After that ordeal, he seemed almost relieved to be taken into custody.

Fifteen minutes later, as soon as things had settled down at the arrest scene, someone realized that the recruit chasing the Corvette's passenger was still not accounted for. We rushed back to the area where he'd last been seen to start a search. We knew he had no portable radio with him; it was still in the police car.

I drove down dark side streets, and after several anxious minutes of searching, finally located the recruit. He was proudly standing at curbside with his handcuffed prisoner at his feet. He had the happy look that police dogs get when they catch a crook and want that all-important recognition from their master for a job well done. It turned out that he'd had no problem capturing his suspect after a short foot chase and a brief struggle. He had then just waited there patiently with his prize, confident that a police car would show up sooner or later.

***

One of the most incredible chases I ever observed began one weekday evening when an East End patrol unit attempted to pull over a Dodge sedan. The car bolted, and the pursuing members called for "Code Four," which gave them priority on the radio channel in order to broadcast the pursuit.

Judging by the broadcasts, it sounded to me like the vehicle was traveling at a relatively high rate of speed. Since much of the route they traveled was through residential side streets, it was clear that the chase would have to end quickly, one way or another, before somebody got hurt.

I followed the progress of the pursuit as they sped through the East End. I stayed clear of the action until I heard the only police unit still in the chase broadcast that he was westbound and about to cross one of the major thoroughfares. At the time I was a block away on the same street. As a result, I was a spectator to the unusual end of this chase. The suspect vehicle, with a marked police car locked onto its rear end, blasted across the main street at well over the speed limit. They left a trail of smoke and assorted car parts in their wake. I watched a civilian car proceeding down the thoroughfare hit the rear bumper of the suspect's Dodge as they met momentarily in the intersection. Both cars continued on without stopping. The innocent citizen never did report the collision to the police.

I pulled in behind the cavalcade. The two cars, still locked together, continued down a crowded side street which was just wide enough to allow one-way traffic. I knew they couldn't keep this up for long, so I was not surprised when the two cars finally veered into a parked van. There was a horrendous crash, and both vehicles were demolished as they crushed one side of the van.

The incredible spectacle unfolding in front of me was so fascinating that I neglected to apply my brakes as quickly as I should have. My brakes locked up but it was too late. I remember seeing the policeman brace himself for the impact as I plowed into his car's back bumper at slow speed, causing minimal damage. As the two of us hauled the suspect out of the smoking ruins of his car, we discovered, much to my amazement, that nobody was hurt.

The suspect's only comment to police about the incident was that he had been in car chases all over Canada and the United States and had never run into a policeman who could drive like that. He'd had the misfortune to be followed by one of our more tenacious members, a good, aggressive street policeman who seldom lost a car he was chasing. Under normal circumstances, the suspect would probably have been successful in eluding his pursuers. I know I couldn't have caught him. He eventually received a year in jail after a dangerous driving conviction.

***

I would never buy a used police car. They take incredible punishment during their years of service, primarily because most po- licemen treat them as disposable tools of the trade, readily expendable if the situation merits it. While exploring a remote path in Stanley Park one night, I managed to get a brand new unmarked car stuck on top of a fallen log. It took us over an hour to pry it free. By that time we had managed to tie up our entire shift to help push us, as well as two tow trucks which both managed to dig themselves axle deep in the mud. One tow truck driver was trying so hard to help us that he rammed a tree in the process and demolished his passenger side door.

My favorite story about damage to a police car happened well before I joined the department. It apparently began when a policeman skidded out of control on black ice during a quiet night shift. He sideswiped a pole, causing damage to one side of the car. Concerned that this act of negligence would hurt his promotional chances, he woke up a friend who owned a body shop and informed his radio dispatcher that he'd be tied up for a while. By the time his night shift ended, he and his friend had repaired the damage and slapped on a new coat of black and white paint. According to legend, nobody ever noticed the repair job, and the story only emerged after a long evening at the bar.

***

A particularly quiet rainy evening was interrupted by a broadcast that one of the public transportation supervisors was reporting that his car had just been stolen. He'd left his keys in the ignition while he was out assisting a bus in the skid road area. I started in the direction of Hastings Street, anticipating that the suspect would head toward the West End.

Within a matter of seconds one of our units spotted the stolen car heading westbound on Hastings through heavy traffic. As the car approached the intersection of Cambie and Hastings, it was blocked by cars stopped at a red light. A police car pulled in behind it.

Coming from the opposite direction, I stopped beside it to assist in the arrest. For some reason I felt a little uncomfortable about the look of this particular suspect. As a result, I made the decision to draw my service revolver in case he was armed.

I needn't have bothered. The driver looked at me contemptuously when I pointed my revolver in his direction as several other police officers ordered him to exit the stolen car. He offered us his right middle digit in reply, then raised the driver's side window and meticulously locked all the car's doors.

I could see him looking for a way out, and I realized there were several scenarios that could potentially cause us a lot of trouble over the next few seconds. If the civilian cars blocking his progress from the front pulled out when the light turned green, we could quickly find ourselves involved in a high-speed pursuit. In any case, if he turned his wheels to the right and pulled up onto the sidewalk in order to bypass the traffic jam around him, we would be off to the races again. Several of us approached the stolen car at the same time. Something had to be done before it was too late.

I got to the driver's side first. I had never broken a car window before, so I decided that a considerable amount of force would be necessary since safety glass is stronger than normal glass. I put my revolver in its holster and grabbed my three-cell flashlight. Using a full roundhouse swing, I closed my eyes and struck the window with all my strength.

When it shattered it showered broken glass all over the thief and the inside of the car. When I pulled the door open, he still refused to give up without a fight. At first we weren't able to force him out of the car, even with several officers pulling him in different directions. He was finally taken into custody after someone realized that the thief still had his seat belt on.

He was not hurt by the shattered glass or by our exertions during his arrest. Because he had a long history of mental illness, he was eventually returned to a hospital for treatment. After he was taken into custody, I discovered one of the disadvantages of this dramatic method of pulling people out of stolen cars. I had tiny razor cuts all over my right hand from glass fragments. Police work goes much more smoothly in television shows, and the cops on TV never seem to get cut up during an arrest.

***

"Four Alpha Fourteen, Code Four! We're in pursuit of a hit and run vehicle, westbound on Hastings from Campbell."

A sunny winter Sunday afternoon was soon enlivened by the sound of a car chase over the radio. Officers on routine patrol observed a battered Datsun rear-end another car in the area of Clark and Hastings. The Datsun didn't bother to stick around, even though the damage was relatively minor. The driver simply backed up and then sped off in the opposite direction, refusing to stop when the police pulled in behind him with its emergency lights flashing.

The chase proceeded through the waterfront area and took a bizarre twist when the suspect sped through a parking lot situated beside the harbor. It was full of policemen's personal cars because this was the only downtown parking lot available to us at the time.

I followed the pursuing units to the waterfront area and monitored the progress of the chase through the lot. Miraculously, despite his erratic driving style, he didn't hit any of our cars. However, as the suspect headed out of the lot, he sideswiped a police wagon that tried unsuccessfully to roadblock him and then continued on his way. I considered positioning my police car to block his passage, but decided against it at the last second when it became clear that he intended to ram anything in front of him. There was also a police car right on his tail, too close to stop if the suspect hit me. I decided it just wasn't worth the hours of reports that would have followed, although in retrospect I probably should have tried it anyway.

Next he tried to make his escape down the railway tracks beside our lot. He may well have seen cars in movie chase scenes that successfully negotiated railway tracks, but he was no stunt driver. The chase ended when he high-sided his car on the rails after traveling less than twenty feet. He was surrounded by blue uniforms before he could attempt to escape on foot. The suspect, a long-time drug addict with a lengthy record, had stolen the car just before the chase began.

***

Just as we started our morning coffee one Sunday day-shift, our radio operator informed us that an RCMP member from North Vancouver was chasing a motorcycle toward our end of the Second Narrows bridge. A motorcycle has several distinct advantages in a car chase, and the driver of this one obviously knew what he was doing. After a series of maneuvers, which included a U-turn in the middle of the bridge, he finally managed to escape.

The Mountie in pursuit gave his operator a brief description of the motorcyclist, who was wearing a distinctive red rain jacket. This information was, in turn, passed on to us via our radio, in case he decided to drive through Vancouver later. Unfortunately, the Mountie was unable to give us a license plate on the bike because he couldn't get close enough to see it during the chase.

It was a quiet morning, so I decided to sit on our side of the Second Narrows bridge in case the motorcyclist attempted the crossing again. I reasoned that no one would be awake that early on a Sunday morning unless he had an important commitment. For instance, if he had a job to report to, there was always a chance he might be foolhardy enough to retrace his original route after laying low until the excitement died down. His only alternative would be to double back across the Lions Gate bridge, which was at the other end of the city.

Traffic was light, so I had no difficulty eliminating the first few motorcycles that drove past as potential suspects. After sitting there for half an hour, I watched a motorcycle cross the bridge at a speed well below the posted limit. The driver was close to the vague description we'd been given, except that he was not wearing a red rain jacket. He pulled over almost immediately when I activated my emergency equipment. It had been raining all morning, but this driver wore only a denim jacket for protection against the elements.

He was nervous at first, although he was polite and cooperative. He denied involvement in a car chase, and had almost convinced me that he was innocent until I noticed a bulge under his denim jacket. As he sat astride his bike, I unbuttoned the lower half of his jacket and pulled out a full set of red rain gear. The motorcyclist then decided that he did not wish to comment further, so we waited impatiently for the RCMP officer who had initiated the chase to attend so he could identify him.

The Mountie arrived two minutes later and immediately confirmed that I had stopped the right man. He considered laying criminal charges for dangerous driving against the suspect, who was still not admitting anything, but in the end decided that a criminal charge would be too difficult to prove. Instead, the Mountie laboriously wrote the unlucky motorcyclist a ticket for each offense he had committed during the chase, a grand total of eight different tickets. The biker was quite upset and indignant. Although he complained bitterly to us about the injustice of it all, he never once tried to deny the allegations.

***

One of our police cars was hit from behind by a speeding motorcycle that had been attempting to elude other officers. The impact of the bike left a deep indentation in the car's trunk, almost as if it had backed into a pole at freeway speeds. The biker's helmet crumpled the car's roof almost all the way to the driver's seat. The damaged car sat in the police garage for several days with the wrecked bike positioned at the original point of impact. After examining the wreckage, it was easy to understand why the motorcyclist's injuries ultimately proved fatal.

***

It was just after midnight when I parked my marked car east of Main Street on Terminal Avenue, a business area with a long, straight road that resembles a drag strip. As I wrote a report, I heard a super bike leaving the intersection of Main and Terminal in a big hurry. Super bikes are the powerful, high performance motorcycles that can accelerate to well over a hundred miles per hour in the quarter mile. I put my car in gear, ready to follow him if he decided to run. His front wheel actually left the ground as he accelerated, but when he saw me looking at him, he instinctively backed off the throttle.

After hesitating for a moment, however, he changed his mind

again and accelerated away from me. I pulled out after him, but he quickly reached incredibly high speeds and I soon lost sight of him. I terminated the chase and gave our radio operator a description of the bike and rider in case any other policemen happened to be in the neighborhood. Although another officer observed the biker and tried to catch him, he was also outrun.

The motorcyclist had another close encounter before he finally made good his escape. One of our police dogs happened to be out of the car tracking on an unrelated case when the biker roared down a narrow street, heading directly toward him. The dog's handler barely managed to drag his animal off the road before the bike raced past, narrowly missing them both. After that, he disappeared for good.

***

Several of our units were chasing a motorcycle through heavy traffic in the vicinity of the old Expo 86 site one afternoon. When traffic blocked the intersection ahead, the suspect started driving down the sidewalk, forcing some pedestrians to jump out of his way.

He would have escaped, but the intersection he chose to disrupt was manned by a Reserve Policeman directing traffic. The officer had already endured a great deal of abuse from the public that night. He had no police radio with him, but he could hear the sirens and see the flashing red and blue lights of our police cars as the biker left them behind in snarled traffic. It would have been safer for the Reserve Policeman just to jump out of the path of the speeding motorcyclist, but after a difficult evening of dealing with impatient and downright negligent motorists, he decided that this jerk on the motorcycle was the last straw.

Wielding his flashlight, which has a red cone on the end for directing traffic, he waited to make his move until the bike was beside him. Then he deftly clubbed the biker off his mount, knocking him to the ground. As soon as other policemen arrived on the scene, he immediately resumed his duties directing traffic as if nothing untoward had happened. The biker, a penitentiary escapee described as armed and dangerous, was soon handcuffed and returned to jail.

***

Motorcycle accidents are all too common these days, as more and more drivers with minimal experience push the envelope while piloting machines capable of outperforming some race cars. I've seen more than my share of demolished bikes and shattered bodies at accident scenes, and like most people who have owned a motorcycle, I've had a fairly serious accident myself. As a firm believer in freedom of choice, I do not agree with banning high-powered super-bikes as some would advocate. However, I would certainly be in favor of a mandatory comprehensive training course for everyone buying their first motorcycle. There are just too many serious accidents involving super-bikes where low odometer readings indicate novice riders.

One accident I attended illustrates just how dangerous super-bikes can be in the hands of inexperienced riders. It occurred along an overpass on the boundary between Vancouver and Burnaby. Although it happened during the day, there were no witnesses. The first impact was with a guardrail. Some of the driver's severed fingertips were found there. Further down the road there was a trail of clothing and body parts that led to the victim's shattered corpse. He ended up on the pavement beside the demolished bike.

To the best of my knowledge investigators never determined what actually caused the accident, although it was obvious that it occurred while the machine was traveling at a very high rate of speed. I took two enduring images with me from that scene. One was of a cheerful Mountie, present because we ultimately determined that the accident had occurred in his jurisdiction instead of ours. He stood over the body, one foot on each side of the torso, and bent over almost double to carry out the necessary search through the victim's pockets for identification papers.

I also remember interviewing the woman who discovered the accident. She was calm at first, but her composure deteriorated markedly after she averted her eyes momentarily and noticed a piece of the victim's brain on the pavement nearby. She made a determined effort not to look at it again, but I noticed her cringing every time her eyes subconsciously began to stray back in that direction.

***

We passed one of the skid road bars just in time to observe a Pinto fly out of the parking lot without any lights on. It then drove eastbound on Cordova at high speed. The driver ignored our emergency equipment for the first two minutes. We were about to declare a full-scale chase over the radio but the car suddenly pulled over.

The sole occupant, a rather attractive young woman, hesitantly stepped out of the Pinto. She was more than a little unsteady on her feet, but what really got our attention was the fact that she wore a skimpy outfit and flaunted her wares unashamedly. She was very friendly at first; she explained that she worked as a stripper at the bar she'd just left. She admitted having a few drinks after her shift ended, although she vehemently denied that she was too drunk to drive.

When we informed her she was going to have to pay a visit to the breathalyzer room downtown, her mood changed suddenly and the smile turned into a fierce snarl. The sultry, seductive pose disappeared altogether, and the fight was on. It was a vicious struggle while it lasted. I was the recipient of a well-aimed knee to the groin as I tried to handcuff her. We eventually convicted her of impaired driving.

Two years later, I stopped the same stripper for speeding again. She hadn't been drinking this time, so we had a much more pleasant conversation, at least until she remembered who I was. She still went to jail, however. This time it was for several speeding tickets she had neglected to pay.

***

In the early seventies there was a notorious Vancouver youth who regularly stole Corvettes and then drove around the city looking for a police car. He would then pull up alongside the car and attempt to provoke the officers into chasing him, knowing full well that, because he was a juvenile, nothing would happen to him in court if he got caught. Apparently many of the policemen he approached simply ignored the young man, and he eventually went on to bigger and better things in the world of crime.

***

We do not get much snow in Vancouver, but when a storm does hit the area, many of our citizens do their best to contribute to the notoriously high accident statistics our province is burdened with. The natural beauty of a snowstorm seems to fill most drivers with awe and reckless abandon. When coupled with inexperience, this exuberance creates mayhem.

I was once involved in a car chase during one of the worst snow storms I ever experienced as a policeman. I followed a small pickup truck south on Oak Street from 41st after its driver refused to pull over. Road conditions at the time were terrible, but fortunately there was only light traffic ahead of us. The idiot driving the pickup kept opening his door and leaning half way out, almost as if he intended to shoot at me. The speeds he reached were not excessive, although his driving was very erratic. I kept my distance, not wanting to risk getting shot if indeed that was his intention. I guessed from what I'd already witnessed of his driving ability that he would skid off the road soon anyway.

After avoiding several near accidents, the pickup truck started building up a head of steam as it approached the Oak Street bridge. Once across the bridge, there was nothing to stop him from running all

58

the way to the United States border. He must have had second thoughts about deserting the warm hospitality of Vancouver, however, because after crossing the bridge he suddenly decided to do a U-turn. I watched in amazement as he swung his car sideways and successfully plowed through a deep mound of snow that separated the divided highway. He then started back the way he'd come. There was no way I was going to lose him now, so I closed my eyes and duplicated his maneuver, hoping that there were no guardrails hidden under the snowbank.

As we headed back to Vancouver, he suddenly stopped his car in the middle of the highway, emerged from his cab with a dog and sat down in the snow to play a game of fetch. When I approached him, it soon became obvious that he was in a world of his own, although he was capable of conversing in a limited fashion. As we handcuffed him, he talked about space ships and interplanetary travel through time warps. I didn't find any weapons. We discovered that he had recently been released from a mental institution and had not been taking his medication since leaving the hospital. We arranged to have him recommitted for the Christmas holidays.

***

The first serious motor vehicle accident I witnessed occurred well before I became a policeman. My job that summer was to deliver interdepartmental mail around the province for the government. I was driving down a rural highway one morning when I observed cars parked along both sides of the road ahead, a sure sign that an accident had just happened.

Of course I pulled over as well, being just as curious as everyone else. There was a car in the ditch with an injured man still propped up against the steering wheel. The windshield was starred where his head had impacted, and it appeared that the vehicle must have rolled over at least once before finally coming to rest on its wheels.

There were at least fifty people gathered around the car when I arrived. They were all standing there quietly, watching the injured driver as if waiting for something to happen. I wandered over to the car, certain that somebody must have already called for an ambulance by now and thinking that I should do something for the victim. As I looked in through the window, the man turned toward me, looked me in the eye, and then collapsed sideways onto his seat. There was blood everywhere. Since I had no first aid training at the time, I quickly decided that there was nothing I could do for him except get him expert help.

I asked the crowd if anyone had left to phone for an ambulance.

Everyone ignored me and continued gawking at the wrecked car while talking to one another in hushed voices. I hopped in my car and drove a couple of miles to the nearest residence to use the phone. I called the RCMP and asked them to send an ambulance. As I was about to hang up, I asked the officer how many people had already phoned about the accident. He replied that this was the first he'd heard of it. I found out the next day in the paper that the driver died at the scene.

I know that most of the people who stood there and watched that man die were decent citizens who would never dream of hurting anyone directly, yet they were either too stupid or too thoughtless to make any effort to help. Was it because they needed someone to take charge, someone to tell them what to do? I saw that often during my career as a policeman. Society has created a solid base of very civilized, very pleasant individuals who act, for the most part, like dumb cattle waiting to be herded.

***

I attended a pedestrian accident during the Christmas holidays after a middle-aged woman was struck by a car as she staggered across a busy thoroughfare. I saw something pink protruding from her skull as the ambulance crew placed her on a stretcher. It was part of her brain. To me that was a good indication she was not long for this world, even though she was still breathing. I chalked the outline of her body onto the pavement after she was moved into the ambulance, and then directed traffic so the Accident Investigation Squad could take measurements at the scene.

She was pronounced dead later that evening. The driver who'd hit her was quite upset about killing the unfortunate woman, although he was relatively sober and unusually cooperative. He was even honest enough to admit that he had been traveling perhaps five miles an hour over the speed limit when she'd stepped out in front of him.

I believe there was nothing he could have done to prevent the accident. The investigators issued him a ticket as a result of his statements to them about exceeding the speed limit. Since an inquest into her death was not held, a traffic ticket was probably the fairest method of exposing the facts of the case to public scrutiny.

The woman, it turned out, was a drug addict who had been drinking quite a bit that day. She was under a court order not to visit her children, but apparently she had decided to disobey the order because she was crossing the street in front of their residence when she was struck.

We were all called to court when the driver disputed his ticket.

I suspect most of the members present were indifferent to the outcome of the trial. I, for one, was hoping he would get off. After all, offenders who actually tell the truth when asked how fast they were traveling at the time of an accident are extremely rare. I very seldom wrote tickets to violators who politely and truthfully explained their side of the story to me when they were pulled over.

A conviction for this offense would also hurt his chances of winning a civil suit launched against him by the dead woman's family. I couldn't help feeling a little bit sorry for him as he sat there in front of a judge in traffic court. The fact remained that he was only there as a result of his own honesty, because without his statement, there was probably not enough evidence to convict him of speeding.

I was on the stand to give my limited share of the evidence for only a few moments when it became clear that his case was going well for him. Up to this point, the judge seemed very sympathetic to his cause, and the prosecutor was only going through the motions. Then the defense lawyer, for whatever reason, began playing a very sarcastic Perry Mason role toward the prosecution witnesses. He made a very insulting attempt to show that I should have been giving the victim first aid instead of chalking her outline, even though there was clearly nothing I could have done that the ambulance staff weren't already doing for her. The judge had a reputation for fairness, but he was obviously growing more and more upset as he listened to the lawyer's stupid tactics. He tried several times to dissuade the defense lawyer from continuing down the cynical path he'd chosen.

The defense lawyer ignored the judge, and eventually his client was found guilty. Although there was more than sufficient evidence presented at the trial to convict him of speeding, my bet is that this judge would have found a way to acquit him had the lawyer not been so obnoxious. I saw the accused crying after the verdict was announced, and, not for the first time, I regretted being a part of a very imperfect system.

***

The radio suddenly came alive, on what had otherwise been a routine evening in the West End, when a motorcycle policeman requested that an emergency ambulance attend a motor vehicle accident he had just witnessed. We were nearby, so we decided to cover him. As we entered the block, we could see what appeared to be a very serious accident ahead. There was already a crowd gathered at the scene. Strangely, the motorcycle cop was just standing there doing nothing as we drove up.

The scenario that greeted us simply didn't make sense at first. A new, high performance Mustang, its engine still roaring and its rear wheels spinning impotently, was sitting on top of an upside-down Datsun sedan. A very frightened lady sat bolt upright in the driver's seat of the Mustang, staring straight ahead as if she still intended to continue her journey toward the second story of a building that stood directly in front of her windshield. There was a young child with a bored expression on his face sitting in the passenger seat. Neither appeared to be injured.

After removing her key from the ignition, we assisted the two of them down from their runaway steed and attempted to find out what had happened. She was of no help at all because she didn't speak English, and the child was too young to talk. A witness from an apartment that overlooked the accident scene eventually approached us to explain what had happened.

The lady had pulled out of a parking spot on the second floor of a parkade that exited onto the street by way of a steep ramp. She apparently floored the gas as she left the lot, roared down the ramp and struck the driver's side door of an unoccupied Datsun parked at the curb. Her Mustang somehow ended up parked high and dry on top of the overturned Datsun. No Hollywood stuntman could have duplicated the results.

***

Even the most serious of police officers can usually find an element of black humor in the calls they are assigned, although admittedly some incidents are just too depressing to think about. A cop's bizarre sense of humor is a defense mechanism, a device used to convey an account of his work experiences to other policemen without appearing too morbid.

One incident with a lighter side occurred years ago on East Broadway when an outlaw biker in the center lane sped past one of our paddy wagons. The motorcyclist grinned in the policeman's direction and extended his middle digit as a sign of his lack of respect for authority. The biker then gunned his motor to draw attention to his gesture, but neglected to watch for traffic ahead in the meantime. As a result, he collided with a truck that stopped suddenly in front of him. The truck was damaged, but not beyond repair. The biker's injuries were fatal.

***

Police-involved motor vehicle accidents are, unfortunately, all too common. Each shift may include up to ten hours behind the wheel, so most policemen accumulate a lot of driving time over the years. When you consider the extra demands placed on them by the excessive speeds and unusual maneuvering required during some types of police work, a certain number of accidents are unavoidable. I was involved in several minor collisions during my career, including two in the space of one week that involved the same paddy wagon. Fortunately, no one was hurt as a result of my accidents.

I have vivid memories of a run I made en route to a serious call one noon hour. I was the front seat passenger in a marked police car driven by somebody I only worked with once. As we entered a busy intersection with lights flashing and siren wailing, we T-boned a city bus that was proceeding slowly through a good green light. Nobody on the bus was hurt.

I was still sitting in the car with my fingers dug deeply into the dash in front of me when the bus driver, a very attractive young lady, leapt out her door to survey the damage. She stared in disbelief at the conspicuous black and white police car embedded in the side of her bus. After ten seconds of shocked silence, she burst into tears. We learned later that it was her first week as a bus driver.

***

My last accident on the job was perhaps the most ironic. I was driving down Hastings Street in the skids when I overheard a description of a possible impaired driver in a Firebird. According to the radio operator, he had last been seen in Burnaby, westbound on Hastings. Apprehending the drunk driver was actually another team's responsibility, although the description was repeated over our radio channel because of his direction of travel. As I signaled to turn down a side street, I turned to my partner and joked, "I guess we'd better get out of his way!"

Immediately after those words were uttered, there was a tremendous crash behind us and our marked police car was pushed violently into the intersection. It was the same Firebird. The report that he was an impaired driver had certainly been accurate. In fact, he was so drunk that he fell out of the car as we opened his door to remove him. He had a very high breathalyzer reading and was later convicted of impaired driving.

Arresting impaired drivers becomes more and more complicated every year. Dealing with drunks is often an unpleasant experience anyway, but on top of that there are invariably complications and problems involved with the charge. Increasingly restrictive procedures make an impaired driving arrest extraordinarily time consuming. When there is a manpower shortage on the street, an officer knows that while he is spending several hours processing an impaired driver, there may not be enough cars available to answer serious calls. In fact, if the police arrested every drinking driver they stopped, very soon there wouldn't be enough room in the jails to hold them all.

There are other options available to the police, so discretion is frequently exercised. If there is a sober passenger in the car, he or she can replace the driver behind the wheel for the rest of the trip. If the driver is at all sensible, and not quite intoxicated enough for a charge, his license can be suspended or he can be sent home in a taxi.

Despite the fact that driving while impaired is currently unfashionable in today's society, anybody with police experience knows there are still plenty of drunk drivers on the roads just by watching for certain erratic driving patterns. Although there may be fewer arrests recently, I think statistics that claim to show an overall decrease in drunk driving are, at best, misleading. When a law becomes difficult to enforce properly, it tends to be utilized less and less.

* * *

My award for the impaired driver who sobered up the fastest goes to the young man who decided to show a hitchhiker how fast his Datsun sports car could travel through Stanley Park one night. The road he picked to demonstrate his driving prowess winds its way around the park, with trees lining one side and a harbor on the other. I was called to the sea wall near a particularly dangerous corner after a report of a car sinking in the water there.

Two very cold and very wet individuals met me on the sidewalk and pointed out to sea about a hundred feet. I could just make out a pair of headlights still shining dimly under six feet of water. Neither occupant was injured, so I drove them back to the West End where they could catch a cab home. The driver appeared to have sobered up by the time I dealt with him. Since he had apparently dived underwater several times to rescue his trapped passenger, I let him go with only a ticket and a stern lecture.

The next day I asked one of our accident investigators to meet me at the scene. After examining the area carefully, he was able to show me exactly how the car had left the road and gone airborne. He found a dent in the sidewalk where a wheel rim had bottomed out, and a grease mark on the sea wall where the oil pan had scraped across it. From there the Datsun had been launched airborne from the sea wall, coming to rest on its roof in mid-harbor. As for the remarkable distance the car traveled through the air until it finally landed in the water, the investigator believed that was due to the extremely high speed it had been traveling before leaving the road.

***

I arrested my share of impaired drivers during my twelve years as a policeman, including one I followed as he drove unsteadily along a sidewalk for half a block, swerving carefully to avoid newspaper boxes and lamp standards. When I stopped him he refused to believe that he hadn't been driving on the road, and he acted insulted when I accused him of drinking too much.

However, there was one drunk driver I encountered near the beginning of my career that I decided not to charge. I arrived at the accident scene and discovered that the morgue wagon had rear-ended another car with enough force to rupture its fuel tank. There were no injuries. Since the morgue employee was standing unsteadily in the middle of a pool of gasoline trying unsuccessfully to light his cigarette, I began to suspect he might have been drinking that day.

I knew the man only from talking to him at several sudden death calls. I'd been impressed by his cheerful demeanor. He seemed like a genuinely nice person, although I'd heard rumors he had a serious drinking problem. I suppose anyone who earns a living picking up decomposing bodies could be excused for using alcohol to insulate his sensibilities from overexposure to the gruesome nature of his work. On the other hand, if he continued to drink and drive, he would eventually create more work for himself, if not his successor.

I spoke to the driver of the car he'd hit and told him that I was inclined to give the morgue employee a break this time, but only if he agreed with me that it was appropriate to do so. Rather than taking the employee downtown for a breathalyzer, I explained that I planned to suspend his license and give him a ticket for causing the accident instead. The other driver also felt sorry for the morgue employee, and after thinking about it for a few seconds he agreed that this seemed fair to him and shook my hand.

As I explained the situation to the morgue employee, I noticed he had not been alone in the wagon at the time of the accident. His passenger, a corpse zipped inside a body bag, had landed on the front seat with its head on the floor and its feet in the air. We disposed of that problem by having the tow truck drop the body at the city morgue on the way to the wrecking yard.

I had a long, serious discussion with the morgue employee about this accident. By the time I left him, I was convinced he had learned his lesson once and for all. I never saw him under the influence of alcohol again. In retrospect, I believe I did the right thing that day, although if something had gone wrong I would have been looking for a new job. After all, of the many thousands of people I caught breaking the law, I only charged a few of the worst and most flagrant offenders. The rest I just lectured and warned.

Years later, in another jurisdiction, something obviously went very wrong with his life. He died alone in a motel room. It was a sad ending for an interesting character who had a unique sense of humor.

***

I liked to write tickets for jaywalking because it was a good way to get to know the active criminals in the high-crime areas. They served no other useful purpose. In the skids almost everyone ignored the traffic lights and crossed the street wherever they pleased. These offenders were well aware that nothing would happen to them if they tore up the jaywalking ticket, unless they happened to do so in front of the policeman who had just issued it. In that case they earned an additional ticket for littering, which was also ignored by the justice system.

Pedestrians were knocked down by cars on a regular basis in the skids, primarily because many of the people there were drunk when they tried to jaywalk. Tickets had no effect on these horrendous statistics because only well-to-do citizens with a guilty conscience ever paid the fine. Many pedestrians met their fate on the pavement of the 100 East Hastings, a block with more than its share of beer parlors and drunks. On one particularly bloody evening, less than an hour after one ped-struck had been bandaged and sent on his way to hospital to die, another drunk was hit by a car at the same location. He landed squarely on top of the blood and discarded bandage wrappers left behind from the first accident.

***

I attended one accident which I guessed would prove to be fatal after one quick glance at the driver. He had driven his car over a highway guardrail at the East First Street overpass, finally coming to rest on an embankment after plowing through a grove of trees. The driver's twisted body was jammed between the front seats, and his head rested on the back floor. The car was totaled and he looked like he would soon be joining it.

The fire department arrived and immediately went to work to free him from the wreckage. First they tried using a long metal bar to pry out the smashed front windshield. That effort went well until they realized they were inadvertently using a particularly sensitive part of the

66

victim's unconscious body as a fulcrum. He didn't show any sign that he objected to the abuse, so it began to look more and more like a "fatal" to those of us watching from the sidelines. The ambulance attendants cut all his clothing off and attached a neck brace. He was not out of the woods yet, because even with the front windshield removed, they still didn't have enough room to pull him out of the car on a backboard.

Consequently, the firemen sent for the Jaws of Life, a sophisticated hydraulic device used to forcibly remove car roofs. Immediately after they fired it up, a fitting came loose. The device then sprayed the car and its occupant from stem to stern with hydraulic fluid during the thirty seconds it took them to fix the problem. By the time the roof was removed and the unfortunate victim was finally extricated, I had already written him off.

I talked to the officer assigned to the call several hours later, fully expecting to hear that the errant driver was no longer with us. I was surprised to learn that after a thorough examination, the hospital was ready to release him in the morning. Other than some bruising around the area that had supported the pry bar, he did not have a single injury. A test of his Blood Alcohol Count revealed that he had been extremely intoxicated when he catapulted over the guardrail. The only aftereffect of the incident would be a massive hangover the next morning.

Chapter Four
HAZARDS OF THE PROFESSION

The job could be dangerous at times, but an incident that I found more frightening than any physical threat to my well-being occurred just after midnight during a particularly busy afternoon shift. While driving the paddy wagon, I was called to the skid road area by another policeman to transport a female drunk to the detoxification center. We put her into the back of the wagon without any problem. I then spent ten minutes covering the officer on another disturbance call nearby.

We arrested another drunk there, and I put him in a separate compartment and drove directly to the detox center to unload. As I opened the door to remove my original customer, she turned to the detox staff member standing nearby and pointed directly at me. "He hurt me!"

We both ignored her, because she was obviously intoxicated. We rolled her into the facility in a wheelchair, and then stood her up in front of the reception desk for processing. I returned to the wagon and retrieved the second prisoner, who by this time was already trying to sleep off his celebration. Having completed my part of the process, I then stood near the counter in case the civilian detox staff had a problem booking the drunks I'd brought them.

I was day-dreaming, staring off into space absent-mindedly, when I heard the female drunk declare, "That big cop. He beat me up and raped me!"

I looked in her direction, very much alert now, to find her pointing a very shaky finger squarely at me. She was in her thirties, and once might have been almost attractive. Now, however, her hair was matted with dirt, and her tattered and filthy clothing had vomit stains front and back from the short wagon trip. I could smell the pungent odor of cheap wine, vomit and filth from where I stood ten feet away.

The staff were nearly as startled at the allegation as I was. Their reactions were all different. Most of them just looked down to their paperwork, clearly embarrassed or upset with what they had just heard. One male staff member shook his head and smiled knowingly in a gesture of disbelief. What worried me the most was a female staff member whose face now mirrored disgust and horror. I knew instinctively she believed the drunk's story.

The atmosphere in the office, while subdued, was clearly strained at this point. The drunk repeated her allegation, then stared at me as if daring me to do something. It was clear the next move was mine, and I made a supreme effort to keep the fear from showing in my voice. "Go ahead. Tell them your story. We're all listening."

She looked around the room as if seeking support. By this time, however, everyone was keeping very much to their own counsel, sensing they might soon serve as witnesses during a very serious investigation into my conduct. When nobody else seemed interested in her allegation, she seemed to sag, and stated plainly, "Okay, I was lying. The pig never raped me, okay. I made it up."

There was no questioning the veracity of this last statement, as it clearly had the ring of truth to it. For me, it was as if a death sentence had suddenly been lifted. I would have been hard pressed to account for every second of my time between pickup and delivery of the prisoner, and of course it would have been necessary to prove the allegation was false. Physical tests, the same ones performed during the investigation of any ordinary rape, might well have shown evidence of sperm in her vagina. She was a prostitute, after all, albeit a bargain discount variety of working girl. I would have to hope that further testing would prove beyond any possible doubt that the deposits weren't mine. On top of that, the staff had all witnessed the allegations she had made about me. Frankly, I had to admit that she had sounded unusually sincere at the time, considering her advanced state of intoxication.

While in all probability I'd have been able to disprove the charge, that was among the least of my concerns at the time. My reputation as a good street cop was the most important thing in my life then. To put it simply, the fact that a sexual assault accusation had been made against me, no matter how frivolous or improbable, would have stayed with me for the rest of my career. It is difficult for someone not on the job to understand the devastating significance of this type of allegation. Frankly, I doubt very much that I could have lived with the disgrace, real or perceived. I know a policeman who took his own life after a similar, unfounded incident.

***

I quickly developed an immense amount of respect for fire and the damage it can do to the human body after spending some time inside burning buildings. Structure fires are downright frightening, especially when viewed from the interior of the structure, and I have to admire the courage of those people whose job it is to fight fires.

69

Having said that, it is important to point out that policemen and firemen have little in common with respect to the jobs they do. Union spokesmen sometimes try to play one profession off against the other at contract time by quoting work-related injury figures and other statistics. These comparisons never really prove very much. Police and firemen work in completely different environments. Frankly, I wanted nothing to do with their world, especially after hearing a policeman explain how he once reached into a burning room to grab hold of a victim lying just inside the door. When he tried to pull the victim to safety, the charred body disintegrated and all he managed to rescue was a forearm.

***

My first fire was one of the worst experiences of my life. It began innocently enough one night when we heard an alarm ringing a block away from our beat. We walked over to investigate and found a man standing outside a derelict three-story house which had a second-hand store at the front. Apparently he was the caretaker there, and he explained in a disinterested manner that he'd just noticed a fire inside the building, although he had made no effort to call the fire department yet. The thick smoke already billowing out of the ground floor windows meant there was a well-entrenched fire somewhere inside the dilapidated, wood-framed structure.

We called for the fire crews to attend and stood on the sidewalk to await their response. It soon occurred to us that this building, like many of the remaining older houses scattered throughout the West End, might have been divided into apartments. We mentioned that to the caretaker, who was now sitting on the fender of a nearby car having a cigarette. He seemed surprised at the question, as if puzzled as to why we would be interested. After some thought, he grinned sheepishly and confirmed that there were indeed tenants residing inside the burning structure. That was not what I wanted to hear.

We entered the house through a door that led into the ground floor hallway. The smoke inside was already dense, but we could still see well enough to make our way from room to room. We immediately started kicking in doors and waking the tenants because there was a good chance the structure could burst into flames at any moment. It was not an easy task. Many of the inhabitants were derelicts who had to be shaken awake because they were in a drunken stupor when we found them. Some stubbornly refused to leave their rooms.

I started inhaling noxious fumes with every breath I took inside the building. As breathing became more and more difficult, my partner kicked in the door to the room where the fire must have started. He and

I stood at the entrance of what we later discovered was a one-room apartment situated directly behind the secondhand shop. There was fire and thick smoke in the room, but we could still see the shape of a person lying on a burning bed to the left of the doorway. He was horribly burned. The flames that enveloped him had transformed him into a charred, shriveled caricature of a human being. I knew instinctively that he had to be dead, because nothing could have survived the inferno inside that room. I yelled to my partner that we should forget him and get the rest of the tenants out. The fire was already spreading through the walls and floors, and I was concerned we would all be trapped inside if we didn't get on with the evacuation.

As we turned to leave, I glanced back inside and caught a glimpse of the victim's leg flexing in slow motion. I realized the movement was probably just the result of his muscle tissue contracting from the heat, but I also knew there was a small chance part of him was still somehow clinging to life inside that charred body shell. I wouldn't go in there after him. I couldn't. Not with the room burning around us. It was my decision to leave the victim where he was, and for the moment that was what we did.

We left for the second floor and continued our attempts to rouse the other tenants. Other policemen, alerted by our calls over the radio for assistance, joined us. With their assistance, we finally managed to evacuate everyone else from the premises. When my partner returned to the fire room on his way out of the building, he managed to grab the victim by a leg and drag him into the hallway in an act of courage that impressed the hell out of me.

When I next saw the victim, he was sprawled on the doorstep awaiting an ambulance. What used to be a face was now just a featureless, hideous blob. A sporadic stream of bubbles emerged from a slit where his mouth should have been, evidence of a fragile spark of life somewhere beneath the charred surface. He never regained con-sciousness before he was finally pronounced dead a short while later at the hospital.

I know there was nothing we could have done to save him because he was burned to a crisp by the time we arrived. That is not to say that I have never regretted the pragmatic decision to abandon him to his fate so we could save the rest of the tenants. Frankly, that choice was made at least in part as a result of my reluctance to enter the fire room out of fear for my own safety. In fact, I always regarded the incident as one of the few times on the job where I was tested and found wanting. As a street policeman, I discovered that the experience of taking calculated risks could be, at times, extremely exhilarating. On the other hand, the consequences of failure during some of the more challenging situations were sometimes extremely difficult to deal with. Happy endings were rare in my line of work. Years of nightmares about this fire served as an unpleasant reminder of my shortcomings.

***

The best thing that ever happened to skid road hotels was the installation of automatic sprinkler systems. Most of the fire calls I attended as a policeman were the result of smoking in bed. Many of these fires would have been disastrous if the sprinklers hadn't extinguished the flames before the fire could spread.

During one fire that quickly filled an old rooming house hallway with smoke, two of us who arrived before the firemen kicked in the door of the fire room. We expected to find a charred corpse inside. What greeted us instead was a soggy mattress and a shower of water that soaked us both through to the skin. There was no sign of the occupant because he had left for an evening at the bar. Best of all, there was little danger that the fire would consume the entire structure, along with many of the residents, after working its way into the walls where nothing could stop it. It was well worth the cold shower not to have to deal with another serious burn victim.

***

It was one of the coldest days of the year. I showed up for work that particular Sunday morning with a mild hangover. I rolled the passenger-side window all the way down so I could inhale massive amounts of cold, cleansing oxygen as my partner for the day drove through the East End. The streets were deserted. It was just after daybreak, and there was a low fog that shrouded the frost-covered houses along our route. Since radio wasn't holding any calls for us, our first stop was to be a coffee shop for much-needed nourishment.

Nobody else was awake at this hour, and the bitterly cold morning air went a long way toward restoring my well-being. I was fascinated by the way mist was drifting around the darkened houses we passed, but a wisp of fog near one half-open window on the second story of an older frame house caught my attention for some reason. I asked my partner to drive around the block so we could have a second look. We stood on the sidewalk for a minute, trying to determine if it was indeed smoke coming out of the window or just fog.

Even from close range it was difficult to tell the difference. We knew it was wiser to err on the side of safety, so we called the fire department and started banging on the two front doors of the house. The downstairs occupants joined us on the porch moments later. When no one responded from the upstairs apartment at first, we decided we'd have to kick in the door. Before we could do so, a young man with fresh burns to one arm suddenly barged out through the entranceway. He seemed stunned, and mumbled something about his room having caught fire. According to him, there was no one else inside. Because he seemed to be quite intoxicated, we decided we should check the apartment ourselves.

We ran upstairs and found the bedroom just starting to burst into flames around the area of his bed. As soon as we were sure there was nobody else left behind, we ran outside to wait for the firemen. They were able to extinguish the fire quickly before it had a chance to spread to the rest of the house. When they threw a smoldering mattress out the front door, it was obvious that smoking in bed had caused the fire.

As the freezing air sobered up our victim, he readily confessed that there had been a minor mattress fire hours earlier when he'd stumbled into bed after a night of power-drinking. He had apparently fallen asleep after lighting a cigarette. Instead of calling the fire department, he had simply thrown a glass of water on the mattress and then passed out in a drunken stupor until we woke him up by banging on his door.

We had driven by just as the smoldering embers burst into flames again. The young man would undoubtedly have died from smoke inhalation if we hadn't awakened him when we did. He never even bothered to thank us as he was led off to the ambulance for treatment of his burns, although the downstairs tenants were grateful that we saved their house and their lives.

***

If only I had a dollar for every time a suspect told me, "You're only doing this because I'm _____!"

You can fill in the blank with all the common colors, races and professions. Nobody ever wanted to accept the simple fact that they had been arrested, or otherwise dealt with, primarily for the same reason people climb mountains: "Because they're there." No, whatever happened must have happened because all cops are racists. Stupid people rationalize their actions in stupid ways.

Allegations of racism always get prominent media attention. When a member of any minority group happens to get shot by the police, critical headlines are inevitable, regardless of the actual circumstances of the incident. Extremist groups claiming discrimination against their particular race or religion tend to use such incidents as a focal point for media attention to their cause. The issue of racism quickly overshadows the facts of the case, especially where controversial allegations can be distorted and exploited to further the aims of unscrupulous activists.

Individual police officers must face a form of trial which is frequently conducted by members of the media. Reporters will discuss the case as if they have done a complete and impartial investigation, and of course they usually haven't. Often evidence of dubious value or relevance will be produced in news stories in an attempt to prove the police officer has erred in some way. During this process the officer finds himself serving as a visible representation of society's real or perceived sins against its minorities, and the press are fully prepared to sacrifice his career for the greater good of society, even if he is completely innocent. For instance, any previous allegations of racism against a policeman will be held up as undeniable proof that he is a bigot, and therefore undoubtedly guilty of whatever current allegations he faces.

The reality is that police officers are no more prejudiced than the society they are drawn from. Having said this, it is important to note that officers cannot allow their prejudices to influence their judgment or decisions. There is a good reason for this. With the possible exception of political office, there is no other line of work where an individual's treatment of everyone he deals with is more carefully monitored. The necessity of fair and even-handed police behavior is regulated by the criminal and civil courts, human rights commissions, royal commissions, internal review boards, the media, peer pressure and vigilant supervisors.

What the activists seem to be saying, if their accusations are to be accepted at face value, is that policemen as a group are deliberately killing minorities at random in situations where, in theory, a WASP suspect would merely walk away undisturbed. That concept defies logic and is directly contrary to my experience on the job. Without corroborating evidence, how can any rational person conclude that a policeman who defends himself against a man attacking him with a knife is prejudiced, solely because the person he kills happens to be of a different race? Unfortunately, few in the media see fit to defend individual police officers against this type of vicious and unsubstantiated allegation. By the time a policeman is cleared of all accusations during a trial or inquest, it is usually too late to repair the damage done to his reputation.

I find it less than amusing to hear the left-wing lunatic fringe calling for all police officers to be tested for racist tendencies, and then fired or not hired in the first place if they don't pass. Social scientists believe they have come up with methods of analyzing test subjects in order to weed out those whose ideas don't match their own concept of the ideal new-age, public-relations oriented police person. This concept is impractical and unrealistic when a person's career may depend on someone's interpretation of an ink blot. Such a blatant violation of their own privacy and civil rights would, of course, be unacceptable. Despite this, they seem more than willing to subject a policeman to such indignities. It always reminds me of ancient times when people accused of witchcraft were tested by dunking their heads under water. Anyone who drowned after several minutes without air was deemed to have flunked the test and posthumously pronounced guilty.

There is no such thing as a reliable test that can prove a policeman is racist. There is no litmus test for racism other than the quality of the individual policeman's work itself. There are, at present, more than enough safeguards built into the system to monitor each policeman's actions on the job and weed out those who would abuse their authority.

**

Whenever I hear a debate about freedom of the press, I always flash back to the disturbing image of a newspaper photo we were shown at the Police College. It was obviously nighttime when the picture was taken. Two of our members had been photographed holding an explosive device they were examining while standing beside a garbage can. The incident must have dated back to a time when the department didn't have the well-respected RCMP bomb squad to call on, because from one blue-uniformed arm dangled all the components of a genuine time bomb. It consisted of several dynamite sticks, batteries and a clock, connected with a length of wire.

Most of the details of the object they were examining so intently have blurred with time, but not the expressions on the faces of those two policemen. A news photographer had apparently crept to a position beside the cops while they were cautiously removing the device from a garbage can. The instant the bomb emerged from its hiding place was also the moment he chose to take his picture.

The policemen, with their concentration resting solely on the deadly object they were examining, must have thought their lives had suddenly come to an end. The brilliant fireball of light as the camera's flash went off in their eyes must have seemed like the last thing they would ever see, because the sheer, stark look of terror on their faces was unmistakable. It would seem clear to me that this photographer had been willing to risk their lives just to capture a good photo opportunity. Sadly, that kind of attitude is not uncommon.

***

My first run-in with the media came during a warrant attempt at a house on the East Side. We had information that a robbery suspect, believed to be armed, was holed up inside the house. When a supervisor asked for additional units to surround the house so the suspect wouldn't be able to escape, TV crews were monitoring the broadcast with their scanners.

Even before we had a chance to set up for the arrest attempt, one marked TV van had already parked directly in front of the house and another was sitting nearby with its engine running. Even the stupidest crook knows what overt media presence outside his home means. The element of surprise, often the best protection a policeman has when attempting to arrest an armed suspect, was now lost.

We had to leave our positions behind cover in order to ask the TV crews to move. The cooperation we received was minimal at best. Their attitude was particularly galling since the media know that if the suspect somehow twigs to their presence before police on the scene have an opportunity to get organized, there is a good chance of provoking a premature and violent response from the criminal. Naturally this could result in some spectacular footage, especially if somebody gets shot.

The media's justification for inserting cameramen into the middle of serious and volatile situations is that the public have a "right to know". Of course what they are really saying is that the public have a "right to be entertained," since the footage obtained at great risk to the cameramen as well as to policemen nearby is valuable only when it contains graphic scenes of violence and mayhem.

The facts underlying the original incident could quite reasonably be reported without the accompanying dramatic footage that serves only to entertain and titillate. The reality is that nothing grabs viewer's attention better than controversy and the sight of blood. A news show without ratings does not sell advertising.

***

I once saw footage of a cameraman who was nursing a slight gunshot wound, inflicted while he was filming an incident involving a barricaded gunman. I was shocked to hear him deny on camera that police, who had surrounded the area of the gunman's house, had ever

76

asked him to stay out of harm's way. I found his story a little difficult to swallow. He obviously must have known the nature of the call and the address where the suspect was calling from, because he wouldn't have been there in the first place if he hadn't heard the details on his scanner. How much warning does a normal person need before moving out of the line of fire? When the injured cameraman then suggested that somehow the police were not working hard enough to protect him, my blood boiled.

I remember experiencing similar problems with the media at many of my man-with-a-gun calls. It was a constant battle to keep some of the most aggressive cameramen out of range of a potential firefight. We also had to worry about citizens drawn to the scene out of curiosity. Most importantly, we had to stay out of the line of fire ourselves, while at the same time maintaining a vigil on the suspect's location so that we didn't bump into him unexpectedly, or inadvertently allow him to escape.

There is seldom enough manpower to safely cordon off and evacuate an entire neighborhood. However, when a shootout does occur, the media will always ask why this was not done. They never mention the fact that some of the policemen at the scene who could have been used to contain the suspect had instead been kept busy herding adventuresome cameramen safely out of the way.

One of the most reprehensible techniques employed by certain members of the media involves what I call "grieving widow" interviews. This technique is utilized to best advantage after a police-involved shooting. Anyone who witnesses an incident where deadly force is used against a suspect will naturally be excited and upset immediately afterward. If that witness happens to be the person responsible for summoning police to the scene, or perhaps a friend or relative of the deceased suspect, he or she will often experience overwhelming guilt because of their role in the incident.

Before the initial shock has a chance to dissipate, bystanders are naturally susceptible to manipulation by unscrupulous reporters who shove a microphone into their faces. Conversely, a policeman obtaining a statement from a witness must be careful not to taint that statement in any way by coloring it with his own viewpoint, as best illustrated by the classic "Just the facts, ma'am" of Dragnet fame.

The reporter's questions will be anything but neutral. "How do you feel about the police gunning down your nephew right in front of you? Do you think it was necessary for the police to shoot that young man, since he was only threatening them with a knife, while they themselves had guns? According to you, the man the police emptied their revolvers into was a quiet tenant; don't you think they might have over-reacted? Do you think it is right for a human being to die like that?"

An unethical reporter can easily create controversy or raise at least one contentious issue at even the most straightforward of police calls. At the tail end of the piece, he or she need only state that the police have many questions to answer in order to suggest that something is amiss, even if that is clearly not the case. Only those eyewitnesses whose accounts contain controversial viewpoints will survive the editing process to make it to the evening newscast. The more emotional their response, the greater the impact.

Bystanders who haven't actually seen enough of the incident to make a reasonable judgment about the appropriateness of actions taken by police officers are often subsequently portrayed as neutral eyewitnesses by inept reporters. The possibility that their opinion may be influenced by mitigating factors, such as drunkenness or a lengthy criminal record, is seldom mentioned. On the other hand, the police must interview these witnesses before their story can be influenced by others. Investigators must get a coherent statement from them that will eventually form part of the evidence for a trial or inquest. I saw coverage of a local police-involved shooting that featured eye-witness accounts from two grubby-looking bystanders. Subsequent investigation by the police revealed that neither of them had actually been present during the incident.

A thorough investigator could take weeks to piece together the complete story behind a serious incident, but the media demand a neat and tidy solution in time for their next deadline. Because the police will not or cannot comment on the investigation before all the facts have been gathered and analyzed, an information vacuum is created. It is a void that some unscrupulous members of the press are happy to fill with malicious speculation. Whenever I was involved in a serious incident and then heard a completely different story emerging from the well-paid lips of a talking head during the next newscast, I couldn't help but question the credibility of everything else I saw on their show.

I've met a few reporters socially. They always profess to be surprised when they discover that many policemen regard the profession of journalism as somewhat less respectable than prostitution. Many of them are decent people, and they usually just shrug their shoulders and remind their accusers that, after all, it's only a game, isn't it?

I also had an opportunity to peer into the private lives of some prominent media types during the course of my police duties, and I was always appalled by the way they could cheerfully invade the privacy of others while zealously protecting their own dirty linen. The most revolting human character trait has to be hypocrisy.

***

The Granville Mall beat men had heard rumors about a particularly flashy pimp who had just moved up to Vancouver from the United States. Since he had allegedly been flashing handguns in front of various street people, we were eager to talk to him. My partner and I were traveling through a quiet neighborhood on an errand when we unexpectedly spotted the distinctive Lincoln Continental that this pimp was reported to be driving.

We pulled him over without incident. After a thorough search turned up no sign of the weapons, we arrested him for being in the country illegally and turned him over to the immigration department. His car was left on the street, parked legally. We knew he enjoyed hurting the prostitutes he coerced into working for him, and after talking to him for a while we confirmed to our own satisfaction that he was indeed a thoroughly despicable person. We were also well aware he had a good lawyer, and that he could potentially prolong his stay in Canada indefinitely by appealing any deportation order. That meant he could continue his lucrative trade as a pimp in our city.

There seemed to be nothing we could do about this pimp, until a senior detective who overheard us discussing our dilemma began carrying on a rhetorical conversation. What if, he speculated, our pimp friend had not bothered to make his bank payments back home, now that he had moved his operation to Canada? What would happen if someone notified an American repossession company just across the border that there was a beautiful Lincoln parked on a Vancouver street that belonged to an American bank? What indeed!

As we had anticipated, the ugly American was released from custody later that week. I have no idea what happened to his car, but I do know that he never saw it again. We learned the story of the rest of his stay in our country through the police crime bulletins and the local newspapers. Apparently much of this pimp's status and manhood emanated from his flashy car. Now that he traveled everywhere by taxi, he lost any chance he'd had of gaining a substantial foothold in the lucrative prostitution business in Vancouver. In fact, his associates on the street now shunned him and his girls began to mock him openly.

His stay in Canada finally ended after he rented a cheap sedan and tried to run over one of the local working girls who had just rejected his latest business proposal. She took exception to being struck by a lowly Chevy and called the cops. The pimp was eventually sentenced to a lengthy jail term, after which he was slated to be returned forcibly to his native land by immigration officers.

***

One pimp who developed an instant dislike for me made his feelings known by punching me as my back was turned to him. I was at the jail attending to another matter when this particularly unsavory individual, part of a load of prisoners already destined for Oakalla prison, slugged me for no reason. I wanted dearly to repay him in kind but circumstances in the form of an attentive supervisor conspired to protect him from immediate retribution. He laughed in my face as I stood there impotently nursing a bruised side.

I checked his records before he left, but as far as I could tell I had never arrested him before and it seemed the attack had taken place solely because of the uniform I happened to be wearing. He was currently appearing in court on a vicious rape charge, a fact that his fellow prisoners were not privy to. There is a good reason these matters are never discussed. Convicts are well known for their hatred of sex offenders, a part of the inmate code that seems to have survived intact over the years.

I mentioned the circumstances of our altercation to the sheriffs escorting him to Oakalla. I realized afterward that another convict had moved unobtrusively to a position beside us and might have been eavesdropping on the conversation. Apparently, word of his status as a sex offender had indeed leaked to the prison population. Shortly after his arrival at Oakalla, he suffered an unfortunate accident when he somehow tripped and fell down a flight of stairs, breaking both his legs.

***

Siphoning gas is the preferred method of refueling for downwardly-mobile crooks who haven't got the nerve to fill up at a self-serve station and then drive off without paying. Because sniffing gas fumes, and sometimes even drinking gas itself, is a cheap but deadly high, siphoning gas from other people's tanks has more than just the obvious side benefits. Most people who regularly park downtown have some form of locking gas cap to prevent such thefts, so you can imagine the joyful expression on one youthful offender's face when he discovered an unattended Recreational Vehicle with no lock whatsoever on its tank.

He quickly pulled his stolen car alongside this unexpected prize. Under the cover of darkness, he removed the cap, inserted one end of the plastic siphon tube into the opening and sucked deeply to start the flow of gasoline. Unfortunately for him, the tank he had chosen to pilfer was in fact a waste-holding tank full of sewage.

***

I have never been much of an athlete. In fact, I tend to carry around far more weight at belt level than I should. For many years my idea of exercise was walking ten feet to the bar to order another beer. That was why I was particularly amused at the scene I witnessed on Hornby Street one busy Friday night. Two of our most athletic members, a well-respected male and female team from our shift, were handling a routine call on the sidewalk. A particularly cocky young man had emerged from the crowd of partiers that had gathered to watch. Obviously feeling the effects of too much booze, he began taunting the police.

As drunk as he was, he could still run fast enough to elude the frustrated police officers each time they gave chase. He would run away until they gave up, and then follow them back to the sidewalk to resume haranguing them while they attempted to finish their report. The members were, of course, carrying a heavy load of equipment and they were understandably tired after a long night on the street. However, they were also joggers, and the bottom line was that they simply couldn't catch him.

The young man, emboldened by his success, became increasingly more annoying. It was like waving a red flag at a bull. By the time I dropped by in the wagon to cover the call, he was still at large and there seemed to be no sign of an early end to the impasse. Any thought of surrender was unthinkable at this stage of the game, because the situation had gradually evolved into a direct challenge to police authority. I suggested shooting the runner in his kneecap to slow him down, but the officers were not amused.

I watched the spectacle for a while until I noticed that the runner's attention was fully focused on the two frustrated police officers on the sidewalk. I walked quietly onto the roadway on the outside of a line of cars until I was well past his position. I then doubled back to the sidewalk as quickly as my overweight body would allow, knowing full well that if he got away from me now, the story of my presumptuous stratagem would quickly be related to the entire shift.

He actually caught sight of me out of the corner of his eye as I lunged for him, but the alcohol had dulled his senses and he hesitated just long enough that I had the opportunity to grab him by the collar. His feet never touched the ground as I walked him to the wagon and tossed him into the back for safekeeping later in the drunk tank. In the violent world we policed, this particular skirmish was unremarkable and trivial. In the end, however, it was the little victories that made the job so enjoyable.

***

Rumors about an incident with a darker side made the rounds of our department several years ago. A well-respected policeman who was known for his effectiveness at arresting crooks suddenly began receiving threats from a group of active criminals who frequented his beat. The threats were taken seriously after he learned that one of the crooks had discovered his unlisted home address from a baby-sitter. The rounders openly boasted to their associates on the street that they planned to pick a night when the policeman was on duty to visit his home, pour gasoline around the circumference and burn it down. They were well aware that his wife and children would be inside the house at nighttime, thanks to the baby-sitter, but they made it clear that this would not deter them at all.

The policeman did everything in his power to discourage the threats, but the rounders just shrugged off his warnings and put word out on the street that the only way they would drop the plan was if he stopped interfering in their criminal activities. The criminal justice system could do little to protect his family, and in the end it was clear he would have to take care of the problem himself.

More by luck than anything else, he happened to spot the suspects parked in a vacant lot across the street from his home. It was a dark night, and they had no idea he'd spotted them. They seemed to be discussing their plan of action, secure in the knowledge that until they actually committed a crime there was nothing the police could do to stop them.

The policeman considered calling 911, but in the end left his phone on the hook and instead went to his gun cabinet. Moving quickly under the cover of darkness, he left his house by the back door and made his way to a position near the car. He then fired one 12 gauge shotgun round into the trunk.

He was surprised at the amount of damage he caused. As he watched, the trunk flew open and the tire nearest to him exploded dramatically. The driver did not need further prompting. His car sped off with one bare rim leaving a trail of sparks to mark its progress away from the quiet neighborhood. The cop later learned from his sources on the street that the rounders had apparently decided to call off the vendetta. In fact, they never returned to his neighborhood. When he checked the communications center the next day, he discovered that none of his neighbors had bothered to call in the shots fired, even though the single shotgun blast had sounded to him like a small nuclear detonation.

***

One of my favorite stories about the justice system concerns a pleasant-looking but obviously distraught young lady who approached a policeman on a quiet West End street one afternoon. She had been raped, she sobbed, and the suspect was still holed up in her apartment.

The policeman called for a cover unit as the victim led him up the stairs to her suite. He knew the chances of a rapist remaining at the crime scene were remote, but he had to give it a try before traveling to the hospital to begin the complicated process of investigating the rape. He opened the door cautiously and discovered a very surprised young man sitting on the couch having a coffee. The complainant instantly shrieked out a positive identification of the young man, and he quickly found himself handcuffed and under arrest.

It is a rare crook who doesn't make at least a token attempt to deny the charges against him, no matter how overwhelming the evidence to the contrary. This one was no exception. He said he'd just met the victim on the street that very morning while window shopping. She had befriended him and invited him up to her place for a sociable coffee, and he had readily accepted. He emphatically denied that sexual intercourse had ever taken place. He claimed the victim had excused herself to shop for the ingredients for dinner at a corner store just a few minutes earlier.

The investigator found his story more than a little incredible. Still, something about the case troubled him, although he couldn't say for sure what was wrong at first. The victim was still adamant she had been raped, so he sent her to the hospital for tests. He then called for a wagon to transport the tearful suspect to jail. While they waited for transportation to arrive, the desperate suspect had one last inspiration. He begged the cop to take him to his apartment nearby. According to him, they would find irrefutable proof of his innocence there, although he would not elaborate further.

By this time the policeman's instincts were telling him that something was very wrong, and he agreed to accommodate this one last request. At the door of the suspect's apartment they were warmly greeted by an effeminate youth who spoke with an exaggerated lisp punctuated by gestures from a particularly limp wrist. The lad took one look at their handcuffed prisoner and immediately began begging the startled cop not to take his lover to jail. All the prisoner could say was, "See! See! I told you I didn't do it. This proves it. I'm gay!"

He was released shortly thereafter when his story was confirmed. Further investigation showed that the female had traveled all across the province making false rape complaints against complete strangers. She was mentally ill, of course, but not sick enough that she could be confined to an institution for treatment. The damage she had done to innocent people's lives was incalculable. Our department took what limited steps it could to make sure she would never again be able to repeat her offense.

***

On one occasion we ran into trouble when we arrested a crook in his hotel room after we discovered there were outstanding warrants in his name. The man's landlord packed all his possessions into suitcases because he knew the crook was now vacating the room for other, less comfortable accommodations at the jail. When his belongings were forwarded to him in prison, however, his prized hash pipe was nowhere to be seen.

His defense lawyer accused us of stealing his client's hash pipe during the arrest. He threatened to sue us, and he bragged that he would use legal aid funds to cover the cost of dragging us before a civil court. The suit never went ahead because the budding young Clarence Darrow realized his client, who was already on probation for another offense, was prohibited by the conditions of that probation from possessing or consuming drugs. In order for the civil trial against us to proceed, his client would have to explain why he had been in possession of the drug paraphernalia in the first place. We never did hear from the lawyer after that revelation.

***

Three of us were called to a comedy club where the live entertainment had been rudely interrupted by a table of neatly-dressed drunks at center stage. The two couples were told several times to shut up or leave, but they responded by threatening the staff. The meanest of the two men was particularly big, so the bartenders had good reason to be concerned. The heckling continued unabated for an hour until management finally decided to call the police.

The whole bar was watching their antics with disgust. The couples were obviously very drunk or very stoned. We tried the polite approach first by warning them that they were headed for jail if they didn't leave immediately. This attempt to defuse the situation was markedly unsuccessful, and they escalated their misbehavior by

84

screaming obscenities and threats into our faces.

Most of the crowds we encounter at these incidents are neutral, if not downright hostile toward the police. This audience, a full house, had obviously listened to the yahoos at center stage for long enough, because they began to yell out support of our endeavors.

The two couples still refused to leave. Consequently, we arrested the loudest and biggest male for assault by trespass, since he had ignored the bouncer's original request to leave. He was totally out of control by this time, so I was not surprised when he swore at us and refused to come without a fight. In fact, he threw a roundhouse punch that narrowly missed rearranging my face. A policewoman and I removed him from the club by grabbing his arms and pushing him forcefully toward the door. The patrons gave us a standing ovation as we left, which was a first for me.

Once outside, we handcuffed our prisoner and tossed him into the paddy wagon. The second male was wise enough to keep his distance and passively monitor the situation, but both wives went berserk and had to be arrested. The wagon was rocking from side to side on its suspension as the three prisoners tried to kick their way out through the locked doors. I followed the wagon to the station, and heard them screaming threats against us all the way to jail. We had a fair amount of trouble processing the arrests, but to me the standing ovation we got from the audience was well worth the effort.

***

I traveled the width of my district at high speed one night to an emergency call, only to be canceled at the last second and diverted to investigate a stabbing that had just occurred back at the other end of my area. Two men at that location had interrupted a prowler breaking into their car. When they confronted him, he attacked them with a bayonet. One victim had been stabbed in the chest, and by the time I arrived on the scene with my brake linings smoking, his blood pressure was too low to measure. He was sent to hospital as soon as paramedics could stabilize him for the trip.

His friend had wounds to his neck and head that didn't appear serious at the time, but we sent him to hospital as well. Later it was discovered that the tip of the bayonet blade had penetrated his skull. Both victims survived, thanks to the prompt response by Emergency Health Services crews.

A dogmaster found the suspect responsible for all this mayhem nearby. I whipped around the corner to cover him when I heard his radio broadcast. As I drove up I could see the policeman wrestling with our stabbing suspect on the ground. The scene was surrealistically illuminated by the flashing wig-wag headlights of a police car. The blood-stained bayonet was on the ground beside them. A very excited police dog maneuvered frantically to try to help his master, although he was definitely having trouble finding an opening as the two combatants rolled on the ground during a desperate struggle.

I could tell when the dog finally found what he was looking for by the sound of a piercing scream unlike any I'd heard before. By the time I emerged from my car to help subdue the attacker, I could see the dog had chosen to bite the suspect's most vulnerable and sensitive area. Once he'd sunk his teeth into solid flesh, he started shaking and tugging at it, as if attempting to tear a chunk of flesh from between the man's legs. The screams signaled the end of the suspect's attempt to resist arrest, however, and we had no further problem handcuffing him.

I have talked to a number of violent offenders who have had run-ins with police dogs. The vast majority of them freely admitted that after these encounters, they never stopped looking over their shoulders while committing crimes. I would be willing to bet that the worst of their nightmares featured a massive German Shepherd lunging out of the darkness.

***

Mistakes are something a police officer must eventually learn to accept as part of the job. Modern police work is incredibly complicated at times. The number of different and challenging situations a cop now encounters makes it inevitable that things will not always go as planned. He can only hope that these errors will turn out to be minor and will pass unnoticed. A wise police officer learns from his mistakes and then puts them behind him, regardless of how embarrassing they are.

And yes, they can be embarrassing. Early one Sunday morning after the bars had closed, I was assigned to attend a nightclub on Hornby Street because the janitor had recovered a stick of dynamite from under one of the tables. This came at a time when there seemed to be a lot of dynamite circulating throughout the underworld. In fact, one enterprising individual had recently been using a stick of the explosive to convince bus drivers that he should ride for free. Not surprisingly, nobody argued with him and he traveled several bus routes without paying his fares until he was eventually apprehended by the police.

I soon identified the red cylindrical object recovered at the night club as a real stick of dynamite. Procedure dictated that the Royal Canadian Mounted Police bomb squad be called for the dangerous task of disposing of all explosives we found, so I asked the radio operator to make the appropriate notifications. Members of the bomb squad had a reputation for coolness under pressure. Most seemed very confident in the way they handled what surely must be one of the most stressful jobs in police work. Fortunately there was no sign of seepage or crystallization on the dynamite, two indications that nitroglycerin might be present on the outside of the red cardboard exterior. In that case the dynamite could explode just from rough handling. I anticipated that there would be no complications and accepted a coffee while we waited for a member from the bomb squad to be called out from his home.

We were there for half an hour until a middle-aged man dressed in neat civilian clothing walked in and greeted us with a confident smile. He walked over to where we had left the dynamite on a table, picked it up, examined it closely and then tossed it casually into the air several times, catching it in the palm of his hand as if it were a beat man's baton made of wood instead of high explosive.

I marveled yet again at the bomb squad officer's casual disdain for danger. When the individual finally sat down to join us for a coffee, I anticipated hearing some interesting war stories. After what must have seemed like a very puzzling conversation to him, I eventually discovered he was not the bomb squad expert I'd been expecting. In fact, he was the owner of the club. The janitor had called him at home and he'd dropped by out of curiosity. He knew nothing at all about explosives, and I was doubly grateful when the genuine expert arrived to safely dispose of the dynamite.

***

We were hot on the trail of a robbery suspect, and we knew he'd just ducked into a skid road hotel on East Hastings Street. We hurriedly described our man to the desk clerk. He nodded knowingly and told us the number of a room he'd rented recently to someone matching that description. We ordered him not to make a warning call to the suspect while we made our way to his room. After running up several flights of stairs, we stood outside the suspect's door for a minute, listening. We were hoping to get some indication of how many people were inside and what they were up to. All we could hear were rustling sounds, as if the suspect had hopped into bed already.

We promptly kicked the door in, hoping to surprise him in the event he was armed and prevent him from disposing of drugs and other evidence out the window. I went inside first with my weapon drawn, but stopped in the doorway as the action in the room froze in mid-stroke. There was a man lying on the bed, but he didn't quite match our description, although I immediately recognized him as a criminal I had arrested before. The prostitute beside him was in the process of plying her trade. She stared at us blankly as the object of her desire slowly retracted to a mere shadow of its former self, leaving her empty mouth frozen open in the shape of an "O".

My partner stepped back into the hallway as I stammered an apology. He was just in time to see the door of a room down the hallway open. The occupant popped his head outside to see what all the excitement was about. It was our suspect! We ran to his doorway and grabbed him before he realized what was happening. The evening ended happily for everyone but the robbery suspect and his frustrated next door neighbor, who probably to this day flashes back to a very traumatic moment in his life every time he goes to bed with a prostitute.

***

Another incident proved almost as embarrassing. We had been called to a dark lane on a Peeping Tom report, but there was no one there when we finally arrived. Several of us then got out of our cars in front of the reportee's address to discuss something that had happened at a previous call. As we gossiped, I glanced over my shoulder and gasped at what I saw through the basement window of the apartment building.

The couple inside were oblivious to the commotion caused by our arrival, and their passion was clearly visible through the open drapes. We had undoubtedly found the object of our Peeping Tom's interest. I made an inane remark as three heads wearing police hats all stared in the same direction, awestruck. "Now we know what got him interested, eh?"

I almost had a heart attack when a male voice rang out loudly from a darkened balcony only a couple of feet above our heads. His words were dripping with sarcasm. "Presumably the same thing you're looking at, officer!"

When I had recovered my composure, I thanked our helpful citizen. He told us he had phoned in the original call when he had noticed a young man staring into his neighbor's window. I could almost hear the grin on his face when he cheerfully wished us a good night as we left.

***

When I started as a policeman, heroin was the drug of choice with street addicts. Hypes used to carry several capsules of heroin inside powdered balloon ends called bundles, which they usually secreted in their mouths. When approached by the police, they would simply swallow the bundle. Often it became a race between us and the addict's stomach as to who finally got possession of the drugs. Most hypes could regurgitate the bundle at will after the police left, but some had to wait for it to complete its dangerous passage through the digestive system.

We were walking through a crowded Granville Street bar when our eyes met those of a very nervous male wandering from table to table. His hand shot toward his mouth as we lunged at him. By the time my hand closed around his throat, he had managed to swallow what he'd been holding in his hand. At the same time I was trying to keep the evidence from disappearing, my partner gave him a love tap to the stomach to discourage him from swallowing.

Even as I realized we were too late, I was conscious of my partner's hand plunging deeply into the hype's belly. I watched as the suspect's already pale complexion suddenly became even whiter and he gasped loudly in pain. I quickly released my grip on his throat to give him a chance to breathe normally, so any chance of recovering the drugs disappeared as he swallowed once and then gasped for air.

After he regained his composure, he lifted his shirt and showed us a massive wound on his abdomen, complete with neat rows of fresh stitches. He explained he was dying of stomach cancer and had just left the hospital after recovering from a serious operation. There did not seem to be any fresh damage as a result of our drug search, and he declined our invitation to have his surgical scars checked out in the hospital.

He cheerfully admitted swallowing the drugs, although he claimed there was only one cap inside the balloon. In fact, he sincerely apologized for spoiling our drug case against him, and graciously wished us better luck next time as we said our good-byes.

***

I was involved in a similar incident one evening while working security for a rock concert at the Pacific National Exhibition. We had been asked not to make any drug arrests that night as we were short-handed and could not spare the manpower to process the charges downtown. Our job there was simply to keep the peace. I saw several drug transactions near me during the concert. It was almost as if the traffickers sensed they had some form of temporary immunity that night, because they were not at all subtle while they went about their business.

On my coffee break outside the stadium, I watched as two young men talked about twenty feet from me, oblivious to my presence. I saw one hand over several bills. In return, the other placed something in his friend's shirt pocket after reaching inside his jacket.

I'd already had a long, frustrating day on the street, along with an extremely aggravating evening at the concert. It was as if they had waved a red flag at a bull. I charged at them with as much energy as I could muster. What they saw was a massive, bellowing figure in a dark blue uniform running at full speed down a slight incline toward them. They froze in their tracks. Before they could move I had both of them turned around and pinned securely against the side of a semitrailer.

The first priority was to seize the drugs before they had a chance to disappear. Unfortunately, when I reached into the pocket where I expected to find the evidence I needed for a drug charge, there was nothing there to find. What I did discover was a plastic security tag hanging from the pocket, and I realized to my horror that what I had seen was one of them attaching the tag to the other's shirt. The tag gave the bearer permission to unload the contents of his truck inside the coliseum, a fact that the man now wearing the tag pointed out to me in a very loud, very agitated voice.

I apologized profusely for my mistake, and explained my actions to them as best I could. Another policeman stood by, watching with an embarrassed expression on his face, clearly anticipating a trip to the Internal office and wishing he was elsewhere. The man who had bounced the hardest off the trailer never did accept my apology. He threatened to sue me for everything I was worth, which at that time would have bought him little more than a month's supply of beer. The second person had a great sense of humor. He'd had several run-ins with the police during his youth. When he realized he wasn't going to be charged with anything, he was so relieved that he burst into laughter. In the end, neither of them made a formal complaint.

***

The easiest drug arrest I ever made occurred during a quiet day shift. We had received information from an informant that the occupant of a basement suite was dealing small amounts of grass through his side door. There was insufficient evidence to obtain a search warrant, and we decided that it was not worth spending time watching the apartment to obtain more evidence. We opted to use more subtle methods to put the trafficker out of business, although subtlety was a quality that was usually foreign to my style of police work.

The occupant was a scruffy-looking kid in his early twenties. When he answered the door, we took advantage of his surprise. Using my best attempt at a stern, officious tone, I said, "We know you're dealing out of this place. You wanna bring the drugs out so we can get this over with as quickly as possible?"

"Yes, Sir!" The suspected drug dealer emerged from his apartment thirty seconds later with a bag of grass about the size of a package of frozen peas. He held it out to us respectfully. In fact, he was so polite that we took pity on him and only charged him with Possession of a Narcotic, although the quantity involved could well have warranted a charge of Possession for the Purpose of Trafficking at that time.

***

I attended a motor vehicle accident in the 3000 block of East 1st one sunny winter afternoon to check a report of a car wrapped around a massive wooden hydro pole. The impact had obviously damaged the crossbars far above us at the top of the pole because I could see occasional sparks emanating from amongst the wires secured there. As we helped the ambulance crews extract a victim from his wrecked car, I pointed out the sparks to a firemen. He assured me there was nothing to worry about.

Just before the wrecker moved what remained of the car, I stood on its hood to examine the power pole's metal identification tag which was about seven feet above ground level. I needed the serial number of the damaged pole for my report.

As I climbed down, a traffic policeman who had been directing traffic a block away drove up with a warning. An off-duty B.C. Hydro lineman, stuck in traffic nearby, had noticed the sparks at the top of the damaged pole I was standing under. He approached the traffic officer, stating that the wires above us were very high-voltage lines that could snap at any time and begin whipping through the air. According to him, every living thing within a fifty foot radius of where the wire touched ground would fry instantly.

I believed him, but when I warned the firemen they just laughed and continued their discussion, which happened to be taking place directly under the damaged pole. I left them to it and completed my reports several blocks away.

I was curious as to whether or not the employee had been exaggerating, so I phoned the emergency line at the power company the next day. Their representative made some inquiries, and I subsequently learned that they had obtained high voltage readings almost halfway down the pole. In fact, the electric current had apparently reached a level just above where I had been rubbing dirt off the ID tag with my finger. The company representative told me that if it had been raining that day, our conversation would not have been taking place.

***

My partner and I were cruising aimlessly around the area of

headquarters when a ghostly apparition suddenly appeared out of the misty night air in front of us. The individual was running awkwardly down the middle of Cordova Street at full tilt. I needed another jaywalking statistic toward my monthly quota that night so I jumped out of the passenger side as our car came to a stop. The midnight jogger seemed less than enthusiastic about meeting us and desperately attempted to flee. As we grabbed him in mid-flight, it became obvious that we would not have to handcuff him because he was already wearing somebody else's cuffs.

We returned him to jail just as reports of an escapee on the loose started filtering over our channel. One of the wagon drivers had apparently been knocked over by his prisoner as he opened the wagon doors at the rear of the jail. We locked the escapee up for the night, but not before giving him his jaywalking ticket. I always regarded this incident as the only occasion when the ticket quota system ever accomplished anything worthwhile. Fortunately for us, the cautious bureaucrats who monitored our performance could or would never define in writing the specific number of tickets necessary to meet the quota. Consequently, it was often possible to duck and weave at the end of the month if calls and arrests had left insufficient time to fulfill traffic enforcement obligations, but only if you had an understanding supervisor.

***

After taking numerous Breaking and Entering reports during the one month period we worked day shift, it was always a pleasure to switch to nights so we could have a shot at the burglars while they were most vulnerable to arrest. Although most break-ins in the suburbs occur during the daytime hours, the situation is reversed for the downtown areas. There was, of course, never a shortage of incompetent or unlucky burglars to be caught because Vancouver has more than its share of break-ins.

I happened to be working during one particularly unlucky night for the criminal element. Four young men smashed out the garage door window of an automotive repair shop. They then entered the premises one by one through the opening to look for tools. We were lucky. An alert citizen called us immediately after hearing the sound of breaking glass, and we were already en route to an unrelated call in the same area when he phoned. As a result, we arrived in plenty of time to watch through the windows as the panicking burglars frantically searched for a hiding place. They soon realized they were surrounded with no way out, but they refused to leave the building when ordered to surrender.

Unfortunately for them, the garage interior was well illuminated, and we could see every move they made. For a change we were able to bide our time and bid for whose criminal career we were about to put on hold. The dogmaster got first preference, because nobody there wanted to argue with his enthusiastic police dog. The rest of us, like successful shoppers at a fire sale, ferreted out our chosen targets from their poorly-concealed hiding places and sent them downtown for processing. Mine was shielding his eyes from the light that betrayed his presence, as if the darkness underneath his coat sleeve could somehow keep him hidden from us. We left well satisfied with our night's work.

***

One night, a burglar with a warped sense of humor entered a building on my beat through a skylight. He arrived at the plate glass front doors to make his exit, only to find the law waiting for him because he had tripped a silent alarm inside the premise. We had to wait for a reference, in this case the building manager, to arrive with keys so we could take our suspect into custody. Meanwhile, the burglar explored the building methodically, leaving a trail of lights behind him to betray his progress until he was finally satisfied that all possible means of escape were blocked.

When all hope was lost, he contented himself with standing in front of us in the doorway, making faces and obscene gestures. He was comforted temporarily by the knowledge that he was protected from the wrath of the law by a quarter inch of plate glass. However, when the keys arrived he threw up his hands in a gesture of surrender and became the epitome of tact to avoid any chance of retaliation for his rude behavior.

***

Another burglar was confronted by the police as he emerged from the smashed-out plate glass window of a posh Gastown restaurant. He too had tripped a silent alarm during his break-in. He had probably spent most of his time inside standing at the bar, because he greeted us with a volley of unopened Scotch bottles. We retreated out of the line of fire, so none of us were hit by the barrage.

Fortunately, the burglar had not noticed me hiding to one side of the window, choking back tears of sadness at the tragic loss of good scotch. When he stuck his head out to taunt us, I grabbed him by the jacket and flipped him face-first onto the sidewalk. He gave the restaurant mediocre reviews during a subsequent interrogation, but that may have been because of the poor service.

***

Sometimes, when I had to search a building for burglars, I preferred to have my revolver in my hand, at my side. It depended on how I felt about the call, and what I observed as I drove up to the building. Even with a police dog checking the premise ahead of us, it was wise to be prepared for the worst. Surprises occurred just often enough to maintain a healthy sense of paranoia. One foolish burglar hit a Police Dog over the head with a two-by-four as the dog searched a room we were about to enter. The dog took it personally, and his master was just as upset. During one search of a jewelry store which had been broken into through the front entrance, I peered around a half-opened inside door to find a burglar staring at me. His face was only a few feet from mine. He was arrested without a struggle, but the thought of what might have happened if he'd been armed with a knife or a gun stayed with me for a long time.

Such encounters are rare, but they do happen. Attending numerous false alarms over the course of years of routine police work tends to condition a cop to expect that burglars are usually long gone by the time police arrive to check the premise. Two friends of mine were searching inside a building when a burglar suddenly jumped out from behind a door and screamed at them. The surprise effect, and the fact that his face was painted jet black at the time, was enough to frighten even the bravest policeman. Under the circumstances, the burglar was lucky he didn't get shot.

***

During my first month on the road, I was on routine patrol late at night with a senior policeman when I heard the plaintive voice of an inexperienced officer working a one-man car talking excitedly to the radio operator. He claimed he was being followed by a suspicious vehicle. To the best of my recollection, this was at a time when American police were being ambushed by snipers. Frankly, the thought of a cop in a marked police car worried about someone following him seemed illogical to me at the time, although many years later a similar, and more sinister incident happened to me while I was working a one-man unit.

We sped off to cover him anyway, in case he really did need assistance. He informed the radio operator of his location periodically and made it clear that he could not shake the vehicle, no matter which way he turned. Several cars arrived on the scene simultaneously, and we boxed the suspect vehicle in so it couldn't escape.

We yelled at the six occupants to exit the car one at a time so we could check them out. Although there was much gesticulation and emotion on their part, they simply ignored us. It was not until we finally opened the passenger side door and removed one of the young men that we realized everyone in the car was Deaf. They were hopelessly lost in an unfamiliar city, according to the explanation one of them wrote in my notebook. Their first instinct had been to stop a police car to get directions. I doubt they ever understood what happened next. We apologized to them as best we could and drove away as quickly as possible.

***

Like the Deaf tourists, I too had difficulty finding my way around town when I first started working as a policeman. I had only spent a total of three days in Vancouver before I joined the force. Because I grew up in a small town, I had trouble coping with the busy city traffic I encountered for the first time in my life. My difficulties were compounded by the fact that I had a hard time with street names, so my street map was often the only thing that saved me from getting lost. More than once, when I was particularly pressed for time, I resorted to pulling over startled citizens to ask them for directions.

The first time I was ever assigned to work a one-man patrol car was a very proud moment for me. One of the first things I did was find a deserted street in a warehouse district and squeal my tires, just to see what it felt like in a police car. After committing this one illicit act, I began the process of learning to drive a police car, an art that is completely different from normal motoring . In addition to dealing with all the usual hazards of city driving, police officers must simultaneously monitor their radios, scan their computer terminals, and watch for anything out of the ordinary. It can get pretty hectic at times.

After the first few hours of driving aimlessly around my area, I started to relax a bit and enjoy the experience. My confidence quickly deteriorated, however, when I was assigned to drive a Calgary detective from the police station to the airport. We drove for ten minutes in circles before he tactfully mentioned the fact that we were headed in the wrong direction. By pooling our limited knowledge of the geography of Vancouver, we finally managed to make it to the airport in time to catch his flight. He was very understanding, but I caught him shaking his head in disbelief once when he thought I wasn't looking.

My navigational difficulties became a serious liability when my training assignment switched from the confines of the West End to the wide open spaces of the suburbs. One of my training officers, an excitable man with a great sense of humor, used to laugh out loud as I wandered endlessly through darkened streets like a blind man in a maze.

He was a superb training officer, and he usually waited until I was inadvertently crossing into another municipality before tactfully pointing me back toward our jurisdiction.

One night as I attempted unsuccessfully to transport a prisoner downtown to jail, my training officer became more and more exasperated and finally refused to give me further directions. In fact, he just sat there and covered his eyes with his hands as we headed aimlessly through Burnaby toward Alberta. The prisoner was anxious to settle into a warm jail cell for a good night's sleep, so after a while he started guiding me through the maze of cul-de-sacs and dead-ends until I finally reached a familiar-looking street that I knew would lead me to the station. My training officer's eyes rolled back into his head every time he looked at me for the rest of the shift, but he submitted a good report on my performance to the academy anyway.

***

The conversation on a busy police radio channel seems almost impossible to comprehend when you first hear it. With experience, it is eventually possible to decipher useful information from a jumble of conversation, acronyms and static. Messages occasionally get garbled and misunderstandings occur from time to time, but after a while the subconscious takes over and monitors the radio for relevant information. It is not just a matter of listening for your own car number to be called, because you also monitor what other units in your area are doing so you can help out if necessary.

I was working the wagon one afternoon along with a reserve policeman when I heard our radio operator assign a West End car to a man-with-a-knife call. The suspect was standing in front of the reception desk at St. Paul's Hospital emergency department.

We were close by, so I grabbed the mike, informed radio that we were covering the call and switched on my emergency equipment. The reserve officer was bold enough to inquire over the sound of the siren as to why we were in such a hurry, and I remember wondering to myself why he would ask such a stupid question. After all, we considered the staff at the emergency department equivalent to family, so when they called for help we made a point of getting there as soon as possible. They didn't phone unless we were really needed. I had no idea what his problem was, but I intended to find out after the call was handled.

We were first on the scene. The wagon had barely stopped when I was out and running through the automatic entry doors of the hospital. There was only one man standing at the counter with his back

96

to me. He was dressed like a typical rounder from Granville Street, which told me all I needed to know at the time to form a plan of action. I simply used my considerable weight to pin him up against the counter and handcuff him with one fluid but forceful move.

The prisoner was screaming and swearing by the time I got him cuffed. The only thing missing for the prosecutor's report was his knife, but I was confident that it would eventually turn up after a thorough search. I just hoped it hadn't inadvertently become lodged in his midriff when I threw him up against the counter. I looked up from my labors, ready to accept the expected accolades from a grateful public. Instead, I was greeted by stares that varied from bewilderment to downright amazement. Puzzled, I finally asked one of the nurses if this was indeed the man-with-a-knife they'd phoned in. Nobody said anything until my reserve piped up respectfully. "It wasn't a man-with-a-knife call. It was for a man with a knife wound."

Judging by the blood I now noticed on his stomach and my hands, this version of the call was starting to look more and more accurate. For a moment I was actually at a loss for words. Fortunately for me, our stabbing victim had already shown himself to be intoxicated and obnoxious by virtue of his rude treatment of the nursing staff before our arrival. We all agreed that he would be more comfortable in restraints until he calmed down enough to have his superficial wound treated. Meanwhile, I snuck out of the hospital as unobtrusively as possible, hoping that by the time the victim sobered up he would forget about our abrupt introduction.

***

Some mistakes were more serious than others. In the latter part of my career, the shift system made it impossible to work consistently with the same partner for any length of time. When I started out on the beat, however, I managed to pair up with a constable who had an excellent reputation as a street policeman and was still very interested in catching crooks. A good partner does more than just watch your back, although that basic precaution is important when you are walking through hostile bar crowds.

When you and your partner handle stressful situations together, you soon learn whether or not you can trust each other, and how each person thinks and handles different situations. We had already been working as a team for quite a while when we stumbled into a hotel room full of heroin addicts as a result of a radio call. One of the hypes was sick, so an ambulance crew we had worked with many times before was summoned to the scene to check him out.

Another of the room's occupants was well known to us because of his size and his propensity for using his fists against anyone who upset him. My partner singled him out for attention, and the two of them left the room two minutes later without saying anything. I guessed that my partner was pumping him for information but doubted he would be successful because of this particular criminal's violent reputation. Meanwhile, I had my hands full watching the rest of the crooks on my own.

When my partner burst back into the room with the rounder he'd been talking to, they were scuffling as if ready to start a fist fight. As soon as I saw that, I knew the altercation would have to be resolved quickly or we would find ourselves fighting our way out of the room. I used my flashlight to make an impression on his skull, but that only made him more upset. He turned on me with a bottle in his hand and raised it as if to strike me. It all happened very quickly, but not so fast that I didn't have time to draw my service revolver and point it at his nose. Fortunately, that got his attention, and we had him under control and handcuffed moments later.

My partner's eyes were rolling back in their sockets, so I knew instantly that I had screwed up somehow. It was not until ten minutes later when he very subtly rooted out a federal prison escapee from amongst the room's remaining occupants that I finally realized what had happened. The aggressive hype had used the trip to the hallway to tell my partner about the escapee, no doubt as a result of a dispute between the two thieves over a drug deal. The altercation had been staged to mask the informant's role. That kind of misunderstanding never occurred before or after this incident, and our partnership was very productive and rewarding right up to the end.

***

Another officer and I found ourselves becoming increasingly frustrated one afternoon as we sat a block away from a man-with-a-gun call. The call should have been relatively straightforward. Two ambulance attendants had attended a second floor apartment after a man phoned 911 stating that his roommate was sick. The roommate had refused treatment when they arrived; he wanted to be left alone for awhile. To reinforce his request for privacy, he informed them there was a handgun in a briefcase in the next room. He threatened to use it to shoot them if they didn't leave immediately. The ambulance crew, having quite wisely retreated to call for assistance, were now sitting in their car around the back of the building, waiting for the police to attend.

The procedure in these cases called for all the officers attending to meet a block away from the scene to formulate a plan of attack. The next step was to move in and surround the apartment in question so the suspect did not have an opportunity to hurt innocent passersby or to escape. Officers would then talk to the witnesses and obtain a floor plan of the apartment and the adjacent hallway. Obviously the sooner that was done, the better, because once the scene was under control, we could negotiate an end to the incident without taking any unnecessary risks.

Unfortunately, the supervisor in charge of this particular incident was well known for his propensity to take charge of one call each shift, no matter how insignificant, in order to establish his presence and authority. He would then disappear for the remainder of the shift. The calls he seemed to prefer were, to put it nicely, usually less than challenging.

On this occasion, the supervisor quite properly used his radio to establish a command post one block away from the building. I have no idea where he was broadcasting from. We all met at the command post and awaited his next order. He seemed to be handling the call well, but at the point where he should have ordered specific units into the apartment building to secure the scene, nothing was said. As the call progressed, the members attending the call found themselves still cooling their heels a block away, waiting for instructions to move in. Those instructions never came.

The two of us decided that at the very least someone should join the ambulance crew. They were still waiting patiently behind the apartment building for someone to listen to their story. They greeted us with very puzzled looks. Although from experience they knew the police should have had the area surrounded by now, we were the first blue uniforms they had seen. They didn't believe us when we told them nobody else was anywhere near the apartment. We obtained the appropriate information from them and they cleared the scene in a big hurry.

When we attempted to broadcast the information we had just obtained, we were cut off by the supervisor. He was in the process of having the radio operator phone our suspected gunman and order him to leave the apartment and surrender. Our jaws dropped in unison. That meant the gunman would have to exit his apartment, take an elevator or stairs to the ground floor, leave the building and walk several hundred feet down the sidewalk until he ran across a policeman. The missing element of the plan was that there was no one anywhere near him to accept the surrender.

I could picture the suspect agreeing to leave his apartment after a little coaxing, but he would then have to push the elevator button with his nose since he was under orders to keep his hands in the air. Because no effort had been made to keep innocent civilians from entering and leaving the building, we would only recognize the suspect by the fact that he was the one holding his arms over his head. Once he'd made it outside, we figured his best chance of getting arrested would be to wait for a police car to drive by and then flag it down, because none of the officers actually assigned to the call were close enough to accept the surrender.

Because we were standing beside the building even though we'd been told specifically not to move in until ordered to do so, we had to decide what to do next. We looked at each other and started laughing. Neither of us was particularly fond of this supervisor, and we would have been more than happy to see him fall flat on his face once again. On the other hand, both of us prided ourselves on our professionalism, although on our own terms. We realized without saying anything that we had to make sure no innocent bystanders got hurt.

Accompanied by another police officer who had wandered by out of curiosity, we entered the building. Luckily, we were just in time to grab the suspect as he walked out of his apartment. Someone else was assigned to do the paperwork, and we drove off for a much-needed coffee.

***

One incident that illustrates the perils of working with an incompatible partner occurred on a quiet Sunday afternoon. At this point in my career I was accustomed to working alone; in fact, I preferred to work a one-man car whenever I had the option. My partner that day was an experienced policeman who also preferred to work alone and still enjoyed catching crooks. The decision to assign us to the same car was a temporary measure instituted that day because of manpower requirements. Although we were good friends, we had only worked together once before.

I was working the radio and he was driving. We were assigned to the skid road area that day, but when a report of an armed robbery came in from the East End, we decided to cover the call even though it was outside our patrol area. The suspects were described as two drug addicts with a handgun. The thought of these two idiots getting away with such a blatant crime on a quiet day like this just didn't seem right. I made a decision that we were going to scoop these two, no matter what.

This was the first of a series of robberies the two men committed over the next two hours. The thieves stole a distinctive Volkswagen Bug after one of their store robberies. They then used the same car to attempt several other hold-ups, with each incident being reported further and further away from our assigned area as the suspects headed south toward the Fraser River.

I quickly found myself becoming obsessed with catching them. They were literally doing everything wrong, and it offended me to think they might pull off so many robberies without being apprehended. We tried to anticipate their next move, and for a while it looked like we were going to be successful. There was a lull in the action as we gravitated to the area of Southeast Marine Drive, near the city limits. A dog squad member thought he'd spotted the stolen car in that area, but he lost it before he could take a closer look. We started searching the Marine Drive area ourselves.

As we drove by a grocery store perched on a slight rise on the north side of Marine Drive, my heart almost stopped. At one corner of the building there was an individual peering cautiously around the corner. A second person was standing to one side of the front door, looking into the interior. The scenario had the classic appearance of a holdup in progress, and I knew instinctively that they must be the two robbery suspects we were looking for.

As the suspects stared open-mouthed at me, I shouted at my partner to stop the car. I didn't want to broadcast, first because we were well out of our patrol area without permission, and secondly, inexcusably, because I didn't know exactly where the hell we were at that moment. Unfortunately, the more I yelled the more confused my partner became, because he hadn't actually seen the suspects and had no idea what I was talking about at first. Instead of stopping, he turned down a side street in an attempt to circle the block.

I was apoplectic by this time. When a citizen pulled out of his driveway, blocking our progress for several seconds, I screamed at him. Had I been driving, I would probably have pushed him off the road. By the time we arrived back at the store, I was totally out of control. Without waiting for my partner, I barged through the front door with my revolver drawn, only to find a puzzled clerk who had seen no sign of the robbers. Apparently, they hadn't even entered the store after seeing me. They had disappeared again.

By the time I dropped back into the passenger seat, the two of us were no longer talking. We gave up the search and drove back to our own area in silence. I decided that it was too late and too embarrassing to broadcast what I'd seen. I was so upset by then that I was almost convinced I'd imagined the entire incident. It was like waking up after a horrendous nightmare: you know you have to do something to save yourself from harm but cannot, no matter how hard you try. Then a unit from the area announced that he'd just recovered the stolen car we were looking for in the parking lot of a nearby temple. We checked, and sure enough the lot was less than a block away from the store I'd just invaded. The car was parked so it was not visible from the street because of a thick hedge. According to a witness, the suspects were last seen running into a wooded area on the south side of Marine Drive. A subsequent search by the dog squad was unsuccessful, and the robberies were never solved.

Fortunately, our friendship ultimately managed to survive the incident. I wrote our failure off to bad karma on my part, as well as poor communications in general. We never discussed what happened to us that day.

Chapter Five
LIFE AND DEATH

Police officers frequently assist people who have serious physical or mental health problems. They witness the spilling of gallons of blood, and observe countless people suffering from injuries that vary widely from routine cuts and scrapes to dismemberment. They may even find themselves using first aid techniques to save someone's life, although that is usually left to the ambulance crews.

A middle class upbringing doesn't prepare young constables for their first encounters with the bizarre behavior of individuals suffering from severe mental illness. Because mental institutions have been emptied of the patients they once sheltered, it is now commonplace to see mentally incapacitated people wandering the streets, homeless until they commit a crime and are sent to jail. The lucky ones are allowed to return to the institutions where they were traditionally warehoused for most of their adult lives.

While it is difficult for me to understand what goes through the mind of someone who commits suicide, the unsuccessful attempts can usually be classified as either sincere or insincere. Offhand, I can only remember one individual who qualified for both categories in the same day. A young man who had been sent to hospital with cuts to his wrist was released after treatment because nothing else could be done for him. He promptly broke into a construction site across the street, fired up a table saw, and cut his forearm off. Because he didn't choose a more indispensable part of his body to amputate, he lived to tell the tale.

***

One attempt I felt was genuine occurred on the Second Narrows bridge one afternoon. I was assigned to investigate a possible jumper. I pulled in behind several cars parked mid-span alongside the guardrail. Bystanders stood nearby watching a gentleman in a suit sprawled on his hands and knees with his head poking through the guardrail over the side of the bridge. He seemed to be having an animated conversation with someone I couldn't see, although I could hear a female voice responding to his questions.

I made my presence known during a lull in the conversation. The man in the suit informed me he was a psychiatrist. He explained that he had been driving toward Vancouver when he noticed a young lady crawl under the guardrail and disappear. As he approached the side of the bridge, expecting the worst, he found her dangling from a girder below and outside the guardrail. The harbor was hundreds of feet below. If she lost her grip, the fall would almost certainly kill her.

It really was a long way down. Since I don't care much for heights, I was happy to let the psychiatrist deal with the would-be jumper and contented myself with directing traffic around the parked cars. I was glad I didn't have to talk to her as she clung to the side of the bridge. I have never had a problem handling the sight of a jumper's shattered body after a suicide plunge, but I didn't want to have to watch someone fall to their death from a great height. It was one vision I had no desire to add to my repertoire of nightmares.

The psychiatrist must have pushed all the right buttons. Within less than five minutes the girl changed her mind and somehow managed to crawl back onto the roadway and safety. She was obviously still quite distraught, so we led her to a waiting ambulance that took her to hospital for psychiatric assessment. The odds against having a psychiatrist first on the scene at an incident like this must be astronomical. There was no doubt in my mind that if he hadn't been there to talk to her, she would have finished what she had started.

***

People intent on committing suicide have traditionally been attracted to high places. You will notice that bridges often have chain-link fences erected on top of those sections of the guardrail that are directly above marinas and other populated areas. There have been incidents in the past where bodies have come crashing down through the decks of moored yachts. When I was in the academy, we emerged from a training session at the Aquatic Center one afternoon to find a distraught female threatening to jump off the Burrard bridge. She was standing the railing, directly above our parked cars. It was fascinating to watch the by-play overhead as two uniformed policemen talked to her. The situation ended when they suddenly grabbed her and pulled her over the railing to safety, just as she seemed ready to take the final plunge onto our cars.

***

My partner and I received a call to the Granville Street bridge one evening to investigate a report that a young man was poised on the guardrail, apparently preparing to jump to his death. As we cruised southbound there was no sign of anyone attempting suicide, although there was a lone pedestrian walking down the sidewalk. I pulled over where the road divides into an offramp to find out if he'd seen anything suspicious. We were often called to bridges to check similar complaints. Most of the calls were never resolved one way or another, because anyone serious about ending their life was usually long gone by the time we arrived.

My partner rolled down his window. "Have you seen anybody jump off the bridge tonight?"

The pedestrian thought for a second, and then calmly replied, "Yeah, sure. Me!"

He then turned and sprinted for the guardrail, followed closely by my partner, who tackled the jumper just before he reached the sidewalk. They ended up struggling on the pavement, only five feet away from the railing. It was a close call.

I slammed the gearshift lever upward and ran to the sidewalk to help handcuff our would-be suicide. As the last cuff was secured, I sensed movement behind me. When I glanced over my shoulder, I saw our unoccupied black and white accelerating slowly backwards. It was heading toward some traffic that was just now coming over the crest of the bridge. One of the cars carried our new corporal, who had just joined the team that night. He had informed us over the radio just before we stopped the pedestrian that he would be dropping by to cover our call and introduce himself. When I saw a marked car approaching, I knew it had to be him.

Fortunately my partner's door was still wide open, and the patrol car had not had time to build up much momentum. I dove in head first and jammed the gearshift lever back up into park, where it should have been in the first place if I hadn't been in such a hurry to help my partner. To his credit, our new corporal never mentioned the fact that he'd watched me driving our car with my body stretched across the seats and my legs dangling outside the passenger's door. He greeted us cordially, as if nothing out of the ordinary had happened.

I know a policeman who encountered a similar situation on another downtown bridge years later. In that case, however, the jumper was able to reach the guardrail first. Our jumper was luckier. We sent him to the hospital and he was released the next day after a psychiatric assessment. Obviously he was still unable to solve his problems because two weeks later we pulled him off a hotel ledge during another threatened suicide attempt. All we could do was send him back for reassessment. I have no idea what happened to him after that.

***

We rushed to cover a policeman in the skids when he reported that he was dealing with a young woman holding a knife to her own throat, threatening suicide. We arrived to find him attempting to placate an agitated teenager who had been drinking and popping pills all night. She stated drunkenly that she wanted to die, and repeatedly demanded that we leave her alone so she could kill herself. It was hard to judge her sincerity because of her advanced state of intoxication, but I noticed that the buck knife she held to her throat did not waver.

There was no way we could overpower her without the risk of someone getting hurt. Therefore, we stayed several steps away, although we left her no escape route because we didn't want her wandering back inside a nearby bar.

We took turns talking to her. When one approach didn't work, another was tried, until finally she began listening to what we were saying. Five minutes later she quietly handed us the knife and went to the hospital for psychiatric assessment.

Had she chosen instead to slit her throat, there was only a slim chance we'd have been able to grab the knife before she managed to sever an artery, which would probably have been fatal. Still, I would have had no difficulty living with the end result, even if she had managed to kill herself in front of us. Talking to somebody on the brink of committing suicide is a daunting experience until you finally conclude that you cannot take responsibility for someone else's decision to take their own life. Under no circumstances would I ever risk my own safety to prevent a suicide. Every policeman has to make this kind of decision sooner or later, but in my case I never felt a strong need to sacrifice my own life unnecessarily for a cause that is already lost.

***

One incident I found very disturbing started with a call to a modest house in a quiet neighborhood. A middle-aged woman answered the door and escorted us to her son's bedroom. The Asian teenager we found inside the darkened room had been diagnosed as suffering from chronic depression and various other mental problems. His condition had worsened recently and he had just dropped out of university. We found him standing beside a bucket containing a solitary drop of blood and a razor blade he had used to cut his wrist superficially.

My partner and I talked to him, and then phoned his psychiatrist to confirm our suspicions. We subsequently arranged to have him hospitalized so he would have access to the treatment he obviously needed. We did everything we could for him. Both of us made a point of treating him with respect, primarily because he seemed so vulnerable and hopeless. The next day, when we came to work, we were informed that the youth had died at the hospital that night. The young man who could not kill himself with a razor blade had somehow found the will to hang himself with his pajamas when nobody was watching.

***

A situation I encountered early in my career would have made a very interesting internal investigation had a complaint against us ever been lodged. We had been checking the third floor of one of the Granville Street hotels when we unexpectedly stumbled upon a local prostitute in the process of injecting, or "fixing" heroin into her arm. By the time we got to her, most of the fluid in the syringe had disappeared into her bloodstream. Consequently, we recovered only trace elements of heroin from the syringe and the spoon she had used to "cook" the narcotic to convert it into a liquid suitable for injection. As evidence in a drug possession charge, it was minimal at best.

We decided not to charge her with a drug offense. However, we did warn her that if we caught her with drugs again she would end up in jail. Like most criminals she had little to fear from the criminal justice system, and she did not seem overly upset as we left her room. She had already amassed a lengthy criminal record which included several drug convictions, so she was getting a break this time that she probably didn't deserve.

As we walked out the front door of the hotel we heard a blood-curdling scream coming from one side of the building. Simultaneously we saw some very startled looks on the faces of two beat police officers who happened to be walking down the sidewalk toward us.

The object of their attention was the shattered body of the hooker we had just left. She was now sprawled grotesquely on top of a concrete parking abutment beside the hotel's south wall, directly under her room's only window. She was still alive, but her injuries were obviously very serious.

As the ambulance attendants began placing her on a back board they were extremely careful not to further injure her spine and neck. They suspected from the way she had landed that she might have sustained a broken back, and they were right. She was obviously in a lot of pain, despite the fact that she had just used heroin. It looked like she was about to pass out, but she suddenly revived and began screaming in our direction. "They did it! The cops pushed me out the window! They did this to me!"

The ambulance crew continued their work, but I could see they were also shocked at the allegations she was making. Fortunately, we were able to produce witnesses to prove we were exiting the building at the same time she jumped, so the matter never went any further.

107

The story does have a postscript, however. Several months later we noticed a prostitute encased in a full body cast, plying her trade near the Granville Street mall. We both recognized her instantly, of course, but when we talked to her, she had no recollection of ever having met us.

She was obviously very much under the influence of drugs, as evidenced by her slurred, meandering conversation. She told us how she had spent the last few months confined to a hospital bed as her injuries healed. When the doctors finally cut off her supply of prescription pain-killers in a futile attempt to wean her off her latest drug dependency, she signed herself out of the ward against their wishes. She admitted that she couldn't face life without drugs. In fact, she showed us the hole carved in the crotch of her body cast that enabled her to continue working the streets so she could earn money to buy more drugs. Within two weeks she was dead of an overdose.

***

Two of our officers arrested a theft suspect in his room on the third floor of a Chinatown hotel. They handcuffed him just as two more policemen entered the room to assist. There was only one door, so they were fairly confident that he could not escape. As they began examining evidence found inside the room, the prisoner used his bed as a springboard and made a perfect exit through the glass of a closed window.

He was dead soon after he hit the ground three floors below. The officers ran down several flights of stairs only to find a bloody mess waiting for them on the sidewalk. Two tourists, who had been walking nearby when he jumped, were standing near the body, watching intently. Their eyes darted back and forth between the breathless policemen crouched beside the victim, and the victim himself, prostrate on the sidewalk with his arms still handcuffed behind his back. When the police approached them to obtain their names as potential witnesses, they quickly backed away, stating, "No thank you! I think we just saw something we shouldn't have. We'll leave now, if that's okay?" They were eventually reassured that what they had seen was in fact a genuine suicide, but it is not hard to imagine what must have been going through their minds at the time.

***

I was daydreaming as I coasted toward the intersection of Main and Cordova Streets near the police station. I realized that something was amiss when several bystanders on the sidewalk shouted and pointed urgently toward the harbor, a block away. It was surprising how many interesting calls began that way. As I turned the corner to investigate, it quickly became obvious what had attracted their attention. A car had blown the red light while traveling north through Main and Cordova at high speed, just before I pulled up to the intersection. I was traveling eastbound, behind another car, so I didn't see him run the red light.

Despite the fact that it was a Sunday afternoon, there had been fairly heavy vehicular and pedestrian traffic in the area at the time of the accident. The speeding car had miraculously avoided several pedestrians in crosswalks, and then collided with a line of parked cars on Main Street after crossing over the yellow line into the oncoming traffic lanes. In fact, his car came to rest on top of a parked Chevette that belonged to one of our corporals.

I immediately pulled the driver out of his demolished vehicle because I was afraid it was about to catch fire. He was calm and cooperative, but I was left with the impression that there was something going on with him that I could not quite grasp. He did not appear to be injured. Considering the fact that he had just come very close to dying, however, his attitude was surprisingly casual.

As we sorted out the witness reports, it gradually became clear that the driver had been speeding. In fact, one bystander believed he had deliberately tried to crash head-on into a car by crossing into oncoming traffic just before the collision. According to this witness, the driver had swerved at the last possible second as the two cars were about to collide head-on. He hit the parked cars moments later.

I questioned the driver repeatedly about these allegations. Although he changed his story several times, his explanations were logical, if not completely truthful. The most common theme had to do with his gas pedal sticking somehow, but I climbed back into what remained of his car and ascertained that it was functioning perfectly now.

I could smell liquor on his breath, but when we put him on the breathalyzer his reading was close to zero. Having eliminated all other possibilities, I finally concluded that he must have mental problems. I put that theory to him directly, and he readily confessed that this was indeed the case. We confirmed this with his psychiatrist, who requested that we send him back to hospital for more psychiatric treatment. We discovered that he had left his girlfriend's house earlier that afternoon, stating to her that he had decided to kill himself as he pulled away. We put his criminal charges on hold for the moment, and made arrangements for him to be hospitalized until he was fit to stand trial.

***

Two of us were assigned to guard a prisoner who had attempted suicide in his jail cell by slashing both arms with jagged porcelain shards from a demolished toilet. He had then gone berserk when the jail staff tried to stop the bleeding. The guards had placed handcuffs on his lacerated wrists before we got there so he couldn't cause himself further harm. We accompanied the prisoner for the ambulance ride to a hospital outside the downtown area. It was a facility I had seldom visited during my time on the Granville Street beat, because we took most of our calls to St. Paul's Hospital.

The prisoner was still very agitated when we arrived at the emergency ward, presumably because of the drugs he had ingested before his arrest. As a result, we advised the staff in no uncertain terms that it would be wise to leave the handcuffs on until he was sedated. If that was impossible, we asked that they exchange the handcuffs for padded-leather arm restraints.

The people we dealt with in this emergency department could not have had much experience with violent customers. At St. Paul's Hospital, on the other hand, a policeman's opinion was usually respected by the emergency room staff. In situations like this one, they would have made every effort to accommodate our requests when it came to safety concerns, while at the same time providing the best possible care for the patient. At this particular hospital, however, the doctor in charge belittled us and demanded that we remove the cuffs immediately, stating that they would take care of all the patient's behavioral problems themselves.

If this individual had been there solely for treatment of his injuries, I would have been happy to comply and then leave before the excitement began. Unfortunately, he was there under guard because he was already in custody on serious criminal charges. Therefore we were obliged to make sure that he stayed in custody. There are few acceptable excuses for allowing a prisoner to escape. Although it does happen occasionally, it is, at the very least, embarrassing as hell for the police officers involved.

I tried to reason with the staff, but they were adamant that his handcuffs be removed so it would be easier for them to stitch up his wounds. To break the impasse, I reluctantly agreed to unlock the cuffs, although I knew full well there would be problems. This individual had a history of extreme hatred for the police. In fact, in his youth he had shot up a police building with a rifle.

Sure enough, as soon as the first cuff was unlocked, the prisoner began flicking blood from his wounds in our direction. We backed away from him. I didn't want any contact with the blood of a heroin addict, even before the specter of AIDS had emerged as a serious threat. I knew that hepatitis was commonly transmitted through exposure to infected blood, and I was acutely aware that one strain of hepatitis was potentially lethal.

At this point most of the hospital staff scattered, leaving the police to handle the situation. Weakness from loss of blood obviously had not affected his fighting spirit, because as I ducked to avoid being sprayed with more blood, he managed to punch me squarely in the jaw with enough force to send my glasses flying across the room. We grabbed him and struggled desperately to reattach the handcuffs without getting hurt ourselves. While we were fighting with him, I distinctly remember hearing one of the nurses shout something about police brutality. As soon as he was handcuffed, the staff belatedly sedated him so they could do their work without further difficulty.

I was furious. The staff at St. Paul's Hospital would never have allowed this to happen, but at this facility they had no concern whatsoever for our safety. The only person that would talk to us in the emergency ward was a sympathetic orderly who just shook his head at what had transpired as he handed us towels to wipe the blood off our uniforms. I expected to get a complaint from the arrogant doctor, and I was quite prepared to respond in kind. However, the matter never went any further.

***

Only someone who has actually tried to restrain a person who has suddenly gone berserk as a result of some form of mental illness can possibly understand the degree of difficulty involved. Five of us once crowded into a closet-sized cell in the city jail to restrain a violent lunatic, so a nurse could give him his medication. We had watched him through the plastic window before entering his cell. He looked docile and almost normal, until we realized we were looking through a foul-smelling brown sheen of human excrement that coated the inside surface of the plastic window, and all the cell walls, like a coat of beige paint.

Our arrival inside the cell was uneventful until he suddenly turned in our direction and let out a piercing scream. The fight was on. He was short and slight of stature, but that didn't mean we had nothing to worry about. Before we finally managed to put him in restraints, he had ripped the pocket off my uniform shirt and left all five of us bruised and battered. He was as strong as any two men I've ever fought, and obviously he had no control over what he was doing. From what little I had seen of his personality, he seemed more like a wild animal running

111

amok. The irony is that bystanders who witness these one-sided confrontations invariably ask scornfully why it takes so many policemen to get control of a harmless-looking little man.

***

Two of us in plainclothes were assigned to attend a doctor's office to arrest a young man under the Mental Health Act. Police were always called for these arrests, even though procedure dictated that the individual be treated more as a patient than a criminal. We always transported these unfortunate souls to institutions in an ambulance. Police just stood by to keep the peace unless the mental patient refused to cooperate, in which case we were responsible for subduing him and escorting him the rest of the way in restraints. At least two doctors had to agree to the process and sign the papers committing him, so most of the time these people were in pretty bad shape by the time we dealt with them.

This particular patient declined to accompany us willingly, despite the fact that we tried our best to coax him into the ambulance. He dove for the floor and clamped his arms around the doctor's leg in a death grip as he screamed threats at us. I could tell by the disgusted look on the doctor's face that he was not exactly impressed by our bedside manner, but that was the least of our worries at the time. I was wearing a cheap leather jacket that day to conceal my service revolver, even though it was summer time. In the five minutes it took us to release the doctor and handcuff his patient, the sweat was literally pouring down my forehead. In fact, when I put on my uniform the next day, I discovered the entire left side of my revolver was covered with rust.

***

Working in the skid road area involved constant exposure to people with varying degrees of mental problems, especially after the government began emptying mental institutions. There were frequent calls to the clinics and halfway houses that cater to the mentally ill, and many disturbance calls we attended on the street involved former mental patients. Most suspects were not considered dangerous, but you could never really tell. The violent mood swings some individuals exhibited could send a routine call spiraling wildly out of control in an instant.

There were times when the behavior of someone I was dealing with became so bizarre or annoying that I would stop the conversation and ask them if they had any idea why they were acting so strangely. Most would actually make a serious effort to answer the question. A few reacted as if the thought that there could be a logical explanation for their problems had never occurred to them before. One lunatic I arrested after he was found chasing little children through a park was able to carry on a normal conversation until I asked him if he liked kids. "Yes," he replied in a serious voice, "Barbecued!"

One particular woman from the West End used to become sexually aroused by the flashing red and blue lights on our police cars, so much so that she would lovingly fondle the emergency equipment on our roof racks whenever she had a chance. Her favorites were the red fireball lights that unmarked cars display on their dashboards. She was harmless, but annoying.

I happened upon a clean-cut young man crawling on his hands and knees in the gutter one day and stopped to see if he was in trouble. As I approached a little closer, I could see that he was meticulously cleaning the dirt off a manhole cover with a screwdriver. Other than this particular obsession, his behavior was quite inoffensive. I saw him on various streets in the skids over the next month or so, peacefully cleaning grates and manhole covers while dodging traffic in the curb lanes. After a while he dropped out of sight, and I never saw him again.

Encounters with some of the most aggressive weirdos could be unnerving. I was told the story of a would-be sumo wrestler who called the emergency number for help one night. The two policemen who responded were met at the door by the complainant, who was stark naked and covered with grease from head to toe. The only reason he'd called the department was to pick a fight with some of Vancouver's finest on his own terms. The fact that he was now able to slip out of their grasp at will made the altercation all the more challenging.

One of my favorite whackos was a man I referred to as "The Human Punching Bag". He used to come to Vancouver from time to time and pick fights with any policemen he happened to run into on the street. He was never happy until he ended the evening with his face black and blue and bloody. He then returned to whatever hole he had crawled out of.

He was never drunk when I had dealings with him, and as far as I know he never made a complaint after his encounters with the police. Only the fact that he obviously enjoyed pain so much differentiated him from the run-of-the-mill punks who had to prove their masculinity by fighting a cop every time they had too much to drink.

***

People with physical injuries were usually less of a problem for the police, because most of the time all we had to do was call the Emergency Health Services for an ambulance, write a quick report and clear the call. The EHS crews had an excellent reputation, and I learned over the years that I could always count on them to be there when I needed them. They were a pleasure to work with, and they could be trusted to handle any problem with calm professionalism.

We were driving down Hornby Street one quiet Thursday noon hour when we noticed a garbage man leaning into the back of his truck. He had a pained expression on his face, and his weak wave in our direction seemed oddly out of character. Out of curiosity we stopped to talk to him.

It was only when we were beside him that we noticed his arm was jammed up inside the machinery that scooped garbage into the storage compartment of his truck. We could see blood trickling down from where a hydraulic-powered gate had clamped down onto his forearm near the wrist. He was as white as a ghost, and it looked as if much of the blood had already drained from his body.

He told us that if he hadn't managed to hit the nearby emergency switch, the rest of his body would have eventually joined his forearm. It sounded to me like the hydraulic system was still powered up, but he assured us that the emergency switch had disabled it temporarily.

We tried to get on the radio several times to ask for medical help, but we couldn't get through because somebody with an exaggerated sense of self-worth was hogging the channel with a routine but long-winded message. After a frustrating delay we finally managed to arrange for assistance. While we waited impatiently for EHS ambulances and the fire department to attend, we checked the trunk of our police car for emergency equipment. All we could come up with was part of a car jack and some fast-food restaurant napkins.

We could have just waited for the firemen to arrive and rescue him, but we were concerned that the machinery might start up again and devour the rest of his body. Consequently, we decided to use the jack to pry the gate open. After several nervous attempts we were successful. His hand, connected now to the forearm by only some skin and sinew, fell out of the machinery as arterial blood spurted from his wrist.

By now our victim looked like he was going to have a heart attack at any moment. We convinced him to elevate the arm while I jammed my finger into a pressure point inside his armpit. The pressure stopped the flow of blood, but after a couple of minutes I insisted on releasing my grip for a brief period of time in order to restore circulation throughout what was left of his arm. I remember him asking respectfully if I was sure he could spare that much blood. After looking at the amount of blood left on the machinery, as well as our uniforms, I had my doubts, but I still assured him that he would survive.

As soon as fire and ambulance crews pulled up, we ducked into a nearby office building to wash the blood off our hands and arms. Apparently a Vancouver Sun photographer arrived just after we left, because the next day there was a dramatic front page picture of a swarm of firemen working on our victim. The caption made no mention of the fact that police had done all the dirty work. I found out later that the garbage man managed to keep his hand, although its mobility was severely limited. Apparently he had been working the truck by himself and had unwisely tried to use a broom handle to clear a blockage, a shortcut he knew was dangerous but tried anyway because he was in a hurry.

***

I will never forget the first time I heard the distinctive sound of a human skull hitting a hard surface after a fall. It was the last night of a six month assignment to the jail for one of the members I worked with. Despite many busy nights and more than his share of fights, he had survived his jail term with an unblemished record. Tonight, of course, he was delighted to put an end to what most of us considered the low point of our careers. I watched as he propped a drunk vertically up against the wire mesh of the holding cage while he returned to the booking desk momentarily to complete some paperwork.

He had curled the drunkard's fingers around the mesh of the cage to support his weight. I watched in horror as the fingers gave way one by one. Before any of us could react, the drunk lost his grip and fell backwards. The entire room went silent as the sound of his skull impacting on our concrete floor echoed hollowly off the walls. With visions of a nasty jail inquest in his future, the shaken officer dropped his paperwork as the color drained from his complexion.

Meanwhile, one of the experienced jail guards picked up the phone and asked for an emergency ambulance, without even bothering to check on the condition of the prisoner. He had heard that sound before, and knew what it probably meant.

The jail nurses arrived quickly to give first aid. They were shaking their heads negatively as they struggled to put his body in the recovery position and called for oxygen tanks. Firemen and ambulance attendants eventually swarmed out of the jail elevator and surrounded the unconscious drunk. There was a beehive of activity around him. His prognosis did not look too good, and by then we had all written him off as a goner and begun establishing our alibis. Just when matters looked

115

their worst, the drunk suddenly sat bolt upright and screamed, "What the hell do you people think you're doing? Take your goddamn hands off me!"

The policeman who had left him propped against the cage finally started breathing again. The dramatic resurrection we witnessed was the only time I ever saw that particular policeman at a loss for words. The drunk survived to resume his role as one of our best customers at the drunk tank.

***

My introduction to the potential lethality of allergic reactions came during a medical call to a downtown theater. A middle-aged woman had inadvertently taken a bite of her companion's chocolate bar, unaware that it contained peanuts. Peanuts had triggered a severe allergic reaction several years earlier. She apparently realized almost instantly that she had made a horrible mistake, but by then it was too late.

By the time paramedics got there, her head had swollen up like a basketball and her airway had constricted shut. They were doing everything they could for the unfortunate woman when a young gentleman emerged from the crowd of bystanders. "I'm a doctor. Step aside!"

He managed to convince the skeptical paramedics that a tracheotomy was the only way to save her life. Since ambulance crews were not authorized to carry out that type of surgical procedure, the doctor volunteered to do it for them. They were reluctant to go along with his plan, but the woman was clearly past the stage where she could be saved by conventional means. The doctor's calm self-confidence finally won them over.

Her throat was grotesquely swollen, so he started his cut on the scar from a previous tracheotomy. Unfortunately, the orientation of her veins and arteries must have changed due to the swelling, so he inadvertently severed a major blood vessel as he broke the skin with his scalpel. As a result, when the attendants administered CPR, every time they compressed her chest they pumped blood all over the theater floor. The unfortunate woman was pronounced dead shortly thereafter. The doctor felt terrible about not being able to save her life, but there was nothing he could have done to change the outcome.

***

I arrested a drunk one day as I was walking the Granville beat. I stuck my hand into his overcoat pocket to search for weapons, something I have routinely done thousands of times over the years. On this occasion, I discovered to my horror that the drunk had filled his pocket with dozens of hypodermic needles he'd found in a garbage can outside a doctor's office. I managed to get stuck more than once while extricating my hand. The drunk readily admitted that he'd done this on purpose. He'd been on a binge for the last two weeks, and he had spent a lot of that time in the drunk tank. Realizing it was inevitable he would be sent to dry out again as the evening progressed, he had decided to get even with the police.

This occurred before AIDS became so prevalent, but I had still heard plenty of horror stories about people catching diseases like hepatitis after contact with dirty needles. As a result, I was very concerned about the risk of contracting an illness that could cost me years of my life, or even kill me. Unfortunately, there was nothing I could do but wait and see what, if anything, was to happen to me. The drunk went directly to jail, and I learned a valuable lesson about searching prisoners.

***

One of the policemen on my team sustained a work-related injury that turned into a nightmare. A prostitute he was arresting decided not to cooperate so he had to subdue her to get her handcuffed. In the process, she bit his hand just hard enough to draw blood. Injuries during scuffles like this are not uncommon, so he washed the area of the wound thoroughly and returned to work.

Later that evening he began to notice redness spreading in his forearm above the bite mark. By the time doctors managed to arrest its progress, the infection had spread almost to his shoulder. His physician later informed him that, had the blood poisoning continued any further up his arm, they would have had no choice but to amputate.

Fortunately I never caught any serious diseases from the people I dealt with. However, like most policemen and ambulance personnel, I often found myself covered with other people's blood. Policing nowadays is probably more dangerous in many ways than when I started the job. A street policeman is still involved in physical disputes with some extremely violent people, but now he faces additional risks in that he could be injured or bled upon by individuals likely to be infected with the HIV/AIDS virus.

Rubber gloves alone cannot protect a policeman from catching the disease. There is no law that forces anyone who has used violence against an emergency services worker or nurse to submit to tests in order to determine the presence of the HIV virus. This is convenient for Workers' Compensation Boards because the onus is then on the infected worker to prove the origin of his disease, an almost impossible task. The potential damage to the career, reputation and family of those emergency workers infected with AIDS as a result of their jobs is devastating.

Legislation designed to safeguard the rights of policemen, ambulance attendants and hospital staff has little chance of materializing at this time. As is so often the case with dangerous intersections, nothing will be done about the problem until it is too late. Legislators will only consider passing laws to help safeguard emergency personnel after innocent lives are sacrificed.

***

While on a wagon call to the hospital one day, I encountered a character who was notorious for his hatred of the jail drunk tank. This was before the government established a more comfortable detoxification facility as an alternative to housing drunks in a city police jail cell. Every time he was arrested and sent to the drunk tank after a night of heavy drinking he feigned a heart attack, secure in the knowledge that the jail staff could not ignore his well-rehearsed symptoms. In fact, he knew that the staff there would do almost anything to avoid a hostile jail inquest.

He had it down to a science. He would ask to see the jail nurse, at which time he would complain of chest pains and dizziness. The nurse would automatically call an ambulance and send him to hospital. Once in the emergency ward, the physician would of course find no symptoms of a heart attack. The drunk would yell and scream at the nurses until they were forced to kick him out of the hospital. He could then spend the rest of the night in the relative comfort of his own hotel room. When he awoke the next day he would immediately hit the streets and panhandle to raise money for his next drunken episode. Unfortunately, on this occasion he was still so drunk that he couldn't walk, so the emergency room staff called for a wagon to return him to the jail.

I found the derelict sitting in a wheelchair with his eyes closed. I could detect no sign that he was breathing, although there was a faint pulse. Over the years I learned several methods that usually awoke even the most intoxicated drunks from their deepest comas, but I went through my entire repertoire of painful but harmless stimuli without success. Although I knew he was in perfect health, he was doing the best imitation of a corpse I have ever seen.

I pulled the doctor aside and he assured me the man was probably healthier than I was. I explained to him that if I returned this lifeless carcass to jail, he would promptly be refused admission and returned to hospital again. It was a classic case of a vicious circle. The

118

physician agreed that it was a pointless exercise. He stopped for a second to think, then asked me to wait outside as he wheeled the derelict into a private treatment room.

I was curious, of course, so I watched through a curtain as he ordered his patient one more time to return from the dead so we could all get back to work. When nothing happened, the doctor tried the same techniques I had used. The drunk seemed immune to painful stimuli, and he didn't even flinch.

The doctor's next move surprised even me. He clamped one hand over the man's mouth and the other over his nose, and then just waited for a reaction. For a long time nothing happened. Finally the drunk opened his eyes and tapped the doctor on his shoulder in a gesture of surrender. The doctor stepped back with a smile, and his patient willingly consented to an uneventful return to the drunk tank.

***

I was feeling quite content early one Sunday morning as I sat in my idling police car, writing a report. I had just checked a silent alarm call to a residential address in the suburbs, and I was looking forward to a coffee break. A shabbily dressed, middle-aged man walked up to my car and waited politely until I turned my head to talk to him through the window. He apologized for bothering me and then asked if I would mind driving him back to his skid road hotel room because he had no money for a taxi. He had been out for his usual early morning stroll, he explained, and now he felt so nauseous and weak from a flu attack that he didn't think he could walk any further.

Street people who asked me for favors usually turned out to be either drunk or jerks, or both. In fact, many very stupid individuals used to flag over police cars and jokingly ask for a ride, knowing full well that anyone riding in the back of a blue and white was only going to one place, the city jail. Police officers seldom allow citizens inside their police cars, primarily because they find it uncomfortable to have someone they haven't thoroughly searched sitting behind them.

Somehow this man didn't seem like the type to ask for hand-outs. When he began to look a little pale around the gills, I invited him to sit in the back seat, something I had done only a handful of times during my career. His condition deteriorated rapidly. I asked him what was wrong, but the sweat running down his forehead and his agonized expression told me all that I needed to know. I shut off my car radio so he couldn't hear my broadcast and stepped outside to use my portable radio to ask for the Emergency Health Services paramedic unit to attend. I was sure he was having a heart attack. I made a specific request that they shut off their sirens a block away so they didn't alarm him any more than was absolutely necessary.

I talked to him while we were waiting for the ambulance, offering him the kind of meaningless reassurances dying people must get very tired of hearing. A fire truck soon pulled up with sirens blaring. One of the firemen asked in a loud voice where the guy with the heart attack was. By this time the victim was oblivious to the noise, having collapsed sideways onto the back seat, unconscious and very close to death.

The ambulance paramedic unit arrived moments later, making a silent approach as I had requested. They were able to save this victim's life, despite the fact that he'd had a massive coronary and came within seconds of dying. The EHS crews always did excellent work, especially while dealing with heart attacks and other serious calls.

This case was different from most medical calls I attended, primarily because I got to know the victim briefly before his condition took such a dramatic turn for the worse. He seemed like a decent person. I did not want him to die in my car, and I felt like I had a personal stake in the fight to save his life. If I had ignored his request, as I had done many times in the past to avoid talking to drunks and pests, he would probably have died on the sidewalk.

***

During my career I accompanied several different shooting victims to the hospital for treatment. By coincidence there was not a single innocent victim among them, primarily because all of them happened to be active criminals.

None of them died. I watched as an emergency room physician treated one victim who'd been hit with a full load of bird shot while sitting in his car. The shooting had occurred during a drug deal that went sour. He had numerous small wounds to the left side of his face, as well as inside his left arm and elbow. The doctor maneuvered the victim's arms into a position that made what looked like separate and unrelated wounds evolve into a single shot pattern created because the unfortunate drug dealer had thrown up his arm in a last ditch attempt to protect his face.

He survived his injuries, although one of his more persistent symptoms seemed to be a loss of memory. He steadfastly refused to tell us what had happened, stating that he'd take care of the matter himself. That was the end of that particular investigation as far as we were concerned, because without cooperation from the victim there was no point in continuing.

***

We found another shooting victim lying on the ground in a parking lot just off Granville Street. He was suffering from a gunshot wound to the chest. During the short trip to hospital he became increasingly hostile and refused to provide us with any information whatsoever. The doctors took an X-ray and discovered a .25 caliber bullet situated deep inside his chest cavity. They showed us how the projectile had wandered extensively through the victim's torso, causing damage wherever it touched a vital organ. That's why small caliber rounds can often be more lethal than their more-powerful magnum brothers. The doctor informed our victim that his injuries were potentially life-threatening unless he received immediate emergency surgery.

As best we could figure, this gentleman had also been shot while in the midst of a drug deal, although that was only an educated guess based on his reputation as a major trafficker. He'd been arrested many times since his youth for a wide variety of serious offenses. Evidently he had grown to hate policemen with a vengeance. While still inside the emergency surgery room, he began yelling obscenities in my direction and demanded that I be removed from the hospital. If not, he threatened to walk out in the middle of treatment. I had no intention of leaving. Since he was hooked up to intravenous bottles and obviously in a lot of pain, I was quite sure he wouldn't be conscious much longer anyway.

His prognosis must have been rosier than I thought, however. After I refused to leave the hospital, he summoned all the energy he had left, ripped out his intravenous needles and tore the monitor pads off his chest. After one last hateful glance in my direction, he staggered defiantly out of the hospital.

There were several tactics I could have used to force him to return for treatment. Because nobody really wanted to deal with this obnoxious individual anyway, we simply cleared the call and left. The doctor assured us that the victim would be returning to hospital eventually anyway, probably in an unconscious state, and preferably after our shifts were both over. We found out later that the victim did indeed return for treatment, well after we left the hospital. Of course he still refused to tell the police what happened, and the case was soon dropped due to lack of interest.

***

Yet another unhappy victim came to our attention as a result of a man-with-a-gun call on Davie Street. Two of our members soon identified, tackled and handcuffed the suspect. He was drunk and

121

obnoxious, but when he was searched they didn't find a gun. The arresting officers deposited him in the back of the wagon I was driving, while other members searched the area where he'd been standing. Two minutes later he started banging on the door, shouting that he wanted to talk to someone in authority.

When we finally opened the wagon door, he showed us a .45 caliber hole in his torso and moaned that he'd been shot, although he refused to tell us how it had happened. I suspected a botched suicide attempt, but that was only a guess. The supervisor at the scene asked for an ambulance and was told they were busy with other calls. Since we were only a few blocks from the hospital, I was told to drive him there in the back of the wagon. Being inexperienced and very gung-ho at that early stage of my career, I intended to get him to the emergency room in record time. I floored it, and with siren wailing and tires squealing, I made it there in less than a minute.

Unfortunately, I had forgotten that the inside of the wagon compartment was not designed for transporting ailing victims, primarily because there was nothing to hold onto and no way to avoid bouncing from one end to the other whenever the brakes were applied. The journey had done nothing for his foul disposition. In fact, he now refused to exit the wagon for treatment, even after I asked nicely. We had to fight him just to get him into the emergency ward. The doctors assigned to treat him were faced with a hand-cuffed wild man who screamed obscenities while spitting on them as they tried to plug his .45 caliber leak. They were not impressed. He survived.

***

In my experience, whenever a child calls 911, it usually turns out to be a legitimate call. Late one afternoon I volunteered to cover a two-man car that was assigned to investigate an unknown problem phoned in by a very young child. They were coming from across town, so I was reluctant to knock on the child's door until they arrived. We had been told that the child was inside the basement suite, so I made my way to the back entrance and listened through the door while waiting for the other car.

I could hear a woman's shrill voice as she conversed with a couple of young children. They, in turn, were pleading with her not to do something, but I could not hear exactly what it was they were discussing. There was further garbled conversation, and then I distinctly heard the woman's words as she addressed the children matter-of-factly. "Now kids, it's time to die. It's time to end all our problems."

I immediately kicked the door in and was confronted by a

horrific scene. The woman and both the little children were naked, surrounded by mounds of debris and spoiled food in a kitchen that looked more like a battleground. The adult had both her hands around the neck of the youngest child, who must have been about three years old, and she was in the process of strangling her. The other child was frantically trying to break her grip. Perhaps the best way to describe the visual impact of the scene would be to compare it to the famous Vietnam war era picture of a young Vietnamese girl, burned by napalm, running toward the camera.

I grabbed the woman and held onto her until the other officers arrived and handcuffed her. She was maniacal, totally out of control, and she continued screaming and crying until she was taken away for treatment.

I got the two young children dressed and managed to calm them down so they could tell me what had happened. I was surprised at how intelligent and well-adjusted they were, despite the fact that they were both far too young to go to school. They explained that their father was already confined in a mental institution. Their mother had grown progressively more mentally ill after extensive drug abuse and member-ship in the Hare Krishna movement, and the kids were able to detail all her symptoms to me. They showed an amazing comprehension of issues even some adults would have been incapable of understanding.

The two of them had basically taken care of themselves for the last few weeks, scavenging whatever food they could find in the kitchen and cooking it on the stove when necessary. Today, they said, their mother had taken a turn for the worse. After ransacking the apartment and throwing all the food on the floor, she had apparently decided they should all die together. Only the actions of the oldest girl, who had managed to slip away and phone 911 while her mother was distracted, saved their lives. I often wondered what became of these children. When I left them they were on their way to a temporary foster home, relieved to be safe but still wondering out loud if they would ever be united as a family again.

***

Nothing has more of an impact on the human psyche than confronting the specter of sudden death at first hand. Everyone wants to stop and take a close look at an accident fatality, even as their subcon-scious recoils in horror at the gruesome reality of violent sudden death. Nobody wants to be reminded of what inevitably awaits them down the road, yet people are still drawn to the sight of blood and gore and death like moths to a light bulb. Police officers are frequently spectators to the process of death. While experience allows them to work and function in the presence of corpses, it is impossible to ignore the fact that the decaying flesh they are there to investigate once housed the soul of a living person.

Police are responsible for investigating most sudden deaths, with the exception of those that occur routinely at hospitals, so a policeman soon accumulates an intimate knowledge of the concepts and realities of death. Patrol members usually handle the initial investigation and then call in specialists when necessary. These days, it is not uncommon for someone from the coroner's office to drop by and kibitz as well. Incidents that involve suspicious or unusual circumstances are usually investigated by the Major Crimes Squad, and those deaths that occur at the work place are often investigated further by the Workers' Compensation Board. When necessary, the Identification Squad attends the scene to take photographs and collect evidence.

Most sudden deaths, however, are routine in nature and are handled solely by the officers assigned to the call. Police are responsible for determining the identity of the victim, as well as notifying the next of kin. Any details which might help the pathologist determine the cause of death are forwarded through the coroner's office. Police officers are also required to search the homes and belongings of people who have died suddenly. Anything of value is usually left with the next of kin at the scene. If there are no responsible relatives present, valuables are secured in the police property office to be turned over to the Public Trustee.

All victims are transported to a hospital where a doctor must examine the remains to formally pronounce death, no matter how obviously dead the victim may appear. The body is then taken to the morgue, and an autopsy may be performed before it is released for burial or cremation. The coroner's office is ultimately responsible for deciding whether or not an inquest or inquiry into the death will be held.

I attended hundreds of sudden death calls during my career. Although I quickly became accustomed to being in the presence of dead bodies, investigating sudden deaths could, at times, be difficult and challenging. A typical incident in the skid road area where I worked usually involved an elderly alcoholic living in a rundown flophouse.

The body was often discovered as a result of complaints from the neighbors about a strong odor emanating from the room. In our city, landlords are required by law to check each room daily. More than once I was faced with a decomposed body, black and bloated and crawling with maggots, only to hear the hotel desk clerk swear that the victim

124

had been fine only yesterday when he'd checked the room. Since it was obvious that the corpse had been rotting for at least a week, their stories lacked credibility. The rooms are usually filthy and crawling with cockroaches, and the smell inside would be unpleasant even without the odor of decomposition present.

A sudden death report is easier to write if the victim checked into the hotel under his real name instead of using an alias. Sometimes it is possible to find a desk clerk or a neighbor on the same floor who knows the deceased well enough to identify him at the scene. Because some corpses can only be identified by their fingerprints, it is convenient that many of the inhabitants of the skid road area have criminal records. Obtaining the names and addresses of next of kin is often difficult unless family letters are located inside the victim's room. Sometimes the information investigators need can be found on jail booking sheets if the victim had a criminal record. Some elderly people anticipate their own death to the extent that they write down a relative's name and address and leave it in a place where it will be found after they die.

Investigating sudden deaths is one of the toughest jobs society delegates to police officers. The horror stories about sudden death calls are as diverse as they are gruesome. There were two incidents a year apart where individuals jumped to their deaths while aiming themselves at policemen who were walking below them on sidewalks near the police station. In fact, one of the jumpers had just escaped through a security window on the fifth floor of our jail before becoming a human projectile. Fortunately, both jumpers missed their targets. Another of our officers had to identify the corpse of one of his best friends solely on the basis of the skin from his face, which was the only recognizable part of his body after a tragic air crash.

To me, the worst part of these investigations was always the suspense of walking into a room and not knowing for sure whether the victim was dead or not. Once death was firmly established, I had no difficulty completing the necessary investigation, no matter how badly the body was decomposed. At times the relatives would be arguing over the division of the estate before we had even removed the remains, although in fairness most family members were genuinely saddened by the passing of someone who had once been close to them. It was nothing short of tragic that so many of the people whose sudden deaths I investigated had been left to die alone, with no family or friends to care for them in life or in death.

I attended several autopsies during my career, and they were interesting and informative experiences once I got past the original shock of seeing a human torso being cut up like a side of beef. Some of the pathologists were more than willing to answer questions about their work and give impromptu lectures on human anatomy to police bystanders. I could never have faced doing their job every working day. I remember hearing the story of one young pathologist who gradually developed aversions to eating chicken, then other meats and types of food as his career progressed. His problems at work finally led to a full-blown eating disorder. Anybody who has witnessed an autopsy will readily understand how that could happen.

A recruit is given instructions about what to expect during a sudden death investigation, but there is really no way to prepare him for the actual incidents he will face. One of my training officers purposely took me to a call where other policemen were investigating a drug overdose, just to show me what a corpse looked like up close. He was wise enough to understand that the first sudden death I investigated on my own would be difficult enough without the added burden of having to deal with the impact of seeing a corpse for the first time.

The drug overdose victim was lying face down on the living room floor. The grieving family congregated around the kitchen table to await his removal to the morgue. They were all crying. I found it very upsetting just listening to them weeping and sobbing until I eventually learned to tune them out while I concentrated on doing my job. I realized then that these calls were never going to be easy.

I investigated my first sudden death during a heat wave. The corpse had not been discovered until several days after death occurred. The human body begins to deteriorate immediately after death, and extreme heat just accelerates the process. This unfortunate lady lived, and died, alone. She had expired while resting on her back, lengthwise on a bed. The process of decomposition had left her arms standing straight up as if she were about to sleep walk, and her face was obscured by rotting stomach contents that had been forced up through her system as her body decayed and began swelling.

A byproduct of prolonged decomposition is the horrible smell that assaults you as you walk into a room where somebody has been dead for any length of time. I have never heard anyone adequately describe the odor, but you could probably get some idea of what I'm talking about if you think back to the last time you smelled rotting garbage and then multiply the impact by a factor of at least ten. The odor stays in your hair and clothing until both are washed thoroughly. Nothing could be more revolting than the smell of death.

Some experienced policemen would stop off to buy a cigar en route to those sudden death calls where there was some indication from the radio operator that the body had been there for more than a day. We didn't have an opportunity to buy cigars en route to my first sudden death, so one senior policeman who dropped by suggested that I heat coffee grounds in a frying pan to obscure the odor. I soon discovered an important disadvantage to this method, however, when I turned the burner up too high and the coffee grounds caught fire. I had nightmarish visions of the entire apartment building going up in flames because of me, but we managed to extinguish the fire before it could spread.

Having completed my part of the investigation, I began searching through her closets for valuables while we waited for the body removal people to attend. Going through an individual's belongings after they die is never pleasant, but as part of our job we must send any identification papers, medications or cash to the police property office. It was during this process that I discovered how much you can learn about a person's life by the evidence they've left behind amongst their effects. The photo albums, marriage certificates, clippings and other keepsakes collected over the course of a lifetime offer an interesting glimpse of the victim's background. Since so many people die alone, especially the elderly, it is often the only legacy they leave behind.

***

While working an otherwise quiet Christmas afternoon shift, I became involved in the investigation of two very different sudden deaths. The first was a fatal motor vehicle accident. I just assisted the Accident Investigation unit assigned to the call, so my role in the investigation was limited.

The second incident was much more involved. Earlier that Christmas day, police had been called to deal with a disturbance at a rundown apartment where a man and woman were reportedly fighting with each other. The woman they found at the scene was a prostitute who had been arguing with her boyfriend and was bleeding from some minor cuts she sustained during the altercation. The man had a few fresh bruises but the blood on his clothing was definitely hers. They were both rounder types who had little use for the police. Since neither of them wished to proceed with criminal charges, a compromise was reached and he agreed to leave the apartment until emotions cooled down somewhat.

Radio dispatched another call to this address several hours later. This time there was information that a possible homicide had occurred. The male participant from the earlier dispute was standing outside the apartment when we arrived. He informed us that he thought his girl-friend, the same woman he'd been fighting with earlier, was now dead.

He was certainly right about that. While other officers held onto him, we entered the apartment and found the woman lying on her back in the living room with a knife in her hand. She had been struck several times in the back of the head with a blunt instrument, and she was obviously quite dead. We found the murder weapon, a hammer, else-where in the apartment.

There was no shortage of forensic evidence to be found, both inside the apartment and on the clothing of the suspect. He vehemently maintained his innocence, stating that he had returned to the apartment shortly after the police left the original call and apologized to her. According to his story, they then kissed and made up. He left when she informed him that she had arranged for a paying customer to drop by the apartment later for a quickie. Of course the suspect maintained that he hadn't seen the customer on his way out the door. He claimed he returned an hour later, found his girlfriend dead on the floor and immediately phoned for an ambulance.

The fact that the two of them had been fighting earlier meant that any evidence of his involvement in the homicide, such as blood-stains on his clothing, could well have been the result of their earlier battle. The police who had attended the original call could verify that. Therefore, without an incriminating statement from the suspect, there was insufficient evidence for a criminal charge. For this reason, al-though the suspect had been involved in at least one other similar incident in the past, he was never charged with this homicide.

***

Someone called an ambulance to an apartment in the West End for a drug overdose. Ambulance attendants found the body of a young woman on the bathroom floor. When it became clear that the victim was already dead, we were routinely notified to attend to investigate the fatality. There was evidence that showed she had apparently been injecting heroin into her arm at the time of her death.

Her boyfriend and several other drug addicts were still sitting in the living room watching a football game on TV when we arrived. They were too wrapped up in the game to talk to us until we finally pulled the plug on their TV set. According to their story, she had been in the bathroom for the last two hours. They thought she had just passed out, and they'd even stepped over her unconscious body to relieve them-selves during intermissions in the game. When I pointed out to the boyfriend that a normal human being would feel remorse upon hearing that the girl he'd lived with for the past several months had died, he just laughed. He and his friends were only interested in plugging the TV back in so they could see the end of the game.

The girl was pronounced dead at the hospital. I dropped by later to search her clothing for valuables. We learned from our records that she had worked the streets as a prostitute for most of her adult life, and she had previous convictions for drug possession. Although during the last few hours of her existence she had been ignored and neglected, in death she finally managed to attract the attention of those of us who were checking the body for signs of foul play. Advertising is an important aspect of any small business, and this victim must have understood the value of promoting her wares. She had a large and colorful smiling beaver tattooed over and around the principle implement of her trade.

***

My partner and I were driving the wagon in the West End during the last few hours of day shift when we were assigned to check a report of a man slumped over the wheel of his car. We got there moments before the ambulance but there was little we could do for this person. He had been very obese, a massive man in fact, and it took four of us to load him into the ambulance for his final trip to the hospital to be pronounced dead.

We had the unenviable task of notifying his wife. She was waiting for him inside their apartment. They lived in a building across the street from where her husband had just died. She was a very pleasant lady, and when we informed her of what had just happened she seemed genuinely heartbroken. We could not officially tell her that her husband was dead until the doctor had certified the death, so of course she wanted to attend the hospital immediately to check on his condition.

The paddy wagon we were driving stunk of stale beer and vomit, but because a patrol car was not available to transport her to the hospital, we offered to take her there ourselves. She accepted our invitation, so we had her sit in the passenger side while I squeezed into the narrow space between the two seats. At the hospital, the Emergency Room physician confirmed that her husband was indeed dead. We spent a few extra minutes consoling her as best we could.

She explained through tears that her husband was a prominent and successful businessman with a long history of heart trouble and obesity. His doctor had told him over and over again that he urgently required heart surgery, but he had been delaying it for months because of business pressures. The problem was so serious that his doctor had finally informed him earlier that morning that if he did not check into the hospital immediately there was a good chance he'd be dead within a matter of hours. The gentleman had chosen instead to carry on with his business, and when we went through his wallet we found thousands of dollars in cash and cheques that he'd collected during the day from his customers.

The victim's wife actually sent us a thank you note for our assistance to her, the only one I ever received during twelve years of police work. We ran into her again six months later after she called the police to report an assault. She had obviously gone downhill after the funeral, and was now living with a very sleazy man who was in the process of relieving her of what remained of the estate and her husband's insurance settlement. Her apartment was full of empty liquor bottles, and her new boyfriend was drunk and openly contemptuous of her in our presence.

She explained to us that he'd been abusing her and she didn't know what to do about it. She would not charge him criminally, for reasons of her own, but she plaintively asked us if there was anything else we could do to help her. Without her participation in a criminal charge, we were powerless to assist her.

The boyfriend was obnoxious when we asked him for his side of the story, and he laughingly boasted that there was nothing we could do about him because he intended to stay with her until she ran out of money. It is possible that where he came from such behavior was acceptable, but that didn't stop us from sending him to the drunk tank for the night after he was arrested under the "Ways and Means Act," an obscure law improvised for those occasions when we couldn't find an applicable section in the Criminal Code.

On the way to jail I told him what I thought of him, and what I thought should happen to him. I also mentally filed the image of his face for future attention should we meet again. I knew he would go back to her the next day after he was released from the drunk tank, and it was clear that she would or could do nothing to stop him from abusing her. It is particularly sad to see vulnerable people being taken advantage of by such unscrupulous crooks. I encountered many such victims over the years, but because she was the only one to ever write me a thank-you note, it made her obvious distress much more frustrating.

***

I was just finishing my dinner in the parking lot of a fast-food restaurant when the policeman sitting in the car parked beside me was given a call over the radio. It was a report of a jumper from one of the

West End's tallest hotels, although the caller claimed the victim had only jumped from the hotel parking lot, which was just two or three stories high. I volunteered to take the call, since the other officer had just started his dinner and I knew the casualty could not be too gruesome after having fallen only three floors.

Fire and ambulance crews were already on the scene, but as we circled the hotel we could find no sign of the jumper. I got out on foot to search the roof of the parkade and found that there had indeed been a jumper, but he hadn't jumped from the parkade to the sidewalk. He'd actually plunged from a room thirty floors up and landed on a parking space on the top level of the parkade.

As I approached the point of impact, I had to walk through a veritable minefield of body parts surrounding the body. He had apparently landed on his head. The force of the impact from his thirty-floor fall had been so great that his skull had exploded, scattering pieces of bone and brain over a twenty foot radius around the shattered corpse. The fireman with me tramped through the debris without watching where he walked, and I could hear squish-crunching noises as he stepped on bone fragments. There could not have been a single bone in his body left intact, and the destruction was horrible and complete. In fact, there was not enough of his face remaining for him to be identified with any certainty.

We attended the front desk and spoke to the clerk, who informed us that the victim had checked in earlier that day, specifically asking for a room as high as possible because he enjoyed the view. We gained entry to the room and found the jumper had thoughtfully left his jacket, boots and identification neatly piled on the couch, along with a cassette tape outlining his troubles and his intent to end his life. He was a businessman who had finally had enough of life after some serious setbacks. According to the tape, suicide had become the only acceptable option he could think of which would solve all his problems.

The body removal service in those days consisted primarily of one very friendly gentleman who enjoyed the odd drink now and then. He was responsible for the difficult task of cleaning up the mess left by our jumper's rather sudden departure from his room. He played to a large audience that day, because there were several hundred apartments overlooking the parkade. It seemed to me that almost every balcony and window had at least one curious onlooker trying to get a glimpse of the remains.

We were disgusted at the ghoulish behavior of these citizens, especially when we noticed that some of them were even letting their children watch the messy cleanup. The body snatcher, as he was nicknamed, took all this in stride. After putting on surgical gloves, he placed the victim's torso inside a body bag and then pulled out a clear plastic bag which he used to collect the smaller parts.

When the plastic bag was full he turned away from the onlookers for a second, tugged off the glove from his right hand and warned us under his breath to pay close attention. With a theatrical flourish he turned to face his audience once again and slowly maneuvered his right index finger behind the plastic bag so it appeared to be well in the middle of the sack of miscellaneous body parts. After making a stirring motion with his finger, he drew it out and placed it in his mouth while making up and down approving gestures with his face as if tasting a special treat. All the balconies and windows around us emptied as bystanders suddenly lost interest, as well as their lunches, much to the amusement of every policeman on the scene.

***

Well before I joined the force, emergency crews were called to the scene of a tragic accident involving a trainman on the railway tracks. He had somehow become caught between two shunting trains and was trapped in the coupling mechanism. He was alive and conscious when help arrived, but there was no doubt that when the trains were uncoupled, he would die.

His lower body was covered with a tarp and his family was brought to the scene to say their good-byes. They left, and the train was then uncoupled.

***

I was inside one of the better West End hotels dealing with an unwanted guest when one of the staff approached the front desk to report a problem upstairs. Apparently a couple on their second honeymoon had just set their luggage down inside their room when they noticed somebody sleeping in their bed. They had called out to this person several times but he ignored them.

We called for an ambulance and soon discovered the reason why this mysterious intruder had not responded to their questions as he lay there with only his socks on. The elderly gentleman had died hours earlier, probably from a heart attack. There was no indication of foul play. Further investigation showed that he was extremely well-to-do. He'd checked into the room for a noontime nap, apparently, and there was no indication that he had been anything but alone.

The maid was supposed to have prepared the room after his departure so the honeymoon couple could check in later that afternoon.

Because of an oversight she had not done so, and the room had been rented anyway, complete with its own corpse. The hotel staff apologized and moved the honeymoon couple to another room, although I'm sure their celebration must have been subdued after what they had just witnessed.

***

Our Sergeant assigned two members from the team to work a plainclothes detail for crime prevention purposes. They were looking for theft-from-auto suspects that evening, and they had just checked a parking lot at Sunset Beach. As they left the area, they passed the Sergeant who was going to park there to enjoy the ocean view while drinking a cup of convenience store coffee. The parking lot was poorly lit at the time, so cars left there overnight were frequently targeted by thieves. As a result, our cars patrolled the area on a regular basis.

We were intrigued when the Sergeant came on the air a minute later to ask for an ambulance to attend the lot as soon as possible, so we immediately started in that direction out of curiosity. When the Sergeant canceled the ambulance thirty seconds later, and instead asked for the morgue wagon to attend to pick up a dead body, of course we became even more interested.

The scenario as we arrived needed no further explanation. There was a car parked in the middle of the lot with its driver's side door ajar. Its interior light was on because of the open door, and the bright light inside the car was shining like a beacon in the almost deserted parking lot. That light illuminated the body of an elderly man who was slumped half in and half out of the driver's seat. He had died of natural causes, probably a heart attack, and apparently he'd been there for some time.

The Sergeant was still standing beside the car, waiting for the morgue wagon to attend and wondering out loud how his two plainclothes officers could possibly have missed seeing the body. He called them back to take the report, and probably had some pointed questions for them to answer about their qualifications as trained observers.

***

A similar incident occurred several years later. Two of our officers on routine patrol were driving by an East End parking lot when the attendant flagged them over. He wanted to know what he should do about a car he'd discovered in the middle of his lot when he arrived first thing in the morning. Because it was parked sideways, it was taking up three spaces, and he wanted it moved immediately.

The policemen were apparently very thorough, if not observant,

133

that day. They actually entered the car through the unlocked driver's side door to examine papers they found on the front seat. They then obtained the owner's address from the registration documents and advised the attendant to phone the owner and ask him to move his car or face having it towed from the lot. When the attendant couldn't reach the owner, he promptly called for a tow truck.

The tow truck driver took one look inside the car and immediately used his radio to call for an ambulance. He had found what looked like a dead body in the back seat, completely covered by various bedsheets and items of clothing. The person he'd found was indeed deceased, according to the first ambulance crew to arrive. From what they observed inside the car, it was clear to them that he'd been murdered.

I arrived to safeguard the scene for the homicide detectives. When the attendant informed me of the assistance rendered him by the helpful policemen earlier that morning, I tried to raise them on the air to warn them of the approaching storm they were sure to face when their role in the unfortunate affair came to light. They were, to be charitable, reluctant to return to the scene for some reason, perhaps sensing that something was wrong and hoping to avoid trouble. Although I asked them three times as diplomatically as possible to return forthwith, they stubbornly refused, eventually becoming quite indignant on the radio.

The radio operator, well aware of what was going on, grew tired of listening to the exchange and interrupted us with a clarification. "Five Delta Twelve, they want you back at the parking lot because they've found a dead body in that car you searched earlier."

There was a long period of silence after that, as the two errant policemen started breaking land speed records back to the scene. Unfortunately, by the time they arrived there were already several indignant bosses lined up to take turns asking them how they could have missed finding the body while they were investigating the interior of the car. The fact that there was a hole blown through the roof from a shotgun blast should have been their first clue that something was amiss, according to the bosses. Having made more than a few errors myself, I understood only too well how the most insignificant of mistakes could sometimes come back to haunt you.

***

We attended a call one night in front of one of the seedier hotels on the Granville Mall after a report of a fight in progress. By the time we arrived, the fight was over and the only casualty was unconscious, face up on the street. An off-duty ambulance driver volunteered to assist the victim while we investigated the incident.

As usual, there was a great deal of confusion. A witness pointed to a man standing nearby and identified him as the one who had hurt the victim. We arrested the suspect and sent him to jail while we continued our investigation and interviewed the rest of the witnesses.

As best we could tell, the victim and his friend had been walking home from a bar when they stopped to watch an altercation on the street. The suspect had been fighting with two prostitutes. When the victim saw the suspect strike one of the women with his fist, he had exclaimed mildly, "You shouldn't hit a girl."

The suspect had turned suddenly and struck our victim once on the jaw, sending him reeling backwards. The sound of the back of his head hitting the sidewalk was so loud that it could be heard inside the hotel next door, according to the night clerk we talked to later.

Midway through our investigation, we received a call from the hospital informing us the victim's injuries were far more serious than we had originally suspected. In fact, his condition was deteriorating rapidly, and they doubted he would survive the night. The victim never regained consciousness, although he remained on life-support from that day onward. By the time the case came to trial several months later, he was still alive, but only because of life-support systems. The suspect was eventually found not guilty of a minor assault charge, and I expected the matter to end there.

Several months after the trial, however, I was phoned by the Major Crimes Squad and informed that our victim had finally died. Prosecutors were considering laying fresh charges of homicide now that he was officially dead. The detectives wanted me to view the remains so I could later give evidence in court that the individual resting in the morgue was the same person I'd seen unconscious on the street when I attended the call. It was a mere formality, they said, but important for continuity purposes in the unlikely event that the case was to be reopened.

I was a little dubious about the chances of identifying the victim this long after the call, but I agreed to give it a try anyway. Visiting the morgue was always an educational experience, and the atmosphere was not nearly as depressing as I had originally expected. I'd heard stories over the years about the bizarre pranks pulled by some of the colorful characters who worked at the old city morgue, and when I visited the place I could understand why they needed a sense of humor to survive their workdays.

I phoned to tell them I was on the way. When I arrived shortly afterwards the staff were unusually polite, so I knew they were up to something. The deceased's drawer had already been pulled out so I could stand beside it and examine his facial features for any resemblance to my original victim. The process of keeping brain-dead patients alive even when there is no possible hope of recovery is often referred to as "watering the vegetables." I'd never seen the results up close before. The corpse beside me appeared to be a skeleton with skin stretched over its bones. The remains bore little resemblance to what had once been a human being.

As I stared at the victim, an attendant rolled out the drawer on the other side of me to expose what I thought at first was a dead walrus. I forced myself to take a closer look. It was a "floater." That's what we called a body that had been immersed in water for some time. In this case the corpse had swollen up to twice its original size while decomposing. The odor surrounding the bloated cadaver was nauseating.

As I tried valiantly to examine the body on my left, I could not help but turn my head toward the floater on my right each time I heard a crunching noise beside me. It was the morgue attendant using wire cutters to remove all the fingertips from the floater's corpse for fingerprint examination later. That was the only way this particular body would ever be identified, because any distinguishing features had been obliterated by the process of decomposition. I maintained my most neutral expression until I finally found an excuse to leave, disappointing the practical jokers by refusing to admit publicly the nausea I was feeling inwardly. I had a very strong stomach at the time. The homicide investigation was never reopened.

***

When someone called an ambulance to a dilapidated and condemned boarding house for a possible casualty, police were automatically notified to attend as well. We learned that the occupant had failed to turn up at the restaurant he frequented every morning, so the waitress there had called 911 because they were concerned about his poor health.

There was only one suite still occupied in the ancient structure, and it was so full of junk that there was barely room to open the door. The victim was difficult to spot because he was almost entirely surrounded by piles of debris. An elderly recluse, he had been murdered within the last day or so and left in his apartment by the killer or killers.

There were two rooms in the apartment, and the walls were still black with soot from a fire which had occurred years ago in the suite next door. The temperature inside was close to freezing. There was no heat or power in the deserted building, which had been condemned and was slated to be demolished in the near future. With the exception of a narrow passageway from the front door to the kitchen area, the entire suite was filled to the ceiling with a wide variety of junk, painstakingly collected over several decades by the elderly pack rat. Everything was covered with a thick layer of dust or slime, depending on how far it was from the camp stove. With the occupant dead, cockroaches now had sole possession of the suite.

For years the victim had been the subject of vague rumors in the neighborhood, rumors that had him pegged as a wealthy miser who had secreted all his riches somewhere inside the ruins of his apartment. Many elderly pensioners don't trust banks after their experiences during the Great Depression. Instead, they often choose to store their money inside a mattress. The prospect of an easy score has no doubt tempted many criminals to victimize the elderly. No one was ever convicted for this murder, although some likely suspects were eventually identified. The building he died in was torn down a few weeks later.

***

Some calls I handled were simple and straightforward, but others were fraught with complications and hidden pitfalls that made the investigation difficult and, at times, tricky. One call we attended just outside the skid road area was almost certainly a death by natural causes, but there were one or two things that just didn't add up.

The deceased, an elderly woman, was found on the living room carpet wearing a short nightgown that had somehow risen up above her hips. It might have happened as she fell to the floor, but we could not overlook the fact that she might also have been molested before or after her death. The balcony door to her ground floor apartment was open, and the maid who discovered the body told us that the victim seldom, if ever, left the door open overnight, primarily because of the dangerous neighborhood she lived in. The room was a bit of a mess, and this was also out of character for her.

As a result, we decided to investigate the incident with as much care as possible in case there was something amiss. We wanted to make sure an autopsy didn't produce evidence she had actually been murdered, without us having fully explored the suspicious circumstances at her residence. If this was indeed a homicide, it was our responsibility to preserve the crime scene and notify the specialist squads to attend. Otherwise, everyone who subsequently entered the apartment would add their share of contamination to the crime scene, obliterating or obscuring potentially crucial evidence before the specialists had a chance to examine it. If it was just a case of routine death by natural

137

causes, we could then complete the investigation ourselves without causing any unnecessary commotion.

We were still in the initial stages of our investigation when an elderly lady charged into the room as if she was taking control of the crime scene and began ripping sheets off the bed to cover up the corpse on the floor. She ordered us out of the room in no uncertain terms, and by her impolite language managed to imply that we were somehow enjoying the rather pornographic view of her deceased friend's private parts, left exposed by the disarray of her nightgown.

We realized that she was upset, having apparently been a close friend of the victim, so we tried every reasonable method of persuading her to leave the room so we could do our job. She adamantly refused our requests and began rearranging the apartment and cleaning up the mess. I had seen people in shock do strange things, but this woman really started going off the deep end. As a last resort, we threatened her with arrest.

This tactic was also unsuccessful, so we ended up physically removing her from the room and locking the door behind her so we could finish our investigation. She made various threats through the door, including the usual ones about complaints to the department. It was embarrassing to see someone acting this strangely in the presence of a dead friend, so we rushed through the call as quickly as possible. Once we had explanations for all the suspicious circumstances we had encountered at the scene, we sent the body off to the morgue.

The old woman's grief at her companion's death was not entirely overwhelming, however, because she managed to find time in the midst of her mourning to phone the Chief in person to make a complaint against us. We were immediately called into the office to justify our actions during the call, primarily because the lady happened to be a prominent activist in the community. The complaint went nowhere.

***

I was sent to an apartment building one summer when one of the occupants reported smelling a dead body in an adjacent suite. As soon as I walked into the lobby I could understand why he'd called, because even from the hallway the smell was overwhelming. The apartment was at the end of the hallway, but we had no key to it and the landlord was not available to assist us. The reportee was able to show us the apartment in question from the outside, however, and we decided to use a living room window as our means of gaining entry.

The apartment was on the ground floor, and the former occupant, like so many of his fellow citizens, had not bothered to take even

138

the basic security precautions necessary to safeguard his home. As a result, I had only to place my hands on the pane of glass and shift it up and down several times until it came out of its tracks. I placed it on the grass and climbed into the apartment, grateful that for some reason the odor in this room was not as bad as I'd anticipated. In fact, I could hardly smell it anymore.

As I walked down the hallway, dreading what I knew I was about to find, a man suddenly stepped in front of me! Now, the last thing you expect to see in the same apartment with a foul-smelling corpse is a live human being, and I must admit that the sight of this one scared the hell out of me. As I instinctively reached toward my service revolver, he jumped backward, just as startled as I was.

He recovered his composure first and said, "Are you looking for the dead body? It's next door!" The friendly reportee had shown me to the wrong apartment! I apologized and broke into the correct apartment where our corpse was still waiting patiently for disposal.

***

Sudden death notifications are usually an unpleasant experience, because no one likes to be the bearer of bad tidings. They can even be dangerous, as one young policeman found out the hard way. He was assigned to notify an ethnic family that their young son had been killed suddenly. For some reason he had to handle the call by himself, even though it was common practice to ask for another car to drop by to cover. The reasoning behind this policy was soon made painfully clear to the young officer when the family, hysterical with grief, began to vent their emotions on the messenger that had brought them this terrible news. He found himself fighting for his life as one distraught relative tried to relieve him of his service revolver. Fortunately he was able to use his portable radio to call for reinforcements before anybody got hurt.

My most awkward notification came on a cold and snowy Christmas night. Another department had requested our assistance in notifying a woman that her uncle had just died. I almost decided to postpone the notification and leave it for day shift to handle when I arrived at the house and found a Christmas party in progress. However, I knew this kind of news should be delivered as soon as possible, so I parked and walked up to their door. Their house was cheerfully lit up with Christmas lights, and I could hear the sound of people inside singing Christmas carols and having a good time.

As a policeman, I often ended up sharing very personal experiences with total strangers in the midst of a crisis or a tragedy. However,

I never felt as awkward about intruding on someone's life as I did now. I reluctantly knocked on their door and asked the woman who answered if I could have a moment of privacy with her and her husband. The house went silent as everyone became conscious that something was happening in the kitchen, and I felt worse than Scrooge as I delivered the bad news. Their expressions changed from consternation to laughter when they heard about the death of her uncle, and I must have looked puzzled.

"I'm sorry, officer," the husband said. "It's just that you looked so upset, and there's really no need to be. Her uncle was an asshole. Nobody liked him, and no way are we going to let it spoil our party. You look like you need a drink!" He was right, of course. I thanked them and gratefully made an exception this one time to my policy of never imbibing with the customers.

***

After years of experience with corpses, and numerous trips to the morgue, I began to feel more and more comfortable in the presence of dead bodies. My self-confidence was dealt a serious blow, however, by an incident that was later immortalized in a poem by the resident Vancouver Police Department bard entitled "The Night The Dead Man Flew".

We were assigned to a call at a hospital after midnight regarding the routine sudden death of an elderly gentleman in the emergency ward. He had been brought there after becoming ill in his home earlier that evening. I always insisted upon seeing the actual body when I investigated a sudden death, even if the death had occurred under a doctor's supervision, because I was wary of creating or otherwise involving myself in some form of bureaucratic mix-up such as a body switch.

We were informed that the corpse was currently on ice at the morgue, so I insisted we make our way there for my ritual look at the deceased. We walked through darkened hallways only to find the doors to the morgue locked because the staff there didn't work night shifts. My partner laughed as I spent the next ten minutes rounding up a security guard with master keys so we could take one quick peek at the newly departed and thus satisfy my need for confirmation that there was indeed a cold body to go along with our sudden death report.

We gained entry and quickly identified the interim resting place of our deceased in an upper locker. I had seen the qualified morgue attendants handling their customers dozens of times. Although they sometimes used a cart under the roll-out metal trays that held the

140

corpses, I assumed the cart was only used when moving customers from the locker to the autopsy table. Because I was in a hurry, I left the cart sitting in the corner.

"This will only take a second," I assured the bored security guard confidently. I opened the locker and noticed that the body, which was wrapped in a sheet, had been stored feet first on a long metal tray so the head was at the other end of the locker. I couldn't get a good look at the victim's face, so I yanked impatiently on the tray to pull it out further. It was on rollers so it moved much faster than I expected.

By the time the tray emerged halfway outside the locker, past its center of gravity, it seemed to take on a life of its own. Without the customary cart beneath it for support, the tray tilted wildly downward toward the floor. This sudden drop shot the corpse all the way across the room, and it crashed into the wall with enough force to break bones.

Meanwhile, I managed to beat the world record for the backward broad jump from a standing start. It took me several seconds to regain my composure as I gradually came to the realization that the corpse had not suddenly come back from the dead and attacked me. By this time my partner and the security guard were engulfed in laughter, and when I finally began breathing again, I joined them. I knew the only possible way to suppress the story of this debacle would be to eliminate all the living witnesses, but that course of action seemed a little excessive. After some thought I accepted the inevitable, and the story soon made the rounds of the patrol division.

Chapter Six
DEADLY WEAPONS

One of the first knife attacks I investigated occurred in a seedy hotel room on the Granville Street Mall. In response to a radio call, we entered the room through an unlocked door and discovered a female victim apparently unconscious in her bed. The sheet was neatly pulled all the way up over her head as if someone had already decided she was beyond hope. I didn't see any reason for optimism either when we uncovered her. There was hardly any blood flow from the deep stab wound to her chest, which was definitely not a good sign. As well, her face was totally drained of color and I couldn't tell whether or not she was breathing.

I leaned over her seemingly lifeless body while we awaited an ambulance and asked what seemed at the time to be almost a rhetorical question, "Are you there?"

Her reply seemed to come from somewhere very far away, as if she were disembodied and speaking from a different level of consciousness. The words were barely audible, and it gave me an eerie feeling just being in the same room. All she said was, "Janet did it."

The doctors who saved her life at the hospital later explained that the stab wound had penetrated her heart; she must have been balancing precariously between life and death while I spoke to her. Janet, the suspect, was arrested outside the hotel room just after our arrival. In fact, I could hear her screaming hysterically in the hallway as the victim was being placed on a stretcher. The suspect and the victim were close friends before the incident, and we later discovered Janet had stabbed her in a fit of jealousy over a man they had both been dating.

By the time the case came to court, the happy-go-lucky victim had made a complete recovery and showed no signs of the traumatic wound she had sustained that night. That made it difficult to illustrate to the judge just how serious her injuries had been, and how close she had come to dying.

The kitchen knife used in this assault was recovered at the scene. It had been driven into her chest with such force that the blade had bent to one side at almost a ninety degree angle. I thought this was graphic evidence of the brutality of this vicious, unprovoked attack. The suspect had stabbed her friend while she was sound asleep, so there was no possibility of claiming self-defense. Obviously the judge felt differently about this case, however. Although she was convicted, she was only sentenced to a few months of probation.

***

When it comes to offensive weapons, most people probably consider a revolver far more dangerous than a knife. It may have something to do with the fact that people think of knives as kitchen utensils, while anyone who has ever watched TV is familiar with the prominent role of firearms in violent acts. Everyone knows the damage a gun is capable of inflicting, but it's difficult to picture a knife as an effective weapon until you have actually observed its handiwork in person. In Canada, knives are used in more homicides than any other weapon.

There are many factors that combine to make knives the weapon of choice on today's crime-ridden streets. Most importantly, it is usually perfectly legal for criminals to carry knives, at least until they use the knife to stab somebody. Certain prohibited weapons like switchblades are, of course, illegal, but police must have evidence that a knife is to be used for an illegal purpose, or that it is concealed for an illegal purpose, before proceeding with criminal charges. Firearms are a little harder to obtain and more likely to land a criminal in jail for weapons charges.

Despite their benign image, there is no question that knives are deadly weapons. A stab wound to any particular portion of the anatomy is at least as potentially lethal as the damage wrought by a bullet. As well, it is difficult for investigators to prove that a particular knife was the actual weapon used in an offense, while specific firearms can often be linked to suspects or their shooting victims if a bullet is recovered at the scene of the crime.

There is another important difference. A criminal must be within arm's reach of his intended victim in order to do any damage. That makes a knife attack a very personal and deliberate matter, and usually poses some degree of risk to the aggressor.

A street policeman encounters knives almost every day, since most street criminals carry them either in their pockets or in sheaths on their belts. The prevalence of knives in combination with the already volatile atmosphere that exists at night in high crime areas such as skid road bars can only aggravate an already dangerous situation. For instance, fights that used to be settled with fists now tend to be resolved with potentially lethal stab wounds, inflicted in the heat of the moment.

The jail staff always get upset when a prisoner who should have

143

been searched during the arrest process arrives at their booking desk in possession of a knife or any other weapon. Everybody makes mistakes, and I made mine one day during a cursory search of a cooperative prisoner after arresting him for public drunkenness. As I completed the frisk and assisted him into the back of the paddy wagon, my partner suddenly grabbed both his arms and jerked him back onto the sidewalk. He had noticed something I'd missed.

After pushing the prisoner securely up against the side of the wagon, he reached under the young man's T-shirt and pulled out a wicked-looking butcher knife. It had been concealed inside his belt, in the small of his back. Had he used the knife to slash someone while being booked into the jail, I would have been responsible. Mistakes like that can happen to anyone, but I vowed then and there never to let it happen to me again.

***

I learned another valuable lesson late one night in the West End. Two of us were talking to a gentleman as he was sitting in the driver's seat of his car. We suspected there were outstanding warrants for his arrest on impaired driving charges, but there was no reason to believe the stop was anything other than routine.

He was polite and cooperative, although at first he denied having any identification papers on him. Then he changed his mind, stating calmly that he remembered hiding his driver's license under the front seat so no one would steal it. He was not much of an actor, and I knew immediately that something was wrong. As he reached under the seat, we both instinctively grabbed him and pulled him bodily through the car window. There were no papers there, of course. We did find a sharp hunting knife directly under the driver's seat, as well as a loaded rifle hidden under the back seat.

***

I spent five minutes one afternoon watching a prostitute literally holding herself together. She was sitting calmly in a chair, but from the amount of blood seeping through her clothing, I knew she was seriously but not fatally injured. She explained that a trick with a paring knife had slashed her when he suddenly went berserk in her hotel room just a few minutes earlier. There was no sign of him by the time we arrived.

After confirming that he had left the hotel, I asked her to show me her wounds so I could brief the ambulance attendants when they arrived. She first moved her right hand from where it was grasping her left upper arm, thereby exposing a gash that extended deep into the muscle tissue. She was squeezing the two sides of the incision together to staunch the blood flow. Fortunately her left hand was still functioning well, despite the injury to the upper arm, because she was using it to put pressure on another vicious wound, this one on her thigh. She also had a shallow cut to the abdomen, and a "defense cut" on the palm of her hand where she had tried to protect herself from the suspect's knife. If she had fainted before having a chance to call the police, she would surely have bled to death in a matter of minutes.

She survived her injuries. I talked to her briefly at the trial several months later after the suspect pled guilty to an assault charge. The suspect's friends from his alcohol treatment program gave glowing testimonials in his defense, so the judge chose to ignore his violent criminal history and merely suspended his sentence.

The outcome of the trial did not seem to surprise her. When I asked her how she felt about the suspended sentence her attacker had received, she explained that the same thing had happened after another incident several years earlier when she was attacked by another customer. The courts, she had long ago decided, placed little or no value on the life of a prostitute. She fully expected this suspect to attack yet another unsuspecting hooker the next time he fell off the wagon, as he seemed to enjoy such behavior. I had no reason to disagree with her. That is the way the justice system operates.

***

It is difficult to imagine anything more disturbing than the eyes and the facial expression of a seriously-injured child. I was called to a home in a quiet neighborhood one afternoon to investigate a report of a stabbing. The people who met me at the door were hysterical. There were several adults simultaneously screaming and yelling in my direction, so I had to calm them down first in order to locate the victim. They eventually led me to the bathroom, where a tiny preschool-aged girl sat in a half-full bathtub, bleeding from several vicious stab wounds in the area of her vagina. She was crying quietly, obviously in shock.

I ordered her mother to lift her out of the tub and place her on a bed in the next room. I then grabbed a clean sheet and bunched it up so she could clamp it between her legs because I wanted to apply pressure on the wounds while we waited for an ambulance.

The child regained her composure quickly, and soon began reassuring her mother that she was going to be okay. I could not help but be impressed by her pluck under such nightmarish circumstances. I managed to get her talking about the attack as we loaded her into the ambulance. She told me she had been stabbed several times with a pocket knife by someone she didn't know but had seen before around the neighborhood. She had no idea why this person suddenly decided to attack her. By the time she left for the hospital, where she eventually made a complete recovery, we had obtained an excellent description of the suspect from her.

The suspect was later identified as a mentally-disturbed juvenile from the neighborhood. He was eventually arrested by detectives and charged. He already had a history of committing violent acts against other children, despite his tender age, and was probably doomed to continue this cycle of violence. It is doubtful that a brief period of incarceration in a juvenile facility and cursory treatment by whatever experts were available to counsel him would be of much benefit. Only after he reaches the legal age of adulthood will he finally be incarcerated for any reasonable length of time, and of course by then it is too late to change his deviant criminal behavior anyway. The criminal justice system as it exists today is next to useless when dealing with juvenile offenders, and I can only hope that eventually something will be done to rectify the situation. I'm not holding my breath.

***

We attended the second floor of a skid road hotel to check a report that someone had been knifed. By following a trail of fresh blood we finally located the victim, a young native male well known to us for his drug involvement. He was in very bad shape with serious stab wounds in his back. He was obviously not long for this world.

Although I have watched several people die in the course of my police duties, his death throes were by far the most grotesque and shocking. He was thrashing around on the floor like a freshly-landed fish, and the agony he was experiencing defies description. He looked like he was screaming, but incredibly no sound emerged. It was as if the torment was confined somehow inside his body.

Although his eyes flashed from side to side, I doubt he was aware of our presence at that stage of his suffering. There was absolutely nothing we could do to help him until the ambulance arrived. There was something I felt obliged to do as a police officer, however, even though it was a thoroughly disagreeable task. I leaned over him and repeatedly asked who had stabbed him. I was hoping for a dying declaration from him that could be used in court against his attacker, or at least some clue about the identity of his assailant to give us something to work with. Had he been sentient and able to talk, there was no doubt in my mind that he would also have understood he was dying. This knowledge on the part of the victim is one of the elements that

146

must be proved in order for a dying declaration to be admissible later in court. Unfortunately, he didn't, or couldn't, say anything to me.

I helped the ambulance crew carry him downstairs. Although all of his vital signs were lost the moment his body tilted downward during the descent, the attendants did manage to bring him back to life temporarily. I accompanied them to the hospital, and like many such trips this one was a series of loud noises and jarring sensations as the siren blared and the car accelerated and swerved violently through traffic. I did my best to help as the paramedic, balancing himself against the wild gyrations of the ambulance, worked feverishly to keep the victim alive. There was little he could do.

Upon arrival at St. Paul's Hospital, the victim was rushed into the emergency room where doctors made a valiant attempt to save him. One of the stab wounds had penetrated his heart, and his condition deteriorated rapidly. As a last resort, the doctor opened up the victim's chest cavity and massaged his heart. The technique didn't work and he was pronounced dead shortly thereafter.

After the incident I was the subject of some good-natured abuse from other officers who had witnessed the one-sided conversation. They chided me for pestering him during the waning moments of an active criminal career, but it was something I felt was necessary at the time. Had the attempt worked, the statement would have been invaluable evidence if a suspect was ever arrested and tried for his murder.

I often ended up loitering in the emergency room at St. Paul's Hospital, watching the staff work on seriously-injured victims from incidents I was assigned to investigate. I never ceased to be impressed by their obvious dedication and magnificent teamwork. There was a standing joke amongst policemen that if you wanted to avoid the extensive paperwork involved in a typical homicide investigation, you should arrange for your stabbing or gunshot victim to be sent to St. Paul's. If there was even a spark of life left by the time the victim arrived at the emergency ward, the staff would inevitably work some kind of miracle. Assault reports were far easier to write than homicide reports, and you didn't have to make those troublesome notifications to the next of kin.

***

After a busy night shift, I was parked on the 1100 block of Granville Street writing a report when I noticed a very large individual staggering in my direction, clutching his midsection. As he approached my car, I recognized him as a notorious pimp and strong-armer. I knew this very unpleasant individual had been responsible for rolling count-

147

less numbers of tricks lured up to hotel rooms by his wife, a prostitute who was presently in jail. He was a typical bully who truly enjoyed hurting the people he robbed.

I jumped out of my car and grabbed him as he tried to walk past me. As I did so, I discovered he had been stabbed in the abdomen. I was not at all sympathetic to his plight; in fact, I was sorely tempted to just ignore him and drive away. However, I knew that wherever he wandered at that time of the night, people would be calling 911 to report an injured person. I offered to put him in an ambulance, but he looked around to find various street people standing nearby watching and immediately began playing a macho role for the benefit of his audience. After screaming obscenities at me, he tried to wander away.

When an individual refuses treatment for serious injuries, there are few easy options. In his case, I would cheerfully have allowed him to proceed off into the sunset, but the circumstances obliged me to take some action. I stopped him again and informed him that an ambulance was on the way and he would have to ride in it to the hospital or risk trying my patience. He still put on a bit of a show for the street people as we waited for the ambulance, but his resistance deteriorated as blood loss gradually sapped his energy. As soon as he was safely inside the ambulance where he could not be seen by his fellow denizens of the night, this particular tough guy promptly broke down in very unmanly tears and repeatedly asked the famous rhetorical question, "Am I gonna die?"

The trip to the hospital was punctuated by laughter from everyone but our victim. The sight of this vicious criminal whimpering in fear now that the shoe was on the other foot amused me so much that I had to leave the treatment room to avoid disturbing the attending physicians because I couldn't stop laughing. Unfortunately for society, fate eventually chose to award him many more years of criminal activity.

***

I was parked in the 300 block of Columbia Street one night, watching the criminal element at play. Without warning a black male, in obvious difficulty, stumbled into the side of my police car. I shone my flashlight on him to assess his injuries, and quickly filled a page in my notebook trying to catalog the different wounds while we waited for an ambulance.

He had stab wounds to the front and rear of his torso, and serious cuts on the back of his head, the left side of his neck and over his left eye, as well as widespread bruising to his face. He had come up

148

from Seattle, he explained, to meet his fiancee's family. They were members of another ethnic minority, and they had collectively taken exception to his particular birthright. As a family they spontaneously decided to cancel the engagement by murdering him with a barbecue skewer and a wine bottle. In fact, his future mother-in-law was among the attackers.

Luckily, he somehow managed to escape before they could kill him, although they made a sincere effort to finish the job. He survived his injuries after hospital treatment. Subsequent cross-examination at a trial several months later revealed that he had been less than candid with us that evening, withholding certain embarrassing details about his own behavior that night which might have influenced our handling of the case. As a result, the entire unhappy family was acquitted of all charges. Ironically, he married his fiancee anyway, despite the fact that he still had good cause to fear for his safety whenever he met her family on the street. I always pictured him as the epitome of husbands with serious mother-in-law problems.

***

Another stabbing victim managed to get my attention with several blasts on his car horn one evening as I walked into the front of the police station. He emerged from a late model luxury car to display a fresh slit in his abdomen, the result, he said, of picking up a female hitchhiker. He claimed that she had stolen thirty dollars from him as well. That made it a robbery. I gave my radio operator a description of the female suspect while the victim was being placed in an ambulance, and two alert beat policemen picked her up five minutes later at a nearby street corner where she was already looking for another customer.

The investigation went well until I interrogated the suspect. She readily admitted responsibility for the stabbing, but stated it had occurred accidentally during a struggle with a trick who had tried to steal back his money after failing to climax. Her story almost had the ring of truth to it, so when I attended the hospital to interview the victim I was already a little suspicious.

He stuck to his original story that he had been robbed by a hitchhiker he'd innocently picked up in the skids, even after I pointed out inconsistencies in his recollection of the events. He denied that any act of prostitution had ever taken place, or that he had tried to obtain a refund from the hooker by using force. I had him put his version of the story in writing and then sign it.

It was the kind of case that is very troublesome to take to court, in that I knew neither the victim nor the suspect was telling me the whole truth about the incident. Because there was enough evidence to forward the charge to prosecutors, I had to leave it up to a judge to determine what really happened.

There was no doubt that he'd actually been stabbed by our suspect. She admitted that much. On the other hand, it was obvious that the victim was lying, at the very least about soliciting the prostitute. Since he could not be charged with an offense simply by admitting that he'd solicited her, I couldn't understand why he didn't just tell me the truth. The motive eventually emerged in court when he reluctantly showed up with his wife in tow. She obviously didn't know about his nocturnal dalliances yet. She was there when the threads of his story inevitably unraveled under cross-examination.

***

Even a trip to jail to do paperwork could prove interesting. One night as I was walking by the holding cage where recently-arrested prisoners wait to be searched and booked into cells, I heard a slurred voice cry out, "Hey pig, I've been stabbed and I need help!"

The other prisoners sharing the cage with him quickly shuffled as far away from him as possible. I stopped and explained to him in terms he could easily understand how I felt about being compared to other species. When I asked him if he was telling the truth, he reluctantly opened his jacket and showed me a large incision in his stomach that had exposed some of his innards. He explained that he hadn't mentioned the injury to the officers who arrested him for causing a disturbance because he didn't think it was important at the time. Now he was beginning to worry about dying, so he wanted his wounds treated.

He did survive, but he refused to explain how he came to be stabbed in the first place. This reluctance to assist the police in their investigation is surprisingly common when dealing with street people. Sometimes they do not wish to violate the convict code, which says you never squeal to the cops about anything. In some instances, the victim intends to settle the score himself if he survives his injuries. Nevertheless, it is always nice to have a policeman present during critical medical treatment, if for no other reason than to offer the uncooperative victim an opportunity to unburden himself at the last minute if doctors deliver bad news regarding his life expectancy.

***

Knives are commonly used in street robberies, although a firearm is probably far more menacing. Up close, however, a knife with a prominent blade can be very frightening when it is held by someone

150

with evil intent. I have taken reports from several wide-eyed robbery victims who showed me a red mark on their throats where some robber had pressed the point of his knife for effect. It takes a very brave or foolish person to ignore that kind of intimidation.

I recall interviewing a female prosecutor who had just been robbed outside the parkade exit to a department store one Christmas Eve. Her description of the suspect was fairly sketchy. On the other hand, it was obvious from her detailed depiction of the six inch dagger he waved in her face that she would never forget her view of the robber's weapon from close range.

***

Every emergency call on the radio was preceded by a warbling alarm tone to get our attention. When the alarm sounded one quiet Sunday afternoon, I learned that someone had just used a knife to rob a West End drug store. I was working an East End car, so I had no reason to get involved in the investigation. Because nothing much was happening in my area, I decided to cruise the Chinatown district, looking for anyone matching the robber's description. Because there are so many ways to leave the West End, the odds of him heading my way were slim. Furthermore, his description was rather vague and seemed to fit many of the people I passed on the street. The only good news was that he was wearing white pants instead of jeans.

After a frustrating hour of driving through Chinatown traffic, one individual I spotted hitchhiking at Keefer and Main caught my eye. As I drove up he made a determined effort to pretend he hadn't seen me, but his attempt to look nonchalant was instead translated into an unnaturally stiff stance. When I finally approached him he became more and more nervous.

Then when I stood directly in front of him, questioning him aggressively, he fell into the trap of attempting to answer all my questions as quickly as I could put them to him. I just increased the pace, cutting off his answers immediately when I sensed he was attempting to mislead me. After circling around the issue of where he had been for the last few hours, he made the mistake of admitting that, yes, he had been inside that particular drug store earlier that afternoon. He hadn't noticed any robberies taking place, he stated innocently, and he tried unsuccessfully to act as if he was shocked that I would accuse him of doing something illegal.

That admission, coupled with his resemblance to the suspect description, was enough reason to handcuff him and put him into a lineup at the police station. When I searched him, I found a knife in his pocket that was similar to the description of the weapon used during the robbery. I also seized some money from his wallet, which happened to be the same amount stolen from the drug store. A positive identification by witnesses completed the case, and a check of his criminal record disclosed that this was not the first time he had committed a robbery.

***

When I first joined the force, I covered a dog squad member who was following a getaway car from the scene of a holdup at a West End hotel. The suspects had used a knife to rob the desk clerk. I was the only car available to assist in the area, and since there were several suspects inside the vehicle, we were particularly careful about where and how we stopped them. By pulling them over in the middle of an elevated viaduct, we could be relatively sure the occupants wouldn't be able to escape until we sorted out the situation.

The stop was done by the book. We pulled in directly behind the vehicle and, at gunpoint, ordered the occupants to exit one at a time. Before the first passenger had a chance to open his door, however, an unmarked car from another patrol area screamed up the viaduct ramp the wrong way and screeched to a stop beside the suspect vehicle. Two policemen in plainclothes emerged from their car, ran up to the passenger door and yanked it open. They then pulled the closest occupant out, bundled her into their car, and left the scene before the brake dust from their sudden stop had settled. We were left with the rather anticlimactic task of sorting out the rest of the prisoners ourselves.

What had transpired, we found out later, was the result of pressure from their boss to produce an arrest that night. After stealing our prisoner, they had simply booked her into the jail under their badge numbers in order to collect credit for the arrest. She would have gone to jail anyway, at least until we sorted out who was actually involved in the incident, but of course their arrest procedures were outrageously flawed. Every time anyone suggested compiling meaningless arrest statistics as a way of monitoring a policeman's productivity, I used this case as an example of why any form of arrest quotas was a bad idea.

***

Although possession of a switchblade is clearly illegal, there wasn't a crook in Vancouver who couldn't find some unlawful use for a knife which they could open with one hand, if for no other reason than the dramatic impact. Street people used to attempt to circumvent the law by modifying a standard folding knife so that a flick of the wrist would snap the blade out and lock it into place, ready for use. Years ago, the courts used to accept criminal charges against people carrying these modified knives as long as one quick flick of the wrist was sufficient to expose the blade. The only catch was that a policeman had to be able to demonstrate the illegality of the weapon in front of a judge in court.

As a result, on some of the less civilized streets in our city, it was not uncommon to see officers flapping their arms wildly away from their waists as if they were brushing off angry hornets. Each weapon had to be tested individually on the street before an arrest could be made, and some policemen worked up a sweat before they discovered the exact wrist motion necessary to flick the blade open. When the case made it to court, the knife had to open the first time or the charges went nowhere.

In the hands of criminals, these flick-knives posed an obvious danger to potential victims, but they also caused more than a few police casualties. Testing them to determine how easily they opened was a science mastered only by a few expert witnesses, and the rest of us often lost control of the knife during the demonstration. I was once struck in the stomach with the handle of an open flick-knife as it spiraled through the air, and I know of one incident where a courtroom demonstration ended with the flick-knife embedded rather dramatically in the judge's bench.

We were on our way to a coffee shop one noon hour when we overheard a policeman we knew ask for an ambulance over the radio. When the radio operator asked him for more details, he mysteriously refused to explain his request. Something about the way he talked led us to believe he was in some kind of trouble, although he definitely didn't ask for any assistance during his conversation with the operator. That just made us even more curious, so we made our way to his location as quickly as possible.

We found him standing on a busy street corner, putting pressure on the inside of his thigh to stem the blood flow from a knife wound. It was self-inflicted, the result of testing a folding knife that worked all too well, and he had been too embarrassed to ask for help over the air.

I will never forget the horrified look on the face of a middle-aged female witness who approached me as we put the officer in an ambulance. She was in tears, and obviously extremely moved by the sight of an injured policeman. "Excuse me, but is he going to be okay? I have to know." I wanted to reassure her, but because I was in a hurry I didn't. It was rude and it was a mistake. In retrospect, I regretted not stopping to explain what had happened because of her sincere concern and the fact that we have so few fans as it is. Fortunately his injuries proved to be fairly minor, but all it takes is one nick of the femoral artery to bleed to death in a matter of minutes.

***

Three of us were waiting outside a business premise in Chinatown for the owner to attend after a false alarm. It was after midnight and the street was quiet. While I was busy talking, one of the officers with me wandered away without saying anything. I turned around to find that he had crossed the street and was approaching an elderly Chinese gentleman walking toward him in the dark. I followed the policeman across the street to find out what was going on.

From my angle I could see the elderly gentleman suddenly pull something shiny from inside his coat. I just had time to grab his wrist as he jabbed a long and very sharp butcher knife in the direction of the other policeman's stomach. Between the two of us we managed to wrestle it out of his hand without anyone being hurt. It was not as easy as I would have expected. Although the gentleman was very old, at least in his seventies, he was still surprisingly strong.

Because he could not speak a word of English, we were relieved when an Asian male stepped out of the darkness on his way to a parking lot. We needed help. "Can you please translate for us? I don't know if he speaks Mandarin or Cantonese."

The young man grinned. "I'd love to, except that I'm Japanese."

We were soon approached by a responsible member of the Chinese community who helpfully offered his assistance as a translator. It turned out that the elderly gentleman liked to walk late at night, even though he had been strong-armed several times recently. The alert policeman had heard something metallic hitting the ground across the street and walked over to investigate. We learned through the translator that the old man had accidentally dropped his knife on the sidewalk. The knife, he stated with a grin, discouraged all but the most aggressive of robbers. Because his eyesight was poor now, he had mistaken the uniformed policeman for a strong-armer, and he decided to defend himself from this perceived threat the same way he always did, by pulling out his knife.

Even a bullet-proof vest would not have helped this policeman very much, had he been wearing one. All of us had heard the story of a protective-vest salesman demonstrating the effectiveness of his product in front of a room full of law enforcement officials. He had successfully used the vest to protect himself from a pistol bullet, but when he had a volunteer from the audience stab him with a knife, the blade penetrated his vest and he died.

The Chinese community was usually pretty good about taking care of its elderly citizens. On this occasion, our translator cheerfully volunteered to see that the gentleman got home safely, even though he had never met the man before. We thanked him and went about our business, grateful for a happy ending to what could have been a disaster.

***

My partner and I dropped by a rundown hotel just off Granville Street one evening in an attempt to locate a fugitive. When we walked into the second floor hallway, we found wall-to-wall wet blood trails everywhere we looked. There were a couple of large pools of blood still coagulating on the floor. The biggest looked like it contained nearly half a pint. More dramatically, there were grotesque blood smears and bloody hand prints on the walls and around almost every door in the corridor.

It was obvious that someone was in imminent danger of bleeding to death. Because there had been no recent ambulance calls to the address, we were relatively certain our victim was still somewhere nearby. We began knocking on doors in an urgent attempt to find him before it was too late.

When no one responded, it was clear we would have to start breaking down doors in case the victim was already unconscious. A supervisor who dropped by out of curiosity asked us to try knocking on all the doors one more time, primarily because he was anxious to avoid having to write reports on the inevitable damage that would result from wholesale kick-ins of every room on the floor. We did so, and our efforts were rewarded when a bloody apparition finally stepped out into the hallway and shouted in our direction. "What the hell do you want?"

He was literally covered in blood from head to toe. The flesh around one eye was hanging from the socket, supported by his bloody glasses. There were a number of deep stab wounds to his face and several more elsewhere on his body. Although his injuries obviously required emergency treatment, he drunkenly refused an ambulance ride to the hospital.

We had a good look around his room while waiting for him to change his mind. My partner found a bloody paring knife in the sink. It was liberally coated with fresh blood, like everything else in the room. As best we could tell, the victim had apparently been stabbed during a drinking party around his kitchen table. He must have wandered drunkenly up and down the hallway looking for help, and then finally returned and flopped face down onto his bed. Blood had soaked right

155

through his pillow, blankets and mattress, and was pooling under the bed even as we watched.

We finally convinced him to visit the hospital. Once the blood was cleaned off his face, we were able to recognize him as a drunk we had arrested several times before. He survived his injuries, which was not surprising because the derelicts we usually dealt with were a hardy breed from decades of living on the streets. Their battered bodies could often absorb a tremendous amount of abuse before succumbing to the inevitable pitfalls of their chosen lifestyle. Many had interesting stories to tell about their backgrounds, but only if you talked to them before they consumed their first bottle of the day. Our victim never did tell us what actually happened that night, either because he didn't want to incriminate a friend or because he couldn't remember.

***

I remember listening to a veteran officer reminiscing about his career just after I joined the police department in 1975. He had plenty of the usual war stories to tell, but one of the things he said surprised me. In over thirty years of police work, he claimed, he had never drawn his service revolver except at the range during annual qualification. He was the exception to the rule, even in those gentler times, and any policeman who works the streets today knows that only too well.

While firearms are not nearly as common here as they are in the United States, Canadian criminals still have no problem equipping themselves with as much firepower as they want. Idiotic gun registration laws will do nothing to change this.

***

My first potentially-dangerous gun call began with a routine license plate check of an Ontario car I was following. The radio dispatcher informed me that this particular vehicle was on file, associated to a group of jail escapees from eastern Canada. The antiquated paddy wagon I was driving was on its last legs, so I had my hands full just trying to follow the suspect vehicle through the crowded West End without losing it. I also had to decipher the street signs I was driving past in almost total darkness so cover units could locate me if I managed to pull the car over. There were at least four occupants, so I preferred not to try arresting them on my own.

The suspects made no attempt to lose me, but instead turned into a parking lot on a dark side street before my cover units had a chance to arrive. Nothing happened for about thirty seconds. I blocked the only exit from the lot with my wagon and waited for them to make the first move. I knew there was a good chance they were armed, so I had to be prepared for the worst.

I was still attempting to give the radio operator a better description of my location when suddenly all four parties in the car simultaneously opened their doors and began to exit the vehicle. Several cars from my district were on their way to cover me, but so far they were nowhere to be seen. I had to do something instantly or face the humiliating fate of losing all the suspected escapees.

I jumped out of the wagon, pointed my service revolver in their direction and threatened in a loud voice to open fire unless they all got back into the car immediately. Amazingly, they all complied without any sign of resistance. I saw the passenger in the front seat duck down for about thirty seconds, but I couldn't tell what he was doing. After cover arrived and all the suspects had been arrested without a struggle, I took a good look through the car for any evidence the passengers might have hidden. I came up empty.

We determined that one of the parties inside the car had nothing to do with the escapees, so he was sent on his way. We had to keep the other three in custody until we could determine which of them was wanted because they all lied about their names and criminal records. I transported them to jail where a strip-search of the prisoners led to the discovery of a handgun magazine containing several rounds of ammunition in one of the suspect's socks.

I remembered seeing him crouch down under the dash on the passenger side as I waited for cover, so I searched the interior of the car one more time. I still came up empty. We had reason to suspect that the car was stolen since its Vehicle Identification Number was obscured, so we had it impounded to the police garage for safekeeping. I asked the detectives to tear it apart in order to locate the weapon I felt certain was still hidden somewhere inside the car. The next day, after an exhaustive search, they finally located a .32 semi-automatic pistol jammed deep inside a heater vent under the dashboard. The detectives found my fingerprints inches away from the weapon. When I had reached in to search the heater, I had not gone quite far enough. The escapees were sent back to prison in Ontario. I never did find out why they decided not to attempt another escape while I waited for cover units to arrive.

***

I often hear police officers described as trained observers. That involves making observations, perhaps during the investigation of a crime scene, and then accurately reproducing those observations later for reports or for use inside a court room. A good street policeman will often see things of relevance to his work that a civilian might miss or misunderstand. Unless he has reason to focus his full attention on a specific individual, most cops during routine patrol tend to develop the habit of constantly scanning their surroundings for anything out of the ordinary. For instance, a male officer giving directions to a tourist while standing on a busy sidewalk will probably be paying more attention to his surroundings than to the person he is talking to, unless, of course, that person happens to be an attractive female tourist.

It is of course important for police officers to keep their eyes open at all times, although there is a tendency to relax a bit while on a coffee break, or while interviewing crime victims after the suspect has left the scene. I learned that particular lesson one evening during my second year on the job. I spent five minutes talking to a landlord who wanted to report an altercation he'd had with one of his tenants earlier that night. The interview went well until the policewoman that covered me on the call suddenly reached over and pulled a semi-automatic pistol from the front of the landlord's belt. It had apparently been displayed there prominently throughout our conversation. It was not loaded. He explained that he was wearing it for protection around the building because of unruly tenants. I resolved to pay more attention to my surroundings in the future.

***

One of the most valuable and disheartening lessons a young police officer learns is that pointing his service revolver at a suspect does not necessarily command the kind of respect they might anticipate. On television cop shows, a glimpse at the hero's gun is usually sufficient to control even the most unruly of suspects. In real life, it turns out, many of the people a police officer runs across have a tendency to ignore all forms of authority, even at gunpoint. Some of these individuals are drunk or drugged, others suffer from some form of mental illness, and more than a few lead such a troubled existence that they could care less whether they live or die.

Early one summer morning, just after daybreak, I covered a supervisor who had just arrested an impaired driver. The supervisor asked me to process the driver, who was still sitting in a truck parked across the street, while he investigated another incident that had occurred nearby. I approached the impaired driver and asked him politely to step out of the pickup truck to talk to me. He responded by drunkenly informing me what I could do to myself.

As I leaned into the cab to repeat the request in a more forceful manner, he became increasingly hostile. I was about to drag him out when he informed me that he intended to shoot me and then began rooting around under the driver's seat as if searching for a weapon. As I drew my service revolver and pointed it at his head, I yelled for him to put his hands on the dash where I could see them.

The supervisor returned upon hearing the commotion and told me to keep my voice down because there were tourists nearby who might complain about my language. I continued yelling at the suspect, who just ignored me as he rummaged around the truck's interior, screaming repeatedly that he planned to kill me as soon as he found his gun. I went so far as to use my left index finger to direct his attention to my service revolver, which was still pointed at his head, while explaining that if he emerged with anything in his hand I would shoot him. He was not impressed by my threats.

I finally got tired of waiting for him to come to his senses. I reached inside the cab when he wasn't paying attention and dragged him out by his hair. I holstered my weapon as I forced him down to the ground and handcuffed him with a little help from the supervisor.

As soon as the suspect was safely inside the paddy wagon, we checked him on the computer and discovered that there were warrants for his arrest originating from another jurisdiction. He had been involved in a break-in several days earlier where several rifles and handguns were stolen.

However, a thorough search of the truck turned up no sign of the weapons. The only intelligible statement we got from our suspect was that he'd forgotten the stolen guns were no longer under the seat because he was too drunk to think straight at the time I arrested him. He refused to tell me where he had cached the stolen firearms, of course, so I left it to the detectives to investigate further.

***

A similar incident happened to me a few months later as I was driving through the skid road area with a civilian ride-along in the passenger seat. We were assigned to check a report of a man sitting inside a nearby bar with a handgun concealed in his belt. The reportee, a bartender who was still on the line to the communications center, supplied us with a detailed description. I memorized it as best I could while we sped toward the bar.

We drove to the front of the building to keep it under surveillance while awaiting cover units. As we pulled up, we heard over the radio that the suspect was about to leave the bar through the front door. Seconds after the broadcast, the door opened and a man who matched the description perfectly stepped outside. My eyes were instantly drawn to a conspicuous bulge that was clearly visible under the left side of his jacket. He walked westbound, and then north along a side street, ignoring our marked car.

Other police cars began pulling into the area, and I noted with relief that the street he was walking along was otherwise clear of pedestrians and traffic. I parked my car about twenty feet behind him and stepped out. After taking cover behind my car door, and urging my ride-along to stay low, I yelled at the suspect to put his hands up.

He turned in my direction and looked at me sullenly as if I was interrupting something. I told him that my service revolver was pointed directly at him, in case he couldn't see it because it was dark. He made no attempt to respond to my requests. I warned him repeatedly that he would be wise to do as he was told. Instead, he ignored my orders and continued to stare at me blankly.

Within a very short time the suspect was surrounded on two sides by police. They were positioned to cut off his avenues of escape while at the same time not creating a crossfire situation where police on one side would be shooting in the direction of other officers. I yelled at the suspect repeatedly while unashamedly using the type of street vernacular I hoped he would understand. I had to convince him that I was serious because I knew what would happen if he did something stupid in front of this many policemen with their service revolvers pointed his way. I did everything I could to persuade him to raise his hands and surrender, but he only responded with an occasional obscenity directed at me.

A dog squad member arrived and took up a position nearby in case the suspect decided to run for it. We maintained the standoff situation for several minutes until finally the suspect turned abruptly and started to walk away. The police dog instinctively grabbed him by the leg and several officers then pinned him to the ground so that he could be safely searched.

We found a container of margarine under his jacket. There was no weapon. We asked him why he hadn't cooperated and he immediately launched into a tirade of indecipherable gibberish, the product of a very disturbed mind that was incapable of understanding what had happened. We released him and sent him on his way. Witnesses inside the bar still swore that they'd seen the suspect concealing what looked like a gun in his belt. We searched the table he had been sitting at, and double-checked the bushes he'd walked past on his way out the door, but the gun they thought they'd seen was never recovered, if indeed it ever existed in the first place.

Had he reached under his jacket for any reason, I'd have been

160

faced with a difficult choice. If I waited to see if he had a real gun, he would have time to get off the first shot. On the other hand, if I protected myself by shooting him as soon as it looked like he was about to pull a weapon from his belt, I would risk killing an unarmed man.

I was involved in several similar situations during my career as a policeman. Often we had only a few seconds to decide whether or not to shoot. In the end I always made the right decision, although often that was due more to good luck than anything else. When facing an individual who might be armed, the consequences of poor judgment, or just plain bad luck, are truly frightening to contemplate.

Ironically, I was notified weeks later of a citizen complaint made against me as a result of this incident. One of the residents of the block, a woman who had once served as a secretary to one of the department big shots, had witnessed the confrontation that night and wanted to complain about my vulgar, offensive language. She had even provided a verbatim transcript of my futile attempt to talk the disturbed man into surrendering. I was impressed by her accuracy and thorough note-taking, because she managed to capture most of the esoteric words I used, as well as many of my favorite combinations of obscenities, blasphemies, vulgarities, expletives and imprecations, phrases that had taken me years of diligent practice to master. Her complaint concerned only my vocabulary, and no mention was made of the fact that I had almost shot what had eventually turned out to be an innocent man. The complaint went nowhere.

***

We received information from a reliable informant that the caretaker of a West End boarding house was in possession of a sizable amount of drugs. According to the informant, the caretaker guarded his room with several firearms, one of which was said to be a sawed-off shotgun.

My regular partner was off on vacation leave, so I obtained the assistance of two other officers I trusted. Armed with a search warrant, we managed to get in the front door of the house without any difficulty. We had to stop there to regroup, however, because the drug dealer, in a fit of paranoia, had removed all room numbers from the dozen or so doors inside his building.

We decided to knock on doors one at a time in order to locate the correct suite the hard way. We were rewarded with a response from one of the first we tried. A male voice inside asked who we were. When I attempted to fool him by using a fictional name, he promptly informed us that he had a shotgun trained on the door and would blow our heads

161

off if we tried anything stupid. At least we knew we were at the right address!

Understandably reluctant at this stage to kick the door in, we informed him that we were police officers, and that we had a search warrant for his suite. There was a long pause, and then I heard a deadbolt unlock from inside. The handle turned quietly, and from where I was standing beside the door I could see that it now stood ajar. This was not my favorite way to execute a search warrant! When I opened the door the rest of the way with my service revolver, I was greeted with the sight of a twelve gauge shotgun pointed directly at my head from several feet away. Fortunately the suspect chose to lower his gun after a moment of indecision rather than opening fire. He was handcuffed so we could search his apartment.

The shotgun he had pointed at me was not the sawed-off weapon we were looking for, although it was loaded and ready to fire. The only other weapon we found inside was a loaded .22 rifle with its serial numbers filed off. Since the law making it illegal to possess a firearm with the numbers obscured hadn't been enacted at the time, the rifle had to be returned to him. Our firearms specialists couldn't raise the original serial number to find out whether or not it was stolen.

We couldn't find any sign of the drugs we were seeking either, although we searched as thoroughly as possible without tearing up the floorboards and walls. Our suspect had just emerged from a Quebec prison where he'd served a lengthy sentence for robbery and kidnapping. When we began our search, he went berserk and tried to snap his handcuffs by flexing his muscles. The intensity of his anger was frightening to witness, and he made it clear he now wished he'd pulled the trigger when he first saw me.

We charged him with a firearms offense. We eventually lost the case in court, even though he admitted on the stand that he was an active drug dealer as well as the landlord of the boarding house. The defense lawyer argued that his client needed weapons to defend himself from thieves because of the large amounts of money he habitually kept on the premises from selling drugs and collecting rent. A gullible judge bought the story.

***

Occasionally, when nothing interesting was happening on our beat, my partner and I would stop and talk with some of the derelicts and street people who frequented the Granville Street mall. It was surprising how often these individuals would provide us with useful information, but it only worked if we treated them with respect and then asked them the right questions. Many were active criminals who would never overtly help the police unless there was something in it for them. As well, there was usually a lingering fear of being labeled a police informant, although almost all crooks snitch to the police at some stage of their criminal career. However, if the conversation was steered in the right direction and nobody else was within hearing distance, even the most stubborn crooks would occasionally yield good information.

Gun cases were always my favorite, so I usually asked potential informants when they'd last seen a firearm. There were plenty of guns to be found throughout the underworld, and any crook foolish enough to brag that he had an illegal gun in his possession soon became the subject of rumors on the street. When these braggarts actually produced a gun in front of bar patrons to prove their virility, it was not uncommon to find that at least one member of his audience later informed a policeman of what he had witnessed. Some of the people we talked to had actually seen an illegal gun in the recent past, but were too addled or stupid with booze or drugs to remember enough to be of assistance to us. However, sometimes our extra effort paid off.

One of the people we talked to was flattered that we would take the time to listen to what he had to say. After a little coaxing, he informed us that he had just seen a sawed-off shotgun the night before. An individual he'd been drinking with had shown it to him when they went to his hotel room for a nightcap.

Our informant was able to provide us with the suspect's name and address. Another police department supplied us with interesting details from the suspect's background. A gun store in their area had been broken into and our suspect was apparently one of a group of would-be desperadoes who had been responsible. They had stolen enough firearms and explosives to fight a small war, but the RCMP had moved quickly and recovered most of the stolen property. Unfortunately, there was not enough evidence to justify charges against this particular suspect so they had to settle for running him out of town.

The gun was no longer there by the time we arrived. However, we found a box containing five rounds of twelve gauge magnum shotgun shells in his room. One round was a deer slug and the other four contained heavy buckshot. The crooks in those days used to refer to this combination as a "professional load" when it was used in a pump shotgun. The slug was held ready in the chamber to be used to blow a locked door open. The buckshot rounds, containing a dozen or so of the largest lead pellets you could buy, were used next to sweep the room clean of any occupants unlucky enough to be found inside.

We never recovered the sawed-off shotgun, although we were certain he had it stashed somewhere nearby. Unfortunately, nothing short of torture would have convinced him to turn the weapon over to us. We applied as much pressure as we legally could, finally offering him immunity from weapons charges if he would simply hand the gun over to us, just to get this vicious weapon off the streets before someone got hurt. He still refused, although he wouldn't give a reason for turning down our deal.

We made it abundantly clear to him that our extensive and wide-ranging investigation of his criminal activities was only beginning, and although we weren't planning to run him out of town on a rail, he might later wish we had. He thought about that for awhile, and just as we were about to leave he decided to tell us about the person who'd sold him the ammunition. He had seen several handguns in the back room of the man's business when he purchased the rounds, and he willingly gave us a complete description of the man and his associates.

Because the informant was of dubious reliability, there were insufficient grounds to obtain a search warrant to seize the handguns, even though this was before the restrictive new constitution was forced upon us. We decided to simply walk into the suspect's business and sweet-talk him into letting us see the back room somehow.

Our suspect was not hard to identify, as he was confined to an electric wheelchair with a disability that left him the use of only the fingers of his left hand. He was obviously in poor health when we dealt with him, and he admitted that he didn't expect to live much longer.

The suspect willingly admitted to possessing the handguns, and then showed us where they were kept. He didn't seem too worried, probably because he knew full well that in his frail condition he would never have to face criminal charges anyway. We seized three working handguns, one of which was a particularly deadly-looking derringer. The guns, he explained, had been taken in trade for certain services he had provided in the distant past. He claimed he kept them there for his own protection, although in his present condition it is doubtful he could have fired any of them. There were indications, however, that he rented guns out to bikers for special occasions.

As we were about to leave with his guns, he asked us for help with a problem that had been bothering him for the last month. A man he'd hired as a part-time nursing attendant had taken one of his nicest handguns home with him after spotting it in a drawer. The attendant claimed that the firearm was broken, and promised that he would return it as soon as it was repaired. Our suspect realized now that he'd been ripped off. He felt that a little revenge would be in order, so he gave us the nurse's home address.

We agreed to investigate further, and eventually obtained a search warrant for the attendant's home after we verified that he still lived there. Our warrant was successfully executed early the next morning when we treated the occupant to an unusually rude awakening that ended with his arrest. We recovered a loaded Ruger .22 caliber pistol from his closet and charged him with possessing an unregistered, restricted weapon.

Like many crooks who get their hands on an illegal firearm, the first thing the attendant did when he got it home was to test fire it to see if it worked. We found a bullet-riddled stick of firewood that had served as his target, good evidence that he knew the gun was in working order. It was not an earth-shattering case, but we were pleased nevertheless to take these four handguns off the street permanently.

***

My first sergeant was from the old school of policing. He liked nothing better than to encourage the new people on his squad to arrest bad guys, and we learned a lot about police work from him. He came to us one night at the beginning of our shift to pass along details of a homicide that had just occurred in another jurisdiction. The victim was a drug dealer who had frequented our beat before his untimely demise. Because we worked that area, he said matter-of-factly that he expected us to come up with an informant and solve the crime. It was, to say the least, a tall order for two inexperienced beat cops.

My partner and I started checking the beer parlors, talking to anyone who might have known the victim. The most we expected to come up with was an unsubstantiated rumor, because word of the homicide had undoubtedly already reached the bars. As a result of luck and persistence, however, we managed to locate an individual who had been a close friend of the victim. He eventually agreed to talk to us.

After a private conversation during which he tried to feel us out to see how much we already knew, the informant finally relented and told us about the murder. He admitted that he and the victim had worked together on several recent drug deals. As a result of his close association with the victim, and his knowledge of the victim's associates and enemies, he had been able to piece together details of the homicide even though he was not present when his friend was executed. He knew why the victim had been murdered, which type of gun had probably been used, and where the suspects lived.

We told the sergeant what we had learned, and then transported our informant to the nearby detachment responsible for investigating the murder. As much as we would have liked to arrest the suspects ourselves and present the investigators with a complete package, we knew it was best handled by the detectives assigned to the case. They seemed quite pleased to hear what we had done for them, and the informant's story was quickly verified as truthful and accurate. Unfortunately, the investigators never bothered to get back to us to express their appreciation, or even let us know the outcome of their work.

For my partner and I, the worst part was losing a potential source of crime information, because the best way to identify crooks and make quality arrests was through street informants. Consequently, the last thing we wanted to do was hand over a knowledgeable informant to another force because we knew only too well that we would never hear from him again. Our sergeant was impressed by our work, however, and that made the frustration a little easier to live with.

***

My partner and I were in the middle of investigating a motor vehicle accident when we heard an interesting-sounding gun call on our channel. We wanted to cover the call, but there was no way we could leave the accident scene at the time. It was a mess. An impaired driver had run a red light and struck an ambulance making an emergency run down Georgia Street. The ambulance then skidded, knocking down a metal lamp post and wrapping its front end around a tree. Miraculously no one was hurt, but it took us several hours to process the impaired driver and complete the reports at the station.

The first thing we did after returning to our area was to ask around about the gun call. The details were sketchy. A young man had apparently walked into one of the skid road hotels while carrying a sawed-off rifle inside his belt. The desk clerk noticed his gun and called the police as soon as the suspect and his friends left. The assigned unit had obtained a brief description from the clerk but had failed to locate either the suspect or the gun during an extensive search of the area. The members told us they'd been given a direction of travel by one of the street people they interviewed as they tried to retrace the suspect's escape route from the hotel. Unfortunately, after following the directions, the trail had grown cold. They soon realized the street person had deliberately misled them, but by then he had disappeared.

Because the incident had happened on our beat, my partner and I decided we would start our own investigation and attempt to recover the gun. We returned to the hotel and found a bystander who denied knowing the suspect but reluctantly admitted that he recognized one of

166

the individuals who had walked into the hotel with the suspect. After some initial difficulties, we eventually came up with an address for the gunman's friend. The friend was sound asleep at three in the morning when we dropped by unannounced to interview him.

This individual was not eager to help us at first, but after some aggressive coaxing he finally provided us with an address for the gunman. We paid this suspect a late-night visit as well, and eventually recovered a sawed-off .22 rifle from a hiding place near his room. The weapon had been shortened considerably by sawing off most of its barrel and stock. It was now a very lethal and easily-concealed package, complete with a loaded 10-round clip of ammunition.

The case was not without its problems, and we never did get a conviction. Our young suspect subsequently distinguished himself in later years by committing a host of violent acts, including slashing a man's throat with a butcher knife. We took some consolation in the fact that at least there was one less gun on the street.

There was one loose end. Our colleagues had mentioned a street person who'd sent them in the wrong direction by feeding them false information. During our interrogation of the suspect, he spontaneously boasted to us that he was still carrying the sawed-off rifle inside his belt when the officers assigned to the call approached him on the street and asked him if he'd seen anyone matching the description of their suspect. The officers indignantly denied that this was the case when we mentioned it to them later. We believed them, of course. After all, they were both trained observers.

***

I was working alone one evening when an informant my partner and I had developed approached me on Granville Street. He was a heroin addict and his wife worked the streets as a prostitute. He was having difficulty containing his excitement, because he truly enjoyed the challenge of putting a case together for us. According to his story, his wife was servicing a trick in her hotel room as we spoke. He had arranged the date for her, and then monitored the sexual activity from outside the room to make sure his wife didn't get hurt. The client was not one of her regulars, and all he knew about the man was that he had just entered Canada as a tourist.

Ten minutes earlier, his wife had slipped out of the room for a breath of fresh air during a lull in the activity. She informed her husband then that the trick was in possession of a loaded pistol. She explained that he seemed depressed and had told her he intended to commit suicide later in the evening after one last fling. As far as she

167

knew, he'd stored the handgun in the glove compartment of a rental car which was presently parked at the rear of their hotel.

The trick would be up in the room for at least another hour, according to our informant's wife, the prostitute, so I was hoping I'd have plenty of time to prepare for the arrest. I located the proper vehicle and waited thirty feet away for another unit to cover me. Two policemen from my shift drove up a few minutes later. We were just discussing how we would handle the arrest, secure in the knowledge that we had at least an hour to prepare ourselves, when a man walked past us in the darkness and began unlocking the door of the rental car we'd been staking out. As usual, things had not gone according to plan.

We rushed over and grabbed him just as he was reaching toward the dash. The three of us frantically pulled him out of the driver's seat before he could do something we would regret later. I didn't start breathing again until he was safely handcuffed. I reserved the privilege of removing the semi-automatic pistol from its hiding place in the dash for myself. It was fully loaded with one round in the chamber and a full clip. All it would have taken to fire it was one squeeze of the trigger.

The informant poked his head around the corner, curious as to the outcome of his tip. In order to conceal his role in the affair, I went through the charade of manhandling him while he in turn acted as if he was concerned that the trick's rights had been violated. This kind of play-acting seemed melodramatic at times, but I had to make every reasonable effort to protect his anonymity. His life was at risk if his fellow criminals discovered he was providing the police with information.

**

A gun call that almost ended disastrously for me occurred during an otherwise quiet day shift. The communications center had received second-hand information that someone inside an apartment at a Barclay Street address was in possession of a high-powered rifle. He had apparently threatened to use it to kill his mother's new boyfriend, who was due to arrive there shortly.

We volunteered to check out the rear of that address in case he tried to escape via the back door. Other policemen with shotguns, part of what used to be called the Special Weapons Squad, were assigned to attend the front of the building where they would locate the suspect's suite and, if necessary, kick his door down. This was before the Emergency Response Team existed, and the Special Weapons members, armed with 12 gauge shotguns, had only a few hours more training than the rest of us. Consequently, we felt just a little bit safer at the back because that meant there would be an entire building between us and any potential shootout.

Somebody mentioned over the police radio that the building we were looking for was probably the Barclay Manor, a well-known boarding house on Barclay Street we had driven past hundreds of times. I had even stayed there once years ago when I was hitchhiking across Canada. We were certain we could identify Barclay Manor from the rear, so we were confident that we had nothing to worry about until we could actually see the building. After checking the rear for potential escape routes, we planned to take up defensive positions behind cover and wait for the confrontation.

What could go wrong? The two of us, in full uniform, walked nonchalantly down the lane in search of Barclay Manor, but there was no sign of it in that block. We started to retrace our steps, certain now that either we must have been given the wrong address by the dispatcher or we had inadvertently walked down the wrong lane.

It was that fixation we had with finding Barclay Manor which almost cost us our lives. We immediately realized how badly we had screwed up when we caught sight of a man holding a rifle in the second floor window of an apartment building, fifty feet away. He was leaning out through the window, pointing a rifle directly at us. Obviously we were in the correct lane after all! We learned later that he'd been tracking us in his rifle sights the entire time we strolled blissfully down the lane. The address we'd been given for the boarding house was in fact correct, but it was not the address of Barclay Manor, which was actually a block away. Somebody had guessed incorrectly, and we had not bothered to question his false assumption.

In the movies, one has only to seek cover behind a picket fence or garbage can to avoid sniper fire. In real life this does not work since a bullet fired from a high-powered rifle will easily penetrate concrete walls and even pass through entire houses. We had nowhere to hide, so we sought cover as best we could beside a garage and aimed our puny little service revolvers in his direction.

He was still pointing the rifle at us, but for some reason he chose not to shoot. When we shouted at him to drop the gun, he ducked momentarily back inside the apartment. We broadcast details of our situation over the portable radio, and waited for his next move. Perhaps this might have been the best time to run for better cover, but neither of us considered it.

Seconds later he returned to his original firing position in the window and pointed his rifle in our direction again. We ordered him to drop his gun, but he still ignored us. In a gunfight our revolvers were no match for his rifle. Even with little or no firearms experience on his part, at close range it would have been easy for him to shoot at least one of us. That meant that at least one of us would probably die. Even worse, because our revolvers were far less accurate, and our issue ammunition was notoriously ineffective, he would probably get off more than one shot before we managed to disable him.

In my opinion, we would have been legally and morally justified had we chosen to use deadly force to end the situation. We decided to wait him out. It is difficult to explain why we decided not to shoot. In my case, I felt the best chance of both of us surviving was to hold our fire. It was a classic standoff, and I could only hope that he would, in the end, decide to surrender.

It was as if the suspect was reading my thoughts. Without any warning he suddenly let the rifle drop to the ground and then placed his hands on the window glass beside him in response to our shouted commands. Within a matter of seconds he disappeared from sight as the policemen at the front of the building kicked his door in and pulled him away from the window. As he was being taken away in handcuffs, he boasted quietly that he could have killed us both had he really wanted to, and he was right.

The rifle turned out to be a .303 Lee-Enfield, purchased earlier that week. We recovered it beneath the window where he'd tossed it. We were lucky. A shiny, brass .303 round that had been sitting in the chamber was clearly visible because the impact had driven the bolt half-open. The magazine had nine more shells in it, and the safety was off, ready for firing. All he had to do was aim and pull the trigger. We never did find out why he decided not to shoot.

We confiscated the rifle as evidence, of course, and charged him with the appropriate firearms offenses. Two years later, because of a bureaucratic foul-up, I was notified that the rifle would have to be given back to the suspect unless we could show cause as to why it shouldn't be returned. At first I thought it was a bad joke, but according to the memo that was the current procedure I was obliged by law to follow.

The suspect had pled guilty to a firearms charge the day after he was arrested. Unfortunately, a mistake had been made somewhere along the line and the prosecutor had not arranged for the rifle to be destroyed, even though the order should have been made at some stage in the proceedings.

I wanted to make certain that this weapon would never be returned to the would-be sniper, so I spent an entire shift going through old reports and writing new ones. I discovered that he had been sentenced to probation as a result of this incident and ordered to report to the probation staff the next day. He never bothered to show up, and nobody knew where he had gone.

Because of a bizarre but not uncommon legal technicality, he could not be charged with breaching the conditions of his probation, so there wasn't a warrant out for his arrest. In order to be found guilty of the breach offense, it was essential that his probation conditions, which included a requirement that he report regularly to his probation officer, be fully explained to him. This should have happened the first time he appeared at the probation office, which of course he never bothered to do. Consequently he never even served the token sentence meted out by the courts, and he could not be arrested now. I finally managed to have the rifle destroyed, but only because he had disappeared from the face of the earth and could not be contacted. This incident was just another example of how the modern criminal justice system often functions.

***

I have become accustomed to watching futile debates between gun control advocates and representatives from the National Rifle Association. The issue of gun control is recycled every time there is a massacre in the United States or Canada. The same old tired arguments are dusted off by each side to prove the merits of their position, and the show is always introduced by the latest homicide statistics and graphic photos of some of the more gruesome multiple murders.

It is hard for me to relate to the extreme positions of either side, and it is unfortunate that the issue seems to allow no room for a realistic compromise. If I had to single out any argument that I believe is valid, it would have to be the gun lobbyists' call for longer sentences for individuals using firearms during the commission of a criminal offense.

When faced with news of a particularly vicious murder, many people feel more comfortable blaming an inanimate object for insane acts that, in truth, defy logical explanation. Then they can avoid confronting the reality that a fellow human being actually pulled the trigger and killed someone. The gun control issue is probably the best example of how society prefers to deal with the symptoms of a problem, rather than the causes.

Of course we will never impede the flow of arms to criminals, no matter how restrictive we make firearms regulations for honest gun owners. If society were to make a sincere effort to deter and punish criminals, the gun control problem would effectively take care of itself, requiring only a few housekeeping rules to regulate sales and possession. I do believe that a mandatory two-week cooling-off period before the delivery of a weapon might delay some people bent on self-destruction, but over the long run, no lives would be saved. Registering all firearms is a terrible waste of money because it does absolutely nothing to make citizens or police officers any safer.

I find it impossible to understand how people can argue that disarming citizens will deter the use of firearms by criminals. Most citizens, like most journalists and editorialists, are appallingly ignorant about crime and criminals. A national columnist, in a poorly-reasoned piece on gun control, generously conceded that police should be allowed to carry guns, with the exception of those officers on traffic duty. Traffic officers in the real world do police work and write tickets, so it is difficult to comprehend why they should not be allowed to carry their service revolvers.

I loved the story of the nationally-syndicated American columnist who vehemently advocated strict gun controls. This is the same man who then used an illegal, unregistered handgun to wound an unarmed trespasser in his yard after the young man tried to take a midnight dip in his swimming pool. Nothing could better illustrate the hypocrisy of those in the media who would lead us by editorial rather than by example.

***

Because every call a policeman attends is different, each incident must be approached with an open mind. Complacency and false assumptions can lead even the most experienced policeman to handle a call incorrectly, with potentially disastrous results.

I had just returned to work one autumn afternoon after several weeks of vacation, and I was feeling very mellow and relaxed. The call that welcomed me back to the violent reality of police work began routinely enough. I heard a one-man car ask for a cover unit to check a suspicious vehicle he wanted to stop in the East End. He mentioned something about a vehicle resembling the description of a getaway car involved in a string of corner grocery-store holdups that had started just before I left for vacation. I was nowhere near his location, but because no one else was available, I volunteered to help out.

As I was en route, I heard him inform the radio operator that there were two Asian males in the car. In the back of my mind, I made a tenuous connection between his description of the car and its occupants, and a brief summary I'd read in the crime bulletins about another series of holdups. My recollection was that knives had been used during these robberies, and I was sure the vehicle description I'd read was significantly different. Anyway, I decided that this was probably a false alarm, and even if it wasn't, the worst we were facing was two suspects armed with knives. Because of my complacent approach, I started my part of the investigation with a less than professional attitude.

By the time I arrived on the scene, the suspicious vehicle had pulled into a parking lot, and the passenger had already emerged to enter a nearby restaurant. The driver was still sitting quietly behind the wheel, ogling us nervously in his rearview mirror.

The other police officer and I left our cars and stood nearby for a short while, waiting for the passenger to return so that we could talk to both of them at once. There were no other cars nearby to cover us, and we did not want to split up unless it was absolutely necessary. As a result, we chose not to follow the passenger into the restaurant.

After waiting a couple of minutes, we finally ordered the driver to step out of his car. We did a quick frisk as he walked up, just sufficient to make sure he wasn't armed, and then asked him a few vague questions. We wanted to find out his background, but we didn't want to frighten off the passenger.

I did a cursory search of the car for any obvious sign of weapons but found nothing. At this point the passenger finally emerged from the restaurant and calmly approached us. Neither of them looked or acted like crooks, so our guard was down right from the beginning. We talked to them for several minutes until another search of the driver turned up several rounds of .38 ammunition in his pants pocket.

Then, belatedly, I realized what we were dealing with. It was like waking up to the sound of your smoke alarm beeping. We handcuffed them both and then began a more professional investigation. Much to my chagrin, I soon discovered that handguns had in fact been used during the holdups they were suspected of committing. I should have asked at the time of the call, but hadn't. Beneath the driver's seat of their car, an area I had hastily searched earlier, we found a loaded revolver hidden under newspapers. The passenger had just been released after serving time in a penitentiary for armed robbery, and the driver turned out to be a member of a notorious local youth gang. We lodged the two of them in jail for robbery and weapons charges and requested that detectives follow up the case.

When I came on duty the next day, I happened to be in the same neighborhood on another call so I stopped by the restaurant the passenger had visited briefly. Neither of us had thought to check it out the day before. The owner approached me as soon as I walked through the door and asked indignantly why the two suspects we'd arrested had already been released from jail. Citizens involved in police cases inevitably question the fact that suspects we arrest always seem to be released on bail immediately, even before the ink dries on our reports. I started giving him my standard explanation about the system being flawed, until I realized there was something else he wanted to get off his chest.

He informed me that the suspect who had walked into his restaurant yesterday, the passenger we had waited for outside, had returned to the restaurant today. In fact, he had just left the area as I pulled into the parking lot. According to the owner, the suspect had spent several minutes inside the men's washroom again, exactly as he had done the day before while we'd waited for him outside. The owner became suspicious this time and entered the men's room to find out what he was up to. He was just in time to watch the suspect remove an object that resembled a handgun from above one of the panels of the false ceiling and hide it inside his jacket. Now I knew that both of them had been packing handguns yesterday. We never found the second weapon.

The entire episode was mishandled from the very beginning, and as the senior member present, it was my responsibility. It was sloppy police work, and it could have got us both killed. I can only speculate that the two crooks must have planned to rob the restaurant or, in keeping with their usual method of operation, the convenience store beside it. Fortunately, when the first police car pulled in behind them, they evidently decided to try and bluff their way through a routine stop rather than opting for a shootout.

***

Family disputes are often cited as the most dangerous calls police officers have to attend. When members of a family start fighting amongst themselves, the result is a highly volatile situation that is prone to get out of hand without any warning. I attended thousands of them over the years. Most of them were resolved without incident.

I had wasted an entire day in court before coming to work on afternoon shift, so I was already very tired by the time I was assigned to cover another officer at a family dispute call one evening. The fight between a husband and his wife was still in progress when we arrived; their children looked on helplessly at the sad spectacle. The husband was Chinese-Canadian and the wife a native Indian. Judging by the hostility we witnessed between them, their marriage was all too obviously on the rocks. In fact he had just left hospital after recovering from stab wounds inflicted by his wife during their last serious argument. She had been charged with wounding and released on bail. Their marital situation had not improved since the incident, even though they subsequently reunited under the same roof in a final, acrimonious attempt to iron out their differences.

We immediately separated the two combatants. I ended up talking to the female half of the problem. She was intoxicated and quite obnoxious. After listening to her drunken, repetitive complaints for awhile, I just tuned her out. She developed an intense dislike for me, a feeling that was soon mutual. When we brought the husband and wife together in the same room in an attempt to arrange a temporary truce, the fireworks promptly began again. I could see that the husband was nervous about something, and I also noticed that there seemed to be some by-play on the side between the wife and her older daughter. However, I was dead tired and eager to finish off the call so I ignored the indications that something was wrong.

Fortunately, the policeman with me was a little more alert. He sensed that we were missing something and investigated further. As a result, he ended up seizing a handgun the wife had stolen from her husband earlier that night. At some point during our call, their older daughter realized that her mother had secreted the .32 revolver in her purse. Rather than telling the police what was happening, she waited until her mother's attention was focused on me, removed the pistol from her purse, unloaded it and then hid it until we asked her to hand it over. The husband admitted that he too had guessed she had his pistol in her possession, but he had hesitated to tell us about the weapon because he didn't want us to send her back to jail.

It seemed that everybody in the house had sensed imminent danger except me. I could only speculate that extreme fatigue had switched off the internal warning bells that invariably alerted me during other potentially dangerous situations. It was not one of my better moments.

The weapon was properly registered in his name, and therefore perfectly legal. However, we convinced him that, under the circumstances, it would be best for all concerned if we stored it downtown at the police station until they sorted out their family problems. That was where the matter ended, at least as far as we were concerned.

***

I attended a family trouble call where the wife phoned in to say her estranged husband was presently parked in front of their house. She had been told he had a gun with him and was about to break in and kill his family. We were able to arrest the husband outside the house without anyone getting hurt. No weapons were recovered at the scene.

We discovered that police had been there many times before as the husband's mental state gradually deteriorated over the last couple of years. Other officers had previously seized his extensive collection of hunting rifles and handguns after his wife found him one night in a closet, huddled under a blanket and mumbling nonsense while he held the barrel of one of his shotguns inside his mouth. On this occasion we could only put him in the hospital after arresting him under the Mental Health Act. We had to hope he could be treated there and cured somehow before he got another chance to carry out his threat to murder the rest of the family.

This type of case is one of the most frustrating situations a policeman can encounter. The criminal justice system can do little to solve the problem of an individual with a mental illness who threatens to kill someone. The law offers few practical options in this case, although the wheels of the justice system are soon set in motion after an offense is committed. Everyone may be aware, for instance, that an abusive husband intends to murder his wife, but how can a judge sentence him to jail when he hasn't committed a crime?

Jail is not always the best alternative for dealing with a family dispute anyway, because sentences are usually short and the offender is released well before the expiration of his full sentence. With or without treatment, the offender often emerges with even more bitterness and problems. Jail does not soften the hatred created by a marriage gone wrong, and with many individuals all the counseling in the world is wasted.

***

I had parked behind a battered, older model pickup truck while attending a routine call late one evening. While returning to my car, I noticed movement inside the rear canopy of the truck and stopped to investigate out of curiosity. Because it was dark there, it took me a few seconds to discern the silhouette of a man lying amongst piles of debris. I decided to knock on the rear window to rouse the occupant to see what he was up to.

It was not until after I had politely coaxed the elderly man out of his cramped quarters that I noticed the rifle lying beside him under his sleeping bag. It was loaded and the muzzle was pointed toward the tailgate where I was standing. I demanded an explanation, and he replied that he kept it for protection in case someone tried to break in.

He sounded a little strange to me right from the beginning, so when he began talking about the sensors and implants inside his head reacting adversely to various microwaves in the area, I was not surprised to find that he had a history of mental illness. It was fortunate that he had decided not to use the rifle on me, because in his confused state he could easily have panicked and squeezed off a round in the general direction of my face. The weapon was seized and subsequently destroyed with his consent.

***

My partner and I played an insignificant part in a case with interesting ramifications. Our role began when we arrested a man wearing a cast on his arm while he sat inside a restaurant frequented by drug traffickers on the Granville Street mall. There were outstanding warrants in his name for possession of a sawed-off shotgun. After we lodged him in cells we did a little research into his background.

By reading through the police reports, we discovered that the charge originated as a result of a motor vehicle accident. The suspect had been driving a borrowed car through Vancouver when he broke his arm after colliding with another vehicle. Police and an ambulance crew attended and sent him off to the hospital. The staff there noticed that he seemed in a big hurry to get the damage to his arm repaired and leave.

The investigator eventually checked inside the suspect's car to dig out the vehicle registration for his report. He found a sawed-off shotgun hidden in the back seat. Before the officer could make his way to the hospital, the suspect walked out of the emergency room and disappeared into the night. Since the policeman had already obtained the suspect's name and date of birth from his driver's license, a warrant was sworn out for his arrest, the same one we executed after picking him up inside the restaurant a couple of days later.

There was a punch line to the story. We were subsequently informed by detectives that this motor vehicle accident had come at a very opportune time for some unnamed Vancouver underworld figure. The detectives learned through an informant that the suspect had come to town to fulfill a contract killing with the sawed-off shotgun. He was apparently on the way to the victim's house to complete the terms of that contract at the time of the collision.

***

There is often a great deal of confusion during the initial investigation of a complicated gun call. Sometimes you can never be certain of what has actually happened until some time after the dust has settled. I was involved in one incident that illustrates the difficulty of sorting out fact from fiction.

Two groups of Asian men were gambling inside an upstairs apartment on one of the busier East End streets. One group thought the other group of card players was about to rip them off. Someone pulled out a small handgun as the game began to break up. A fight ensued and several shots were fired as two individuals were being chased up the street. The shots missed their intended victims, and fortunately no innocent bystanders were hit.

Numerous police units attended after neighbors called 911. I stayed a block or two away from the area where the shots had been reported until further information was forthcoming because none of the reportees seemed to know exactly what was happening. While I was waiting in a nearby lane, a witness informed me that someone firing a handgun had gone northbound in this same lane only five minutes before I arrived. Judging by the five minute time delay, common sense dictated that the suspects were long gone because anybody involved in a shooting would never stick around after hearing police sirens approaching. I radioed what I'd heard to other units in the area and proceeded down the lane in case there was a shooting victim laying somewhere in the darkness ahead.

At the other end of the lane I saw two Asian males standing at the well-lit rear of a restaurant. Hoping that they might have seen something, I asked them the classic "which way did they go" question. They wordlessly pointed north so I continued my way down the lane, looking for anything out of the ordinary.

Suddenly there was a commotion over the police radio; a unit shouted that he'd just found the suspects getting into a car one block west of my location. By the time I arrived, the suspects were already in custody. A puzzled supervisor was trying unsuccessfully to unload the semi-automatic pistol while officers around him ducked frantically out of his line of fire.

After the firearm was safely stowed in somebody's trunk, I took a closer look at the suspects and noticed with a shock that they were the same two helpful souls that had sent me off in the wrong direction back in the lane. Since they had been arrested with the gun in their possession, there was no doubt they'd had it with them when I talked to them earlier. I saw no reason to clutter up the investigator's report with mention of my embarrassing close encounter, so I decided my services there were no longer required and left.

***

One of the cardinal rules I always followed as a policeman, especially after consuming copious amounts of coffee, was never to pass up a clean washroom. Whenever I ignored that rule, I inevitably found myself assigned to a call where I'd be stuck for hours, miles away from the nearest facility. It was a little-known subsection of Murphy's Law.

Late one evening we had a report of a possible robbery in progress at an all-night convenience store just outside our area. According to the dispatcher, the suspects had been seen watching the store earlier that evening. The reportee had just observed them don their ski masks in preparation for a holdup. Because it wasn't taking place in my area of responsibility, and since it was the end of a very long evening shift for me, I did not immediately head that way. They had lots of coverage already, and I was anxious to go home.

I changed my mind when I heard a unit chasing the suspect vehicle as it fled the scene of the holdup. He informed the dispatcher that the suspects were shooting at him from the rear of their van as they made their getaway. The chase continued until the robbers piled up their vehicle and fled on foot. One of the two suspects was immediately caught by a police dog, and a thorough search began for the other.

I volunteered to take a position on the north side of the area where the other bandit was supposed to be trapped. I stood near some trees to wait and watch in the shadows. The dog track was not going well and thirty minutes later the search seemed to have stalled. In fact, it was beginning to sound like the suspect has somehow eluded the police dragnet.

I could not leave my position until the dogmaster decided it was time to give up the search, but I started feeling a new sensation on top of the night time chill. An overflowing bladder was triggering an urgent need for the appropriate response. I checked to make sure nobody was looking, stepped further into the dark shadows of the nearby tree line and watered somebody's shrubs. By the time I was cleared to head home twenty minutes later, only a few diehard searchers remained in the area.

When I arrived for work the next day, I looked up one of the officers assigned to investigate the robbery and asked him what had happened with the search after I left. He reported that they finally collared the last suspect just ten minutes after my departure. They found him hiding amongst some trees on the south side of the search area. As he described where they had made the arrest, I realized that the armed robber could only have been hiding in the very bushes I'd watered.

Chapter Seven
SHOTS FIRED

I worked a one-man patrol car from seven in the morning till five in the afternoon on October 22, 1984. According to entries I made in my police notebook at the time, I handled several routine calls and wrote a couple of short reports during the shift. I had no way of knowing that I was about to become involved in an incident that would make the CTV national newscast that night, but of course unpredictability is one of the most intriguing aspects of the job. You never know what your next call might involve.

As the shift drew to a close, I drove down the 200 block of East Cordova Street toward the police station to park my patrol car in our underground parkade. At the last second, however, I decided to take one more drive by the food line a block further down Cordova. Down-and-outers lined up on the sidewalk there every day for free sandwiches and coffee. I usually made a point of checking the food line at least once when I worked days.

I was looking for a man accused of murdering a young girl in Toronto a few years earlier. The child had apparently been sexually assaulted before she was killed. Police later recovered her body inside a refrigerator, shortly after the suspect disappeared from his apartment. He has not been heard from since.

This particularly sordid crime was widely publicized at the time. Because of the extensive press coverage, we occasionally received reports that someone matching his description had been spotted in the Vancouver area. The suspect description was so distinctive and the circumstances of the offense so repugnant that I carried a copy of his picture inside my hat for several years as a reminder. I wanted very much to be the one who captured him if he was in fact living here, so much so that I had phoned the Toronto homicide squad once to see if they had any information that might tie him to the Vancouver area. As I write this more than ten years later, the suspect is still at large despite an intensive manhunt across North America.

As I made my decision to go around the block one more time, a native male in his twenties waited peacefully near the front of the food line. He held his two-year old daughter in his arms. Without warning, a stranger standing in front of him suddenly turned and shoved him, causing him to reel backward. As far as we were able to determine, the attack was apparently unprovoked.

The young native was too surprised to react. His assailant moved closer and then struck him twice in the stomach. At first the victim thought he'd only been punched. After he noticed his attacker was holding a knife, he decided to back away from the altercation in order to protect his child.

The knife-wielding suspect kept his place in line. By all accounts, he then acted as if nothing out of the ordinary had happened. He obtained a sandwich from the kitchen shortly after the initial confrontation. A female staff member noticed that the suspect was still holding the knife as he reached for his sandwich with his free hand. She said nothing and did not bother to notify the police.

As the native youth picked up his own sandwich and coffee, he finally noticed blood stains on his T-shirt and realized that he had been stabbed in the stomach. He handed the child to his wife and angrily approached his assailant from behind, determined to seek revenge. Hearing footsteps, the suspect turned suddenly and tried to stab him again. I drove by just as the victim threw his coat at the man attacking him in an attempt to deflect a knife thrust.

The two separated as I stopped my marked police car beside them. The victim looked at me, pointed to the blood on his T-shirt and screamed: "Help! I've been stabbed!"

The suspect, a shabbily-dressed man in his mid-thirties with long, reddish-brown hair, walked away from us. He headed westbound on the north side of the street. I ran after him as I used my portable radio to notify the dispatcher that I was investigating a stabbing at the food line. The time was 1614 hours.

The suspect did not seem to notice that I was in pursuit. The churchyard he walked past was bordered by a sturdy fence. Knowing that he probably still had the knife, I decided to move in quickly from behind and push him off the sidewalk, up against the fence. With the element of surprise in my favor, I hoped the violent impact would knock the knife out of his hand if he was still carrying it. If not, the maneuver would at least leave me in a position where I could restrain him against the fence and eventually force him to surrender the knife.

During my previous ten years of police service I arrested hundreds of violent suspects without serious incident. The thought that this arrest would be any different from the others never occurred to me. Although I was working a one-man car, I didn't dare wait for reinforcements. There were dozens of pedestrians in the area. If I hesitated, there was a distinct possibility he would stab a bystander while I watched helplessly from the sidelines. I also wanted to avoid a foot chase because there was always the possibility he might escape. I hate foot chases.

It was at this point that an off-duty constable in plainclothes, on his way home after working day shift, saw what was happening from inside his parked car. He shouted a warning to me that the suspect was still holding a knife. I was so intent on the imminent prospect of subduing the suspect that I never even noticed the policeman.

As is so frequently the case with even the best-laid plans, this one did not work the way it was supposed to. The suspect went down onto his knees for a second when I shoved him, but then popped back on his feet as if he was spring-loaded and began flailing at me with his knife. I stood my ground as best I could and attempted to fend off the blows with my steel flashlight.

He attacked me frantically as if he had gone totally berserk. There was nothing I could do except hang on for the ride. I couldn't drop the flashlight and draw my service revolver without leaving myself open for a potentially lethal knife thrust. Eventually one of his blows struck home just under my left armpit; in the excitement I didn't feel the pain until later.

After what seemed like an eternity, but must have been only a matter of seconds, his frenzied attack stopped as suddenly as it had started. I was able to step back a couple of paces as the suspect stood there screaming.

At this point, the off-duty policeman joined me on the sidewalk. He and I both drew our service revolvers and pointed them at the suspect, who was still holding the knife in one hand and a bag of sandwiches in the other. He stood with his back to the church fence. With the massive walls of the church as a backstop, we maneuvered to a position on the sidewalk that offered us a clear field of fire in the event we had to shoot. I informed the other officer then that I had just been stabbed.

We did our best to reason with the suspect, but he responded belligerently. We ordered him repeatedly to drop his knife, but he continued to act as if he were deranged. His replies were abusive and nonsensical for the most part, until he suddenly demanded in a clear voice that we surrender our weapons. "You drop your guns and I'll drop the knife."

Of course, there was no way we could comply with his request, but we did lower our service revolvers to our sides momentarily. We then asked him once again to drop the knife. He didn't reply, but instead began stalking me, probably because I was the one wearing a uniform. With each step he took in my direction he tried to stab me again. The plainclothes policeman moved to one side and I began backing up while yelling at the suspect, over and over again, to drop the knife or I'd shoot. At one point I stumbled into an open car door and almost tripped backward over the curb. He continued trying to stab me with a maniacal expression on his face.

I was on the street side of a row of parked cars, still backing up, until I finally ran up against a mirror protruding from the side of a parked van. Suddenly I found myself trapped with no way of evading the knife thrusts anymore. The suspect lunged at me one more time. I emptied my revolver into his chest at point-blank range, face to face. He didn't react at all.

When he continued trying to stab me, I dropped down to a sitting position in a desperate attempt to protect myself from his knife thrusts. I remember bracing myself with my hands and then kicking him in the crotch with all my strength as he stood in front of me. Then I watched as he fell backward, away from me. The ordeal ended just as suddenly and unexpectedly as it had started.

I discovered later that the off-duty officer had been covering me from the sidewalk while simultaneously trying to stay out of my line of fire. When he realized that I was still in trouble, he fired one final round into the suspect, finishing him off. As I reconstructed the scenario later, I concluded that the shot he got off must have ended the attack and may have even saved my life.

I recall swearing and cursing at the top of my lungs as I tried to get my bearings. The situation seemed so unreal that it took me a few seconds to take in what I saw. The suspect had traveled several feet backward and landed on his back with the knife still at his feet. It had a white plastic handle and a three inch serrated blade. I remember having no doubt in my mind that he was dead, simply because I was sure no one could have survived that kind of punishment.

Pictures taken at the scene by the Identification Squad that afternoon showed that the sandwiches he'd carried had ended up beside him on the pavement. One police photograph actually captured several pigeons scavenging the leftovers. The plainclothes officer knelt down and opened up the suspect's jacket to check for wounds, only to find that he was still breathing. Incredibly, he still had enough strength to defiantly push the policeman's hands away. He stopped struggling moments later as death finally caught up with him. Several policemen tried unsuccessfully to keep his heart going until an ambulance arrived.

I pulled the portable radio from my pocket to inform our radio operator of the situation. "Suspect down, officer down, shots fired!" I had to repeat the broadcast, as the first transmission was garbled. I also asked for paramedics to attend. The time was 1615 hours. One minute and twenty seconds had elapsed since my arrival on the scene.

I ignored the action around the suspect's body as my instincts reverted to self-preservation. I knew the most important thing I had to do at that moment was to keep track of the original victim until the detectives arrived. His testimony would help establish my justification for killing this person. I told him he had to stay and wait for an ambulance.

Other police officers from my shift actually watched part of the altercation from our office at headquarters. The images were reflected in the windows of the Remand Center across the street. By the time they left the office, the incident was over.

Another officer was parking his paddy wagon on the street when he noticed me confronting my man-with-a-knife. At the same time, he also saw an unidentified individual in civilian clothing pointing a handgun in our direction. Because his radio was tuned to another channel he was unaware of the nature of the call. Consequently, for several agonizing seconds he was faced with a very confusing, nightmarish situation as shots rang out and he had no way of knowing what was happening. It was not until he approached to help that he was finally able to identify the individual in civilian clothing as a plain-clothes officer.

There were also dozens of civilian witnesses to the shooting. As usual, each had a unique interpretation of what he or she had seen during the altercation. A crowded city bus drove by as the incident occurred. Many of the passengers apparently assumed we were actors filming a movie. One lady from a retirement home across the street was concerned because she thought I was a bus driver being assaulted. I heard a rumor later that one citizen even complained because I was swearing at the suspect when I ordered him to drop the knife.

Soon there was a flood of policemen on the scene because shift change had just occurred at the station a block away. I grabbed one of the first officers to arrive and instructed him to stay with my witness and make sure he was taken to hospital.

It may be difficult for a civilian to understand that the most important thought running through my mind was to preserve the crime scene. Eyewitnesses and physical evidence would help to show that I had been justified in my decision to take a man's life. The presumption that a person is innocent until proven guilty does not always work the way it should. Regardless of what the law, the constitution and the charter of rights might dictate, in reality, a policeman involved in a shooting must be prepared to prove his innocence.

While I stood beside a police car, holding my left side and watching the action, an officer from my shift opened up my shirt to have a look at the wound. I realized then that there was a fair amount of blood staining my uniform shirt. My blood. I sat in the passenger seat of the patrol car as someone stuffed a pressure bandage into my armpit to stop the bleeding. An ambulance attendant also took a quick look at my injury and cheerfully assured me that I would be fine. That was nice to hear, until I remembered that I'd said much the same thing to hundreds of similar victims, some of whom had subsequently died painful deaths anyway.

One of the policemen in the car wrote down my words as I tried to explain what had happened. His notes present the best account of what I said at the time, perhaps even better in some instances than my memory. The form and content are typical of hundreds of statements I've taken over the years from witnesses and suspects. Nevertheless, reading the verbatim account of everything I said immediately after the shooting always rekindles some of the extreme emotions I experienced that day.

"The guy had just stabbed someone and I grabbed him and put him up against the wall. He stabbed me! Me and the plainclothes guy pointed our guns at him. He said that if we dropped our guns that he would drop the knife. He kept coming at me. I stepped back and we lowered our guns and he kept coming at me. We kept yelling for him to drop the knife and he wouldn't stop coming. We kept warning him and he kept coming. We kept backing up and he said I'm gonna kill you or I'm gonna get you or something like that. He clenched his teeth and lunged forward and I shot him six times. The fucker kept coming. I fell down and he kept coming and coming. I was out of ammunition and he kept coming. I started to kick at him to keep him away. I hit the fucker six times and he kept coming. It's not supposed to happen this way. I don't believe it."

I handed my service revolver to another policeman. He later passed it to a supervisor, who tagged it as evidence. I knew the two ambulances already on the scene would each be transporting a patient to the hospital. I couldn't wait for a third ambulance. I wanted to leave before the press arrived, so I asked another policeman to drive me to St.

Paul's Hospital. As we sped through traffic with the emergency equipment on, I began replaying the incident in my mind, trying to think of anything that might conceivably be missed by the investigators.

A television crew filmed the suspect as he was loaded into an ambulance just after we left. That station played the scene several times over the next two years whenever they needed stock footage of a police-involved shooting. Two firemen and a policeman accompanied him to the hospital. As they opened up his clothing to massage his heart, they discovered numerous wounds to his upper torso. I learned later that one of the firemen in the ambulance made several sarcastic remarks about the fairness of shooting a man armed only with a knife.

The same doctor who treated me that day was also called upon to examine the suspect when the ambulance arrived at St. Paul's Hospital. He pronounced him dead at 1640 hours that afternoon. As they turned him over on the stretcher, they recovered a bullet from underneath the body. The policeman seized this slug, placed it in an envelope and handed it to the investigators later that evening.

The body was then transferred to a morgue at another hospital. The Identification Squad also attended the morgue to take photographs and fingerprints. They eventually confirmed his identity by comparing those prints with others already in their fingerprint files from previous criminal convictions.

Morgue personnel removed all his clothing, including two jackets and a shirt, and placed it in paper bags for examination by forensic experts later. The officer recovered a watch, a ring and a necklace. These items, along with a wallet containing a welfare card, his only identification document, were added to a list of effects and sent to the property office. The body was then placed inside a locker at 1814 hours. The accompanying police officer secured the locker with a padlock to maintain continuity until an autopsy could be performed.

An ambulance transported the native stabbing victim to another hospital where he was examined by emergency room physicians as well as surgeons. His two stab wounds were found to be relatively superficial, so he was released from hospital later that night. From his position on the sidewalk near the food line, he had witnessed the entire incident, including the shooting. The policemen at the hospital obtained a complete statement from him while the doctors treated his injuries.

Upon arrival at the emergency ward, I ended up on my back on a gurney as the emergency room physicians examined me to determine the seriousness of my wounds. Nurses shaved the back of my right hand and hooked me up to an intravenous bottle. I would not let them take off my pants or boots, but they removed my shirt with their scissors to check for additional wounds.

I was in the hallway, waiting for X-rays, when I suddenly realized that my parents would have to be told about the shooting before they had a chance to hear it on their local news channel. Both my parents have a history of heart problems; in fact, my mother was already in hospital that day for tests. There were several officers with me, friends of mine, so I ended up making a very emotional call to the east coast on a public phone in the hallway while they listened. It was the same phone I had used many times over the years while on routine calls to the emergency ward. I recall thinking how unnatural it was to be using it under these circumstances. My father and brother took the news as well as could be expected. They thought I should wait and tell my mother the next day.

Meanwhile, I gradually began to realize that I was going into shock. I wasn't conscious of it until I lost all feeling in my arms, almost as if they had gone to sleep. At one point, I saw different muscles twitching spasmodically all across my chest. I remember thinking how bizarre it was that my body would react that way. Eventually these symptoms faded, but they were very disconcerting at the time.

While I waited for treatment I told my story to every policeman who would listen. I repeated it dozens of times as friends from the job drifted in and out of the emergency ward. I couldn't stop talking about it. At one point I got so animated that a nurse walked by and pointedly asked me to keep the noise down.

I also had to move onto my side while an Identification Squad officer took a picture of my wound. It was only after I knew for sure I wasn't going to require surgery that I felt confident enough to refer to it jokingly as "just a flesh wound." Although I had seen hundreds of similar injuries and could look at the most severe of them with nothing more than idle curiosity, this particular wound made a lasting impression on me. I still find myself unconsciously rubbing the area of the scar, even though I usually have to think for a moment just to remember which side it is on.

The Duty Officer and my Superintendent both dropped by to see how I was doing. A policeman told me he'd heard someone at the crime scene claiming that only a couple of shots had been fired. I recall stating emphatically to him that I had fired all six rounds into the suspect's chest. Although a short while later I could no longer remember anything about the actual shooting, I can still recall telling the policeman that I had definitely emptied my revolver into the suspect.

The first time I was alone, or at least out of the spotlight, was when I was X-rayed so the doctors could find out whether or not the blade had penetrated my chest cavity. It was quiet in the X-ray facility, and I started to calm down somewhat. I even managed to joke with the technicians.

It was around this time that a good friend of mine from my academy class arrived and accompanied me for the rest of my stay at the hospital. At one point we were in a treatment room discussing the shooting when two gorgeous candy stripers marched in and made a determined effort to cheer me up. Although at the time the contrast between their lightheartedness and the seriousness of the incident seemed almost surreal, I appreciated what they were trying to do, and they did wonders for my morale.

Before I could leave the hospital I had to undergo one final private examination by the emergency room physician in the minor surgery room. He injected some local anesthetic into the wound and used a blunt probe to explore its depth. It extended no more than one inch, and definitely had not penetrated into the chest cavity. After dressing the wound, he had a long talk with me about my emotional state. The doctor gave me some very thoughtful, valuable advice. He also gave me a pill that I could take that night in the event I had difficulty getting to sleep.

I borrowed a jacket to wear for the trip back to the station because what was left of my uniform shirt had been tossed into the garbage. Walking into the changing room wearing only half my uniform, minus my service revolver and spare ammunition, felt very unnatural and vaguely unpleasant. The weapon had been seized as evidence. I knew it would not be returned until after an inquest, or for that matter, a trial, if I was to be charged with a criminal offense.

I walked upstairs to the Major Crime Squad office that night to see how the investigation was going. The first thing they did, after asking how I was feeling, was read me my constitutional rights from the familiar yellow card we had all been issued. These were the same words I had repeated hundreds of times to criminals. Now they took on new meaning, because there was always a possibility that I might be facing criminal charges myself. I told them I was still shaken up and that I'd give them a written statement the next day. They did their best to reassure me that everything was going well, but I could only think about the official warning they had just read me.

I knew they had no choice; that was the correct procedure under these circumstances. It enables a prosecutor to use anything I said subsequent to the warning as evidence against me in court if I was charged criminally. In my opinion, it is also the best thing the investigators can do for an officer under investigation because, if nothing else, it certainly drives home the seriousness of what he is facing in a way that leaves little room for misunderstanding. Nevertheless, it was a sobering experience to be on the receiving end of those words.

That may sound a little melodramatic, but although there was never any question in my mind that this was a "good" shooting, and nobody ever accused me of acting incorrectly, I know of police officers who have been charged criminally for offenses they did not commit. Sometimes it happens because of pressure from community activists and the media; occasionally it is the result of a politically-expedient decision from the prosecutor's office. In fact, it took months for the department to finally notify me in writing that I would not be charged, so the possibility of a criminal trial stayed in the back of my mind until after the inquest ended.

I watched the local news at my friend's apartment. He and his wife did a magnificent job of putting me at ease. I drove home just after midnight and spent two hours writing a two-page statement for the detectives. I had no difficulty getting to sleep by the time I finished. The next morning, I threw the sleeping pill away.

Chapter Eight
AFTERMATH

I phoned my supervisor to tell him I'd drop by the office that afternoon to deliver a written statement to the investigators. Then I went for a long walk. I spent the entire morning thinking about the shooting incident. I had to determine for myself if my decision to take a life was morally and legally correct. I analyzed my actions from a tactical point of view, and then replayed them as they would appear if presented to a jury during a criminal trial.

I eventually concluded there was nothing I could have done differently to change the outcome. In retrospect, there was nothing I would have done differently either. In fact, I cannot recall ever feeling any guilt or remorse about the decision to use lethal force to defend myself. I was confident I had made the right decision.

When I first started walking I was tense and uptight. The exercise calmed my nerves, and I was feeling much better until I saw the morning paper. The front-page headline was dramatic: "COPS BLAST SLASHER!" I didn't make the connection at first, but of course it was our incident they were referring to.

About the same time I was reading my morning paper, the officer who had accompanied the corpse in the ambulance the day before returned to the morgue and used his key to open the cold storage locker where the suspect's body had been kept overnight. Officers from the Identification Squad and homicide investigators attended to watch a pathologist perform the autopsy. She discovered that five bullets had entered the chest cavity. They had each pierced vital organs, so in effect all five wounds were potentially fatal. Another round had entered his right forearm and passed through a bone, coming to rest just under the skin near his wrist.

The wounds were subsequently compared to the bullet holes in his clothing. When the investigation was complete, forensic experts decided that the seventh round, found on the pavement beside him, must have failed to penetrate his clothing and simply bounced off.

As I walked into the station that afternoon, I ran into someone who was able to give me a look at the seven bullets recovered after the shooting. Several of them were still coated with fresh blood from the autopsy. The rounds were all hollow points without copper jacketing, the same issue ammunition carried by all members of the department at the time. I was shocked to find that none of them had mushroomed, or expanded, as they should have.

In theory, hollow points are designed to expand as they encounter flesh, thus dissipating their energy inside the victim rather than passing through him and endangering others. That effect is commonly referred to as "stopping power." In simple terms, it means that a bullet will not only kill a man, but in the process impact him with enough force that he will discontinue doing whatever got him into trouble in the first place. Ideally, if an attacker is shot in self-defense, the attack should stop and whatever weapon he is holding should drop from his hands.

In my case, the suspect received five fatal hits at point-blank range and still managed to continue his attempt to kill me. He should have collapsed and died from his wounds if the bullets had done their job properly. I felt strongly that since the bullets showed no evidence of expansion after impact, the issue rounds must have been defective. Consequently, I refused to carry them in my service revolver. I immediately bought some powerful, copper-jacketed hollow points and used them in my service revolver until the day I finally left the job. Even though carrying these rounds was contrary to departmental policy, I did not try to conceal the practice. When the non-issue ammunition was finally brought to my attention by a supervisor after a revolver inspection, I refused to exchange my rounds for issue ammo. No disciplinary action was initiated over the incident.

Approximately two years after the suspect was killed, I saw a local TV news clip announcing that the department had finally decided to retire the current issue ammunition, reportedly because some rounds were malfunctioning. In fact, the food line incident was cited as one example where the rounds had not performed up to the advertised standard. I never did hear why it took so long to replace the faulty ammo.

I delivered my statement to Major Crime Squad detectives that afternoon at the police station. I then spent a couple of hours explaining my side of the story to any policeman who happened to be passing through headquarters. This was important to me, because it was an opportunity to ventilate my feelings about the shooting. I also wanted to stop any false or misleading rumors about the incident before they had a chance to damage my reputation.

At that time my good name as a police officer was probably the most important thing in my life. As it turned out, the only harmful rumor that emerged from the episode concerned a detective from the Internal Investigations Squad. I knew him well, and had enjoyed working with him in the past as he was an excellent street cop. Unfortunately, he was incorrectly reported to have harassed me about an unfounded and unrelated allegation while I was in the midst of dealing with the shooting investigation. Nothing could be further from the truth, and I did my best to make sure that everyone knew that. Still, he was the recipient of some undeserved abuse because of this idiotic rumor. That fact alone bothered me for months.

Some versions of the shooting as portrayed by the media left me shaking my head in wonderment. While many accounts were less than accurate, the overall tone was not hostile. For the most part, I just ignored what I read, although I was upset when I first saw my likeness in the papers and on TV. The police department released an out-of-date picture from my academy days to the media without consulting me. Later, when I heard the department planned to release a more recent identity card photo, I went to the Identification Squad and summarily confiscated the negatives and all the copies of the photo from their files.

Later, when the media demanded background details of a personal nature, as well as information about commendations I had received over the years, a senior commissioned officer who knew me was kind enough to ask my permission first. I refused to allow any further details to be released, and the matter was never raised again.

For the next couple of months, until the inquest was old news, I would periodically get a phone call as I came on shift telling me to attend the Public Information Counter immediately. The message was always the same. There was a camera crew waiting there to talk to me, I would be told, and a reporter with them swore that the interview had been previously arranged by Superintendent so-and-so. The pretexts ranged from promises that the interview was about something other than the shooting, all the way to vaguely-worded threats that I was required to participate by order of someone from the senior management level. If they had known my attitude toward the hierarchy, that pitch would probably have been changed. In any case, I always refused to talk to them.

One reporter, I was told later, tried a more aggressive approach to getting a story. The knife used by the suspect to stab me was being held as evidence by the Identification Squad, presumably in case further tests had to be carried out. This reporter apparently wanted a good visual image for his story and felt that a shot of the knife would add dramatic effect. Not just any knife would do, however. He only wanted to see the knife I had been stabbed with, and it had to be produced before a certain deadline.

The detectives informed him they couldn't come up with the knife on such short notice because it was sitting in someone's padlocked evidence locker. The reporter became indignant. He demanded that they produce the knife immediately. If not, he threatened to slant his story in a way that would create some doubt that the man I shot had ever been carrying a knife, and then hint that there was a cover-up. The detectives called the reporter's bluff, and in the end he backed down.

Most people were understanding and sympathetic, but I will always remember the reaction of one particular senior commissioned officer, a man I never had the dubious pleasure of meeting. He appeared in our office area the day after the shooting for the first and only time I'm aware of. As I told my story to bystanders in the office for the umpteenth time, I watched a supervisor who accompanied him nodding in my direction and whispering something. Rather than approaching me to see how I was doing, this officer instead walked right past me on his way out the door without deigning to acknowledge my presence. I felt like someone with a communicable disease.

That is not to say that management ignored me completely. One supervisor called me into his office several days after the shooting. He informed me that another senior commissioned officer had recently witnessed me handling a call on the street without my hat and tie on. Instead of stopping to see if I needed any help, he returned to his office and immediately arranged to have disciplinary action taken against me by my supervisor. Later, while rifling through some old files, I found a copy of the report. It included my official response to the allegation, which consisted largely of one very obscene phrase. The standard joke for that episode was that killing a man was less harmful to one's career than failing to live up to the department's strict dress and deportment standards.

Other encounters the day after the shooting were more productive. One corporal made a point of engaging me in a conversation in the stairwell. I hardly knew him at the time, although later he would be assigned to my team. He had collected some literature that described what had happened to other policemen involved in shootings, and he gave me copies before I left the building. Another supervisor, who was later shot and killed in the line of duty, also said all the right things and went out of his way to provide me with additional helpful literature.

I appreciated their assistance, although I never really had a chance to tell either of them how important their actions were to me. It was comforting to know that some of the things I experienced over the next few years had already happened to others. I have since passed copies of these articles to other officers involved in fatal shootings.

I also talked to the personnel officer the day after the shooting. I was pleasantly surprised when management agreed to my request that I be allowed to return to patrol duty immediately. Even though they offered me time off if I needed it, I declined. Although I would have to admit that throughout my career as a constable I frequently found fault with management decisions and policies, I was grateful that in this instance they had enough faith in me to let me make my own choice. In retrospect, I still believe that returning to work was the best decision in my case. On the other hand, I think that officers involved in similar incidents should always be offered time off before returning to the street, if they feel it is necessary.

The first order of business before I could return to active duty was to attend the range and pick up another service revolver. My own weapon was to be kept as evidence until the inquest was over. I disagreed with this policy, because I felt that once ballistics tests were carried out there was no reason it could not be returned. I really didn't want to carry an unfamiliar revolver on the street, but I had no choice in the matter.

I drew a replacement pistol from stores and tested it at the indoor range. I managed to achieve an average score. This particular revolver had seen better days, and it had a different feel than my own weapon. Regardless, it was reassuring to find that I could still handle a firearm without undo nervousness.

Coincidentally there was a reporter at the range on other business when I arrived. We had met before at a bar, so he knew who I was. Fortunately, he respected my privacy and did not take advantage of the situation in any way.

Patrol work was much the same as before, except for one minor problem. Usually my eyes automatically scanned the streets from side to side. Anything abnormal immediately leapt into focus. For the first few weeks after the shooting, however, every nut case or lunatic I passed on the street involuntarily diverted my attention from whatever I had been doing. I couldn't take my eyes off them, and I found that increasingly disturbing. Each time it happened my adrenaline levels soared for several minutes, and I had difficulty concentrating on my work.

Government policy had recently been responsible for moving hundreds of mental patients out of the institutions that had always been their homes. Of course, most of them gravitated to the skids. To remain effective on the job, I had to force myself to ignore their presence. Fortunately, with time, they soon returned to being part of the everyday landscape of the skid road area and I was able to focus my attention where it belonged.

I was assigned to my first knife call only a week after the shooting. We were summoned to a rooming house in the skids where a man and his wife were scuffling. The fight was still in progress when we arrived. They were both drunk. According to the husband, she had apparently been using him for target practice with her kitchen knives. We were able to arrest her without incident. He survived with only a cut to his right elbow where one of the knives had grazed him. I was pleased to find that I had no difficulty handling a knife call, but the real test was to come a week later.

I was on a transportation detail that took me out of my normal patrol area to the West End. As I passed through the intersection of Georgia and Granville, a prostitute flagged me over at a busy bus stop. She shouted something about a man carrying a knife. A young man had apparently sat down beside her and two of her friends and sniffed glue from a plastic bag for five minutes. He had then suddenly pulled out a buck knife and started menacing the prostitute.

"You owe me money," he had snarled. "I'm not afraid of dying. You can't walk away from it. You're going to get yours!"

As I pulled up I informed the radio operator that I would be out dealing with a man-with-a-knife call. I hoped my voice didn't reflect the apprehension I felt. It soon became evident that the suspect would not surrender his knife voluntarily. He still had it in his hand as I left my car, but for the next few minutes he continually switched its position. It went from his hand to his pocket, and then to the inside of a bag he carried. At one point the blade was housed, but then he melodramatically flicked it open again.

I immediately drew my service revolver and ordered him to drop the knife. While doing so I herded him toward the mall area and away from pedestrians in order to keep my line of fire as clear as possible. He completely ignored my request to drop the weapon. I did my best to stay close enough so that I could intercept him if he made a run at one of the bystanders, and far enough away that he would have difficulty stabbing me before I had a chance to shoot him.

What followed resembled a poorly choreographed dance routine. Both of us waltzed face-to-face, back and forth down the mall, always maintaining a constant distance apart. The suspect challenged me physically and verbally. Keeping track of the knife was like following the progress of one card in a shuffled deck, but I could not afford to lose sight of it for a moment.

I returned to the same state of emotion I had experienced two weeks earlier as I was being stalked. I found myself going through the process of preparing to kill another human being, just like the last incident.

I wanted more than anything to avoid opening fire this time. At one point, I managed to trip the suspect and began struggling with him on the ground while I held my revolver out of his reach. When I suddenly remembered how I'd been stabbed during the last altercation, I instantly broke loose from him and jumped backward. It seemed like we had been facing each other for an hour by the time reinforcements arrived, but in fact two other officers joined me within a minute and a half.

We stood on three sides of the suspect and again tried to talk him into dropping the knife. I continued to cover him with my revolver. We seemed to have reached an impasse. Because I couldn't see where the knife was now, I didn't dare try to overpower him.

Suddenly he turned toward his only avenue of escape and momentarily presented his back to me. That was the opportunity I'd been waiting for. I grabbed his hair with my free hand and yarded him backward with all my strength. He was instantly buried under a sea of blue uniforms. I heard the sound of his knife hitting the concrete just as his body smacked against the pavement. He never realized how close he'd come to dying, although if he'd watched the late news he might have heard one TV station quote a witness as hearing me say: "The last guy who pulled a knife on me is dead now."

The next day I shared the editorial page of the afternoon paper with Ronald Reagan. The editorial misspelled my first name, although it did describe me as "gutsy." The headline read something like: "PUT HIS GUN AWAY." The thrust of this editorial was that whenever a policeman was involved in a shooting, he should be placed behind a desk until his name was cleared. The fact that I'd found it necessary to pull my gun for the second time in two weeks made me the perfect example, although they didn't in any way suggest that I had erred in judgment during either incident.

Even before reading the editorial I knew that if I'd shot the second individual my career would have been destroyed, regardless of the circumstances. Media pressure would have made certain that I was transferred to an inside job at least until the heat died down, but perhaps permanently. For someone like me who loved working as a street policeman, there would be no logical alternative but to leave the job.

Being featured in a hostile editorial had almost as much stressful impact as the incident itself, because among other things I considered it an unwarranted invasion of my privacy. To the department's credit, they ignored the editorial and allowed me to continue doing what I did best.

Another serious incident occurred just before the inquest. This call began as a result of a family dispute. An elderly couple had been baby-sitting their two-year old grandchild while their daughter and her common-law husband spent the night drinking and arguing.

The husband eventually broke into the grandparent's house at two in the morning and angrily snatched his child out of the crib. The elderly couple were concerned for the baby's well-being because of their son-in-law's drunken, belligerent state. When they last saw him, he was staggering down the street in freezing weather toward his apartment building, carrying their grandchild who was dressed only in pajamas.

Another officer joined me at their apartment to help. We knew the suspect was already inside his third floor suite because we could hear him talking to himself from our position outside the locked door. It was unclear at first how much of a threat he posed to the child, although there were indications from what we could overhear that he was in a very agitated state of mind.

We wanted to listen to more of what he had to say to himself before making our move, but that option was denied us with the arrival of his drunken wife. We tried to explain in a low voice what had happened to the child, but she was very obnoxious and in no mood to listen. Instead of cooperating with us to protect her child, she yelled out a warning to her husband that the cops were standing outside.

It took a great deal of restraint at that moment not to punch her, but I resisted the impulse. While we waited for his next move, we heard a series of loud banging noises from inside the apartment. It appeared that he was nailing a board across the inside of the door to prevent us from entering. He continued to scream obscenities at us as we stood outside helplessly.

We had to decide whether the risk to the baby was great enough to justify forcing our way into the apartment. It soon became clear to me that this child was indeed in urgent need of our assistance. With that decision made, I felt that the sooner we made our way inside, the better our chances were of preventing further harm to the child.

The heavy wooden door looked like a tough one to kick in, especially now that the father had barricaded it from the inside. I'd attended calls in the building before, and I remembered that there was a common balcony outside all the apartments on that floor. We gained entry into the adjacent apartment and then jumped over to the balcony outside his front window.

His attention was drawn to us as we crept into the living room, probably as a result of another shouted warning from his wife. With an additional two or three seconds advantage we could have jumped him from behind while he was still hammering nails into the door. Instead he was able to duck into a darkened bedroom as we approached. We could not risk following him inside because we knew the baby was already in the bedroom and the suspect still had a hammer in his hand.

When he emerged moments later, he held his baby under one arm as he wielded a hammer over her head in a threatening manner. He made it abundantly clear that if we approached him he would use the hammer to harm the baby. He continued to use her as a shield between himself and the police while constantly screaming obscenities at us.

I kept my hand on the butt of my service revolver. While trying my best to calm him down by talking to him, I found myself instinctively sizing him up for a head shot. It was the only possible way of protecting the baby's life in the event he decided to strike her with the hammer.

Meanwhile, his drunken wife also managed to make her way into the apartment by way of the neighbor's balcony. She staggered into the living room, making her presence known by screaming at her husband and in general doing her best to provoke him into a violent act. My partner tried to restrain her, but she broke loose and drunkenly lunged toward her husband. He responded with a roundhouse swing with his hammer that only missed fracturing her skull because she stumbled and fell to the floor at the last second.

If he had connected he would almost certainly have killed her. He would then have joined her almost instantly with a bullet to the head from my service revolver, before he had a chance to injure the child. Undoubtedly this baby would have been better off with foster parents anyway. As soon as the other policeman regained control of the wife, we continued our negotiations to release the child. The baby was screaming hysterically by then. I seemed to be making very little progress with the father until suddenly he walked toward me and wordlessly handed me the hammer.

No details of the incident were given to the press this time and the affair ended peacefully in a courtroom several months later. I had originally charged the father with several serious offenses. However, for reasons the prosecutors could or would not explain to me, the charges were all either dropped or diluted. I ended up attending family court to give evidence on a very minor charge that I felt did not come close to reflecting the seriousness of his criminal actions.

The loving couple arrived neatly dressed and sober, arm-in-arm with a defense lawyer. When it became clear to me that the important issues of the case were to be totally obscured by the trivial nature of the proceedings, I simply walked away without looking back. It was the only way to avoid becoming personally involved with the increasingly bizarre inconsistencies of the criminal justice system.

***

As the shooting inquest approached, I spent more and more time walking along the Fraser River dikes while trying to sort out a variety of thoughts and emotions. I ran the incident through my mind constantly, analyzing everything that had happened that day and trying to anticipate what kind of questions we would face at the inquest. I expected to encounter at least one hostile lawyer, because inquests these days frequently become bitter adversarial confrontations, especially when the police are involved.

The department showed no interest in preparing the two of us who were involved in the shooting for the ordeal we were about to face. Lawyers representing the city seemed to have other, more important things to do, so we finally went to the head of our union and asked for help. He was very sympathetic to our plight and did everything he could to make things easier for us. His first move was to check for indications that lawyers or activist groups with political motivations were showing an unhealthy interest in the proceedings. There were several potential mine fields that we had to watch for. We were fortunate in many respects, because no controversial issues had emerged as a result of our actions.

The suspect's next of kin very graciously expressed sympathetic understanding of our role in the incident. Most importantly, there was no indication that they intended to launch a civil suit against us. In America, grieving relatives often take time off from mourning to call a lawyer in order to seize the opportunity to turn a quick profit from the untimely passing of a loved one at the hands of the police. Canadians, of course, are now jumping on the litigation bandwagon.

As well, we still had the threat of criminal charges hanging over

199

our heads until just before the inquest. Although I heard news reports that we had been cleared of any wrongdoing by a prosecutor, I was never fully satisfied until I saw that assurance in writing. That did not happen until after the inquest ended.

Had the suspect we shot been a member of any minority group, I would have expected to find activists using the unfortunate incident to prove somehow that the police were prejudiced against that particular minority, regardless of the circumstances of the shooting. After any controversial incident of this nature, a policeman frequently finds himself the victim of various forms of harassment from activists and the media. All too often a cop discovers that his life has been seriously disrupted, perhaps changed forever.

Because of previous threats from criminals, I always refused to give out my address or phone number to anyone other than family and close friends. I even went so far as to withhold it from the department. As a result, when my incident occurred, no one bothered me at home because no one knew how to reach me. I know of other policemen in similar circumstances who have not been as fortunate.

Any special interest group with even the remotest connection to the victim can, and often will use an incident involving police use of deadly force to further their cause. Controversy brings activist lawyers to court seeking an opportunity to cross-examine the policemen involved, knowing full well that they will automatically obtain media exposure for whatever radical cause they happen to be promoting that day. They have nothing to lose. Any type of publicity is equivalent to free advertising, which will ultimately attract more criminal clients to their law firms.

On December the fourth our union president accompanied us to the inquest. He assured us that if something untoward happened, he would immediately intervene and demand that we be allowed a chance to obtain legal counsel. He arranged to have two competent lawyers available on short notice if they were required.

The city's lawyers finally approached us for an interview just before the inquest. We informed them that it was ludicrous to expect us to explain the entire story of the shooting in the ten minutes left before the proceedings began. We ignored them. Somehow I found it difficult to picture them representing our interests without any input from us. The fact that we now had lawyers on call in case the inquest blew up in our faces was incredibly reassuring.

This particular inquest into the food line shooting went as well as could be expected. There was very little in the way of evidence presented, with no Identification Squad pictures or diagrams, and no weapons or other exhibits introduced. We left as soon as our evidence was complete. When the television cameras followed us out of the courtroom, we politely refused comment.

The coroner's jury eventually absolved us of blame for the shooting, much to my relief. Some media pundits tried to make an issue of the fact that many Vancouver policemen at the time were not currently qualified according to departmental firearms standards, but that had nothing to do with us. As one of my peers reminded me, I had successfully met departmental standards with my service revolver at the indoor target range, the outdoor target range and the 300 East Cordova Street that year.

The only contentious issue raised by the jury was in the form of a recommendation urging that police look into non-lethal methods of subduing armed persons. There were quotes in the papers stating that the Vancouver Police had only two alternatives when dealing with an armed suspect: either negotiate with him or shoot him. If that particular media version of the jury's recommendations was true, then I can only conclude that nobody listened to my side of the story. I did my best to explain that we had done everything in our power to dissuade the suspect from continuing his attack on me before we opened fire. In my opinion, there was no practical, non-lethal weapon in the world that could have saved his life that day.

A policeman stands a better than even chance of being stabbed if he uses a nightstick, flashlight, stun gun or pepper spray to disarm a hostile or deranged person who is wielding a knife, regardless of his own size, strength or experience. An individual who has gone berserk often possesses awesome strength. If he is also desperate enough to attack the police while armed with a weapon, he must be regarded as an extreme threat to anyone who confronts him. It is irrelevant whether the suspect is under the influence of alcohol or drugs, suffers from mental problems, or has simply decided to take out his suppressed anger on the first policeman he sees. There is no guaranteed safe way of disarming someone who is threatening to stab you. Anyone who claims otherwise is just plain wrong.

There is a simple way to illustrate the point. Try to defend yourself against a person who is wholeheartedly attempting to jab you with a rolled up newspaper. Then imagine that each blow he strikes is actually a stab wound. You will begin to understand the difficulty of defending yourself against a determined attack where any successful hit could very well prove fatal.

I have always been a believer in trusting the good judgment of the policeman on the scene as to how he should respond to any given incident. Therefore, I feel that a cop should not be faulted if he finds it necessary to use deadly force when confronted with a knife-wielding suspect.

***

After the inquest, my work continued in much the same manner as before, until one busy night my luck almost ran out. Several of us moved in to break up a noisy party in an upstairs apartment at around two in the morning. I underestimated the size of the rowdy group congregating inside the apartment, and we quickly found ourselves dangerously outnumbered. Luckily we were able to push the worst troublemakers downstairs and out the door before they realized there were only a few officers on the scene. Wild parties like this one had the potential to evolve into full-fledged riots at a moment's notice.

This particular party had all the ingredients for disaster, so I was glad to see it break up without having to fight my way out the door. I stood at the top of the stairs by the doorway to cover the backs of other officers escorting some of the more violent individuals outside the building. As I turned around to take one last look inside the apartment, one of a group of people congregating in the kitchen threw a beer bottle at me. It struck me right between the eyes, bending my glasses into a U-shape and shattering just above the bridge of my nose.

Blood spurted from the wound instantly and I felt as if I'd been struck with a baseball bat. I caught a very quick glimpse of a face that I was almost able to associate with the thrown object. Unfortunately, that was not enough to base a criminal charge on, although I was relatively certain I knew the identity of the person who was responsible. He disappeared before I had a chance to grab him.

I was transported to the hospital by ambulance. I required several stitches to close the wound on my forehead. I bought new glasses but they didn't fit until the swelling subsided a week later. I was lucky because the damage could have been much worse. I know of another policeman from a nearby department who lost an eye after being hit with a thrown bottle.

***

I was working a one-man car when I received a call that people were fighting inside a skid road hotel room. Since I arrived before the assigned unit, I decided to remain outside the room. I didn't intend to do anything but listen until cover arrived. Fights and family feuds were

202

seldom handled by a one-man unit, for obvious reasons. The desk clerk led me to the correct door, but it opened suddenly just as we approached it.

Two males walked out. The second one tried unsuccessfully to close the battered and broken door behind them as they left. They were both disheveled and there was a strong odor of booze surrounding them. Although they obviously saw me, they ignored my presence in a blatantly-obvious fashion that made them look all the guiltier and then started to walk by me in the hallway as if nothing was wrong. The clerk had mentioned that he'd seen blood inside the room as he walked by earlier, so when I saw blood splattered on the nearest suspect's glasses, I instantly decided to arrest them.

I ordered them to place their hands on the wall. Both of them were big enough to cause me problems, and I knew from their appearance and mannerisms that they were street thugs, probably with no great love for the police. Fortunately, they chose to comply rather than fighting me. I took no chances and forcibly pinned the two of them against the wall while I waited for assistance.

While I waited, I glanced out of the corner of my eye through the open door. The room looked like a slaughterhouse. I used my portable radio to hasten the arrival of a cover car and called for an emergency ambulance to attend. I was able to keep the two prisoners immobile until another unit arrived, although clearly they would have rather escaped. I have no idea why they didn't resist arrest, unless it had something to do with my sincere threat to shoot them if they tried.

The first policeman to arrive helped me handcuff the suspects, and then guarded them while I rushed inside the room. There was blood everywhere, but at first I could only see the victim's leg sticking out from under the bed. I pulled the body out from where they had stuffed it, removed two blood-soaked blankets and uncovered an unconscious transvestite prostitute whose face now resembled a raw piece of meat. He had been brutally beaten and stabbed repeatedly.

The victim was no longer breathing, probably because there was a bed sheet tightly entwined several times around his neck. I was sure he was a goner. To my surprise, as I tore the garrote from around his throat he sputtered back to life. His breathing was shallow and sporadic. He did not regain consciousness immediately, and I still expected him to expire at any time. The ambulance arrived minutes later and took him to the hospital for emergency treatment.

We discovered in the course of our investigation that the same two suspects had carried out a reign of terror in the hotel throughout the evening, beating and robbing several different tenants before robbing and attempting to murder our victim. This victim sustained the most serious injuries. He ended up with serious and permanent damage to his brain, although he ultimately survived the vicious attack. The two suspects earned assault convictions, which added only a few additional years to the extensive periods of jail time both had already served in the recent past.

***

I was called to the parking lot of a downtown business near the end of a busy day shift. Bystanders directed me toward the side of one of their company trucks where a drunk had wedged himself in between the chassis and an embankment. I woke the drunk up and told him brusquely to be on his way. He was probably only 25 years old, although it was difficult to tell, and he was covered from head to toe with grime. His clothes were also filthy and he reeked of a substance that I could not at first identify, but assumed might be some kind of glue.

He appeared to be quite groggy or stoned, so I didn't expect to encounter any serious resistance. As I bent over to lift him to his feet, however, he unleashed a kick that narrowly missed connecting with my face as I backed up. He then charged at me with fists flying, no longer just a harmless drunk. The entire work force had left their office by now, and they stood there, watching us fight. I used my portable radio to ask for help as I dodged his blows.

After I tried several times without success to calm him down, I began to wonder if he was under the influence of a drug like PCP, or Angel Dust, which can make the user very aggressive and extremely dangerous to deal with. I had a sinking feeling that this call was going to end badly.

I had no intention of wrestling with him in case he had a knife in his possession. I was certainly not going to hit him with my fists, because of the extreme risk of catching a disease if I skinned my knuckles in the process. As a result, I had no alternative but to hit him in the face with my metal flashlight, something I always tried to avoid doing if at all possible. I hit him hard enough that spittle flew from his mouth, but that didn't seem to deter him in the least and the fight continued.

At one point I managed to push him down to the ground. He crawled away from me and placed his mouth over the opening of one of the truck's gas tanks. He then proceeded to inhale fumes with repeated deep, gasping breaths. I realized then that what I'd smelled earlier was not glue or solvents, but gasoline. All these substances are commonly inhaled by people truly desperate to get high. Inhaling gas fumes destroys the brain and eventually leads to death. From my experience working the skid road area, I was well aware that these abusers often acted in an extremely violent and unpredictable manner. Most of them did not survive very long on the streets.

All the fumes did for this individual was to invigorate him temporarily, and he soon came at me again for a second round. It was not his size that concerned me, or his fighting skills, which were primitive even though he was using what he must have thought were karate stances. I kept wondering if he had a knife on him.

I was relieved when cover finally arrived. We were able to handcuff our prisoner after a brief struggle. As we walked him to a wagon, the other policeman thanked the bystanders sarcastically for not coming to my aid when they knew I was having trouble controlling the suspect. Frankly, the possibility of a citizen helping me during a fight never occurred to me, because these days nobody ever wants to get involved.

I sent the gas sniffer to the detoxification center, but of course the next day he was released from custody and immediately returned to the same truck for another taste of the intoxicating fumes. We advised the company to get locking gas caps. Because he was already out on bail for two previous serious assaults, it seemed pointless to charge him with assaulting me. Prosecutors probably wouldn't accept a criminal charge in this case anyway. Nowadays, they seem to proceed criminally only in cases where police officers are hospitalized.

Even if the suspect did end up in a courtroom, there was always a chance he would be found not guilty because he was incapable of forming the intent to commit the offense. The criminal justice system can't do anything to help individuals like this, let alone protect the public from their violent behavior. They either kill themselves with the fumes they become so addicted to, or commit a crime so serious that the system finally decides they must be incarcerated for a while.

***

There seemed to be no shortage of knife calls over the following two years. Almost everybody I dealt with in the skids carried a knife. Many of them would produce their knives at the least provocation, so stabbings were an everyday occurrence. My partner and I were parked near a bus stop one evening, relaxing after a call, when we heard a disturbance beside us. A male voice was shouting and swearing at bystanders. From the sound of it, I guessed he was trying to start a fight.

This was a common scenario in the skids, of course, something we ran across every time we went to work. I was writing a report, so without looking up from my clipboard I simply yelled out the window as loudly as possible: "Get lost or you're going to jail!"

That threat alone was often enough to end most disturbances. Although most of the street people no longer feared us, they were usually reluctant to risk a direct confrontation with the cops because even in this new age of community policing there were still some policemen who didn't tolerate any blatant challenges to their authority. The policeman I was working with, a gentleman noted for his humor and understatement, looked past me through my side window and stared at the suspect, who had by then stopped yelling.

"I don't think you should be impolite to him," he said to me calmly. "After all, he is carrying a knife."

That got my attention. I dropped my clipboard and made a speedy exit from the car as the suspect started walking toward me. I had my revolver pointed at his face before he took his second step.

For a change the suspect actually listened to what I was saying to him. When I ordered him to drop the knife, he did so well before he came within spitting distance. He was just another mental case, so we sent him to jail on a weapons charge and asked that a psychiatric assessment be done as soon as possible.

***

I was driving up the narrow overpass at the north foot of Main Street one evening when a speeding motorcycle almost struck me head-on. He missed hitting me by inches as I slammed on my brakes and skidded to avoid him. The viaduct there is steep and curved, so oncoming traffic is not visible until it is almost on top of you. As I tried to do a U-turn to follow him, another motorcycle that had apparently been trying to keep up with him came over the brow at high speed. He almost lost control of his machine while trying to avoid hitting me.

I ignored him for the moment. I turned my emergency equipment on and tried to pull over the first bike as it sped east on Alexander Street. Instead of pulling over, he accelerated away from me and drove through a stop sign at twice the legal speed limit. I finally lost sight of him as he went the wrong way down a one-way street, still traveling at high speed.

After I transmitted a description of the bike and rider, a succession of other units tried unsuccessfully to pull him over as he continued eastbound through heavy traffic. At one point he just missed hitting the front of a police car that tried to block his passage at an intersection.

The biker seemed quite willing to risk his life in order to avoid being stopped.

It is nearly impossible to catch a motorcycle in a high-speed chase because its superior acceleration and maneuverability gives it an overwhelming advantage over the under-powered police cars pursuing it. Since none of us were willing to follow him through red lights at the speed he was traveling, he soon disappeared again. I moved over to an area several blocks east of where he was last seen and began prowling the dark side streets. There were soon other police cars in the area, but nobody saw any sign of him for the next ten minutes.

I had almost given up hope of finding him until I caught sight of a single red light that flashed for only a second. It was a motorcycle driving down the lane with no headlights on. He had no way of turning off his brake light, and that bright-red light betrayed his presence every time he had to slow down.

I had to move fast to catch up to him. In doing so, I lost track of my location because there were no street signs in the lanes. The alleys were so dark that I almost missed seeing the motorcycle duck into a driveway. I pulled in behind him just as he attempted to turn the bike around and make a hasty exit in the opposite direction.

I told my radio operator that I was out with the suspect, but unfortunately I was unable to give her my exact location. I knew I had to do something immediately to stop him or the high-speed chase would begin again. I jumped out of the car and pushed him off his motorcycle just as he started to drive away.

I remembered hearing about another high-speed chase years earlier. It had almost concluded when the motorcyclist finally lost control and fell off his bike while rounding a corner. However, because none of his pursuers did anything to stop him, such as parking a police cruiser on top of the motorcycle, he managed to climb back on and escape as the police watched helplessly in his dust. I was not going to let that happen to me.

My suspect was still wound up from the thrill of the chase, so I was not surprised when he got up from the driveway and tried to knock me down. I did my best to fight him off, but my flashlight just bounced off his helmet and he kept coming at me. In the old days I would have tackled him to the ground and wrestled with him until I managed to get him handcuffed. Now, because I didn't know whether or not he had a knife, I simply could not bring myself to get in close enough to gain control of him.

I tried to radio for assistance, but without a location to broadcast there was nothing the operator could do for me. As we struggled, I started flashing back to the shooting incident. I remember wondering if I was going to have to use my service revolver to stop this one from coming at me again and again.

I was lucky that night. Several of the cars searching for me arrived to help me handcuff the suspect before the situation could deteriorate any further. I was completely overwhelmed by fear, anger and frustration during the struggle, so much so that I had to struggle just to regain my composure.

I had calmed down by the time I arrived at the breathalyzer room twenty minutes later to process my prisoner. So had he, apparently. I found him relaxing against the basement wall, engaged in a friendly conversation with the breathalyzer operator, who had already removed his handcuffs. The motorcyclist was rational and somewhat apologetic now. He had no significant criminal history and no explanation for the way he'd acted. In fact, he dismissed his behavior as simply a matter of adrenaline getting the upper hand.

***

During the next two years I gradually became aware of subtle and not so subtle differences in the way I handled certain critical situations at work. I knew something was seriously wrong, but there didn't seem to be anything I could do about it. This feeling of apprehension was heightened one day when I helped stop a car containing two suspects who had earlier been seen carrying a gun. To my horror, I found that when I pointed my service revolver at them, my hand was shaking. That had never happened to me before. It was normal and acceptable to experience a nervous reaction like this, but only after an incident was over and there was no further need for steady and absolute control.

My usual style when it came to subduing a hostile suspect could best be described as aggressive. Not that I went looking for fights! Common sense dictated that if I could sweet-talk a crook into handcuffs without a struggle, I did so. There was never any macho question of proving my superiority against the toughest person on the street, because I knew there was always somebody tougher, bigger or crazier waiting to deflate my ego in a very physical way. Only a fool takes risks unnecessarily.

When I say I was aggressive, I mean that whenever I was faced with an altercation, I preferred to get in close and end the struggle quickly, using sufficient force to effect the arrest but not so much that I caused a serious injury. I liked being in close. If I had a suspect I thought might be concealing a weapon, I felt supremely comfortable moving directly into their face and grabbing their wrists.

I very seldom got into fist fights with the individuals I arrested. Because I had no boxing skills to speak of, the odds of winning a fair fist fight were not in my favor anyway. Besides, punching a suspect is a very messy and inefficient way of gaining the upper hand.

If I stood in close proximity to an assailant, I had a golden opportunity to establish control because I was able to monitor the suspect's hands and facial expressions for signs that he was going for a weapon or about to attack. I could then grab or choke belligerents until I was back in control of the situation. When I encountered an individual in the process of confronting another police officer in a threatening manner, I usually positioned myself immediately behind the suspect. This distracting form of intimidation was usually sufficient to prevent any further escalation of hostilities.

After the shooting, I gradually found myself reluctant to get in close anymore. Perhaps it was because I was always expecting to face another knife attack, although that theory did not occur to me at first. Nevertheless, I was no longer confident in my ability to react to violent altercations appropriately. Without absolute control over my reactions, I soon experienced difficulty handling certain types of calls, specifically those involving violence.

At this stage, I still believed that my judgment was sound. In fact, the overall quality of my work remained at roughly the same level. However, I found myself making mistakes that I would never have made in the past. For instance, on one occasion I was assigned to a call, acknowledged it, and then promptly forgot all about it until I received a gentle reminder from the radio operator later in the evening. I eventually decided that I would have to do something about these problems before they got out of hand.

The symptoms were hard to ignore. I had a horrendous nightmare two nights after the incident where the man I shot tried over and over again come at me through some kind of Plexiglas window. The episode finally ended with him fading away into the darkness. His face never reappeared in any of my nightmares.

In the months that followed the shooting, I had a series of increasingly disturbing nightmares, all of them featuring violent scenarios. Most ended with a death. They were, to say the least, unsettling. Another problem that I found particularly difficult to understand could best be described as an internal twitch or nerve reaction that first appeared shortly after the shooting and occurred more and more frequently over the next few years. It felt like the nerves around my forehead were twitching, almost in a fluttering type of motion. I had no control over when this would occur, or how long it would last. It was a very uncomfortable sensation.

Although the problem did not seem to affect my health, I eventually had it checked out by specialists. I had mixed emotions when tests proved there was no physical explanation for the condition, because to me that meant I had psychological problems that I was unable to overcome by sheer willpower.

As my situation deteriorated, I tried to arrange with the department for an unpaid leave of absence to further my education. In my written request for the leave I made it clear that I hoped to use the time to deal with certain problems that had arisen as a result of the shooting. I could not elaborate on what these problems were because I knew that to do so might mean the department would force me to undergo some type of psychological treatment. I was also acutely aware that rumors about a mental illness could have a devastating effect on my career and reputation.

Going public with my problem was simply not an acceptable option then. I wanted to distance myself from work by taking a year off to write a novel and return to university part-time. Shift work meant that the only practical way I could complete my degree was with a leave of absence anyway. I hoped that over the course of a year away from the job, my problems would somehow fade away.

Similar requests by other members had routinely been okayed in the past, although there was no existing departmental policy governing leaves of absence. Nevertheless, I was led to believe that my application would also be approved without delay. For this reason, I was surprised when I received word one week later that I had been turned down.

The reasoning behind this refusal was never explained to me. However, it was suggested twice that I should instead consider resigning and then reapplying for the job when I wanted to return. This option was unacceptable to me. Since I had no friends at the management level, and because I was a middle-aged, white male, I was well aware that my chances of being rehired were, at best, slim. At the time, the job was still all-important to me. Despite my problems, I could not face losing my career as a policeman, regardless of what the personal consequences might be.

About two years after the shooting everything finally came to a head. My situation had deteriorated so much that I felt my only alternative was to book off work and see a psychiatrist. There really was no going back at this stage, and I subsequently spent six of the worst months of my life trying to deal with all the psychological problems that had accumulated since the shooting incident.

The stress of this process was incredible, even though I wasn't working on the street anymore. I soon found myself avoiding the downtown area around the station completely, and as a result I gradually lost touch with my job and the people I had worked with for nearly twelve years. Although I forced myself to attend two or three social functions related to the job, I was never comfortable and usually felt distinctly out of place.

I sat on my couch at home for hours at a time as the stress and apprehension I experienced grew in intensity. Although I went for long walks in an attempt to relax, my thoughts always returned to the shooting. I reexperienced the incident over and over again, every day.

Strangely, part of my memory of the shooting disappeared shortly after the incident. I do not recall actually killing the suspect, or even hearing any of the seven shots fired. I do, however, recollect telling some of the policemen around me all about the shooting as I was treated for the knife wound at St. Paul's, so I guess I remembered it then.

At times I experienced a tumult of emotions as I came close to remembering what happened in the period of time between the suspect's final lunge at me while I was trapped against the van mirror and the moment I found myself on the ground, kicking him in the groin to stave off his attack. I tried repeatedly to bring these particular events back into focus, but I was never successful in doing so. I eventually came to understand that my recollection of the shooting was no longer accessible to me. Perhaps my subconscious has decided it would be unwise for me to know what actually went through my mind as I killed a man.

I experienced flashbacks that were, at times, devastating. For instance, I would be reading a novel when all of a sudden I would find myself back at the 300 East Cordova, experiencing the shooting all over again. The most unsettling symptom was the overwhelming sense of doom that gradually developed; I had a strong feeling that something horrendous was going to happen if I returned to work.

In World War II, pilots who had flown one too many combat missions were described as suffering from the "twitch." There was often a stigma attached to those pilots who "lost their nerve," and the British classified them in a category known as "Lack of Moral Fiber." When soldiers developed problems during combat, the condition was known as "shell shock."

It was only after the Vietnam War that the experts took these symptoms seriously. Eventually they identified Post-traumatic Stress Disorder, or PTSD, as responsible for the misery suffered by some individuals involved in extremely stressful incidents. The experts decided that I too was suffering from PTSD, but I made little effort to research the affliction or understand its ramifications at first. Even though I avoided facing the diagnosis of PTSD head-on, I gradually made some progress in coexisting with it as time passed.

One of the worst parts of the ordeal was the frustration of dealing with the Workers' Compensation Board. I had read many negative articles in the paper about the WCB. The minor brushes I'd had with their bureaucrats in the past left me less than impressed with their ability to deal with even a simple, straightforward claim. Unfortunately, I really had no alternative but to pursue my claim for PTSD with them. Meanwhile, I just hoped I could work my way through my problems on my own and eventually return to a normal lifestyle.

The WCB assigned an adjudicator to my claim. He talked with me for an hour or so at the WCB office about the incident and what I had experienced since then. I basically told him that I had to leave the job, one way or another, to protect my sanity.

I spent the better part of a morning with one of their staff psychologists. The interview in his office was a humiliating and depressing experience. Since I could hear conversations taking place outside his door, I knew that the secretary and anyone else nearby could in turn hear everything I said. The psychologist admitted that his background was primarily in family counseling, and he did not seem interested in finding out what was really wrong with me. Although he was polite and pleasant enough, he yawned constantly throughout the interview. The experience left me feeling confused and frustrated.

At the end of the morning's ordeal, I was seated in an empty room with a pile of cards and a small box divided into two compartments. On each card was a statement. I was supposed to consider the validity of those statements, then place each card in the appropriate box marked true or false.

Many of the questions were bizarre, to say the least. I remember thinking at the time that this test was preferable to describing ink blots, which was the kind of foolishness I had expected to encounter. As it turned out, interpreting ink blots might have been more meaningful. I subsequently checked in a psychology text book and discovered that the test I took was almost universally regarded as outdated and useless, except in certain carefully-defined situations. My circumstances did not even come close to fitting the criteria they listed.

I was well aware that the WCB would pass along a complete and detailed report about my problems to the department. I knew this meant that everything I told them would become common knowledge amongst the people I worked with. Therefore, I had to walk a fine line by telling the WCB enough to confirm the diagnosis of PTSD, while at the same time shielding from them private details that could destroy my reputation and what was left of my career as a policeman.

My biggest fear, now that my problems were out in the open, was that I would be left abandoned, without a career. The more details I told the WCB about my problems, the more bridges I would burn with the department and the tougher it would be to get hired in any other profession. I had only to think back to my own archaic attitude toward people with psychological problems to understand how a prospective employer might regard someone suffering from PTSD.

It was a classic Catch 22 situation, so I had little difficulty envisioning the worst-case scenario coming to pass. The danger was that the WCB would wash their hands of me, and I would then have to convince the department to let me have my job back. The more I revealed about my problems, the less chance I had of ever convincing the department that they could trust me to handle the extraordinary pressures of street police work again.

Meanwhile, the violent nightmares continued. Now they often included tumultuous dreams where I was in the midst of quitting the job when something catastrophic would happen to me.

Approximately six months after I originally booked off sick, I was finally notified by the WCB that they did not think I was suffering from PTSD. Instead, they claimed I was afflicted with something they referred to as "burnout." Their decision meant that the worst-case scenario I had dreaded facing was now a reality. This meant I was now essentially a man without a country, in imminent danger of losing my job unless I took immediate action to salvage what was left of my career. Treating the symptoms of PTSD was no longer a priority.

Therefore, I had to convince the two doctors whose permission was required for me to return to work that I was completely cured of the PTSD symptoms. Although I was in better shape emotionally than when I'd booked off, I was acutely aware that the original problems were still simmering in the background.

I still believed that something horrendous would occur if I

returned to work, but I soon resigned myself to this inevitability and decided it was a risk I would have to live with. Frankly, if that meant that some individual unwise enough to attack me was going to get hurt in a big way, I was prepared to accept the consequences. I simply could not leave the job at that stage of my life. After all, I had nothing else to fall back on and police work was infinitely more appealing than unemployment. Besides, as much as I hated what the job was doing to my sanity, I still wanted to be a policeman.

I made a conscious effort to appear cheerful and normal, and I am quite certain that anybody who talked to me at the time agreed that I was ready to return to work. After getting clearance from the doctors, I arranged to return to my original job in the patrol division. March 24, 1987, was to be my first day back on the road. I was still determined to fight the WCB's decision not to cover the time I had spent away from work, but I knew that unless I was fighting from within the system I had no chance of succeeding.

On the Sunday before I was slated to return to work, I read the morning paper and noticed that the winning numbers for the 6/49 draw looked similar to the numbers I usually played. With growing excite-ment, I pulled my tickets out and compared the numbers. Although I immediately realized that they were identical, I still checked them several times to confirm that they matched. My wife thought I'd really gone off the deep end when I kept shouting and pointing excitedly to the paper and the ticket sitting on top of it. There was a moment of panic when I realized that the ticket I'd pulled out of my wallet was from the previous week's draw, but I quickly located the correct ticket and confirmed again that the numbers did indeed match.

We immediately shared the news with our families, and spent a sleepless night contemplating the vagaries of fate. My wife went to work Monday morning while I went by the lottery office to pick up a cheque for a rather large sum of money. The other half of the jackpot that week went to someone in Quebec. There were some anxious moments while I waited in the lobby for admission to the inner sanctum. For instance, one man who approached the security guard told him that he thought he had the winning ticket on the last 6/49. His ticket turned out to be only a list of the winning numbers printed by one of the lottery machines, so he went away disappointed. It was a common misunderstanding, according to the guard.

My ticket was verified after half an hour, but picking up the prize was not as simple as I'd hoped. When you see flashy ads for the various lotteries, it is easy to forget the reason for their existence.

Lotteries exist solely as a prime source of government revenue, or more properly as a slush fund used to buy votes. In short, lotteries are run like any other business. I had hoped to keep a low profile for a few weeks to give us time to make decisions about our future, but the reality is that publicizing winners is an excellent form of advertising for the lotteries. I was told in no uncertain terms that unless I agreed to a press conference, they would not issue me my money.

I fought this as best I could under the circumstances. In fact, I became quite vocal in my objections to their tactics. The man in charge suddenly became unavailable when I asked to see him. When a security guard was assigned to keep me company, I realized that it was either give in to their demands or walk out without a cheque. Since they now kept my ticket in their possession, I had no alternative but to agree to see the press just as closing time approached at the banks. As soon as I had the cheque in my hand, I mumbled something vague to the cameras and walked away from the podium before they could ask any silly questions.

I read in the papers the next day that I was planning to leave the job, even before I had a chance to make that decision. In the end I had little choice. I had been given a unique opportunity to start life over again. Considering the circumstances and timing of the windfall, it would have been folly to tempt fate by returning to police work.

On the other hand, it was, and to a certain extent still is, very difficult to put the job behind me. I have never encountered a finer group of people than the men and women I worked with in the Vancouver Police Department. To aspire to be a good street policeman is, to my mind, a fine and noble undertaking.

Being a policeman is much like being a member of a secret society, in that you are involved in a lifestyle that is universally misunderstood by outsiders. You develop a strong kinship with the people who share your belief in what you are doing.

There cannot be a job that is more challenging. Even with the gradual encroachment of restrictive court rulings and mind-numbing bureaucracy, a street policeman has been granted a unique mandate by society which often allows him to exercise discretion, judgment and common sense in the execution of his duties. Although most officers were willing to accept responsibility for their actions, in recent times there is less and less margin for error in a system that can punish a policeman's honest mistakes with ruination and even incarceration.

Nevertheless, leaving the job was the hardest decision I ever had to make. It is a difficult profession to leave behind in many ways.

For instance, I still think like a policeman, and talk like a policeman, and it is impossible to express my true feelings on some controversial issues without betraying my police background to civilians. I am gradually learning to live with the contradictions that come with retaining the values and judgments I acquired while on the job even though I am no longer a policeman. Most of all, I miss the day-to-day contact with the men and women of the Vancouver Police Department. Those associations simply cannot continue on the same level after you quit.

The only unresolved issue remaining from the job was my claim with the WCB to cover the six months I'd been off work. The day after I picked up the prize, the WCB asked if I wanted to close the claim. I was tempted to say yes. I wanted to start a new life, and I was finding it increasingly painful and distressing to deal with the WCB's handling of my claim.

On the other hand, my case could serve as a precedent for other similar incidents involving police-related shootings. I could not live with the possibility that another policeman might be denied help because this flawed WCB decision was allowed to stand. I told them that I wanted to continue with the case. My former union stood behind me and decided to assist me in the appeal process.

I finally got an opportunity to examine the WCB's file on my case during the appeal process. I immediately knew I'd made the right decision. There were things in that file that infuriated me. I spent hours going through it, identifying numerous mistakes and tracing certain ambiguities that might be of use to our lawyers. There were even memos about my case from psychologists I had never met, expressing opinions about me solely on the basis of other people's judgments. All the facets of my case had been dealt with as if they were part of an adversary process in a courtroom, except for the fact that there had been no one to represent my interests. Anyone dealing with the WCB should have access to legal representation right from the beginning of the process.

What I found most offensive was the expressed point of view by the WCB that anyone with problems similar to mine should simply look for another job. It was as if anybody who developed psychological difficulties as a cop should simply be written off as a liability, regardless of their record on the job and, indeed, their own personal interests and desires. I compared the contents of some of these memos with what I read in psychology textbooks. Despite my lack of expertise in the field, I began to form my own opinions as to what the WCB's bureaucratic double-talk in my file really meant.

There was light at the end of the tunnel for me when I finally located one particular chart in a psychology textbook. This one-page chart listed the symptoms characteristic to PTSD. It was then simply a matter of checking off a specific number of symptoms from the list to determine whether or not I had been suffering from PTSD. The results clearly confirmed that I had been suffering from PTSD all along.

I felt an overwhelming sense of relief when I was finally able to identify what had been bothering me all that time, despite a smoke screen thrown up by the WCB that had left me extremely confused. It was somehow comforting to know that others had managed to overcome PTSD. When a significant number of Vietnam War veterans returned with these same symptoms, some of the veteran's hospitals in America dealt with the problem simply by refusing to acknowledge that it existed. Those so-called experts were proven wrong decades ago, of course, and there is no doubt in my mind that some of that enlightenment will eventually make its way across the border into British Columbia.

Scientists investigating Post-traumatic Stress Disorder have only recently discovered evidence that the condition has biological roots. It is apparently triggered by certain catastrophic incidents where an individual experiences overwhelming terror over which he or she has no control. Although commonly associated with combat veterans, police officers and victims of serious crimes, PTSD can also affect people from all walks of life if the trauma they experience is serious enough.

The effects vary from person to person. A traumatic event can actually alter an individual's brain chemistry. Thus the manner and rate at which their brain secretes certain chemicals, substances that the brain normally produces only when influenced by severe stress, may be changed. This means minor incidents can inadvertently trigger the "flight or fight" response, inappropriately alerting the body through adrenaline surges to react to a non-existent emergency.

People with PTSD are thus prone to symptoms like nightmares, flashbacks, irritability and sleep disorders. They may also find themselves overreacting to everyday occurrences, such as car backfires. Another part of the brain that regulates the way individuals deal with pain may cause some people with PTSD to experience emotional numbing, thereby changing the way they relate to others.

Reading the news reports about this research was another turning point for me in the process of dealing with my PTSD. Now that there is proof this condition actually exists, and that it is caused by a biological reaction, I can finally understand why certain unpleasant things happened to me after the shooting. Now I can begin the long process of healing myself.

It is difficult to explain how I feel about the symptoms I experienced after the shooting. For a long time I didn't believe PTSD existed, or comprehend how Vietnam vets could really suffer from it. When PTSD affected me personally, I found it next to impossible to deal with the symptoms, let alone the fact that I was suffering from a form of mental illness. It was much easier to confront a condition that had been scientifically proven to exist than to grapple with abstract concepts such as diseases of the mind.

I went through a difficult year in preparation for the appeal, which in the end meant that I would have to appear in front of a panel of three psychiatrists. They would make the final and binding decision about whether or not I had actually been suffering from PTSD. Before I could face the panel, however, I spent many hours being interviewed by another psychiatrist, an acknowledged expert in the diagnosis and treatment of PTSD and other stress disorders. He concluded that the original diagnosis of PTSD was correct.

In the end, the panel of experts also agreed with his opinion. They decided that I had indeed been disabled for those six months by PTSD, and that it was a direct result of the shooting incident in 1984. Best of all, the WCB cannot overturn the ruling because the decision is legally binding. I wanted this precedent to be established so that the WCB will be obliged to help other police officers involved in similar incidents.

Unfortunately, things at the WCB have only worsened since then, and police officers with PTSD are often not getting the kind of help they need. I was glad to finally put an end to my particular ordeal with the WCB, but there is still unfinished business with regard to this problem. It seems to me that it will take one or more tragedies before the mindless bureaucrats are forced to deal with the deadly-serious ramifications of police with PTSD.

I wrote this book in an attempt to tell my side of the story about police work. I can only hope that as crime rates increase and policing becomes more and more challenging, citizens will realize that individual police officers deserve their support and understanding, especially during times of crisis.